BEST SPORTS STORIES 1988

Edited and Published by

The Sporting News

President and Chief Executive Officer
RICHARD WATERS

Editor
TOM BARNIDGE

Director of Books and Periodicals
RON SMITH

796
BES
1988

Published in the United States by THE SPORTING NEWS Publishing Co., 1212 North Lindbergh Boulevard, St. Louis, Missouri 63132.

Library of Congress Catalog Card Number: 45-35124

ISSN: 0067-6292
ISBN: 0-89204-282-6
10 9 8 7 6 5 4 3 2 1

First Edition

Table of Contents

The Prize-Winning Stories

The Prize-Winning Photographs

Other Photographs

Front-Cover Photograph
Ecstasy

by Bill Fields of Golf Illustrated. Larry Mize leaps for joy after sinking his 140-foot chip shot on the second playoff hole to beat Greg Norman for the 1987 Masters golf title in Augusta, Ga. Copyright © 1987, Golf Illustrated Inc.

The Prize-Winning Color Photograph
Headhunter

by Judy Walgren of the Dallas Morning News. The winning color photograph, which appears on the back cover, shows Dallas Cowboys cornerback Manny Hendrix tackling St. Louis Cardinals wide receiver J.T. Smith by the head during a 1987 National Football League game in Irving, Tex. Copyright © 1987, The Dallas Morning News.

PREFACE

In a strictly geographic sense, the 1987 sports year offered a little of something for everyone. Unlike '86, when championships won by the New York Mets, New York Giants, Boston Celtics and Penn State Nittany Lions gave the sports world a decidedly northeastern flavor, the champions of 1987 were spread throughout the country.

The West Coast found enjoyment in the Los Angeles Lakers, who in 1987 won their fourth National Basketball Association crown in eight years. And the San Francisco Giants, who lost 100 games just two seasons earlier, captured their first National League Western Division title in 16 years and narrowly missed making their first World Series appearance in a quarter century.

The Rocky Mountain area could again find satisfaction in the Denver Broncos, who won their second straight American Football Conference championship. But the Broncos, who are developing a heartbreak reputation when it comes to Super Bowls, lost their second straight National Football League title game by a wide margin.

Sports fans in the Midwest had any number of teams they could follow to championship success. Coach Bob Knight's Indiana Hoosiers captured the National Collegiate Athletic Association basketball championship, the school's third such crown in 11 years. The Minnesota Twins astonished the baseball world by winning the first World Series title in club history. The Twins used home-field advantage en route to their crown, winning 56 of 81 regular-season games and all six postseason contests played at the Metrodome in Minneapolis. Minnesota knocked off two more Midwestern teams, the Detroit Tigers and St. Louis Cardinals, in postseason play.

While the East Coast was shut out in baseball, that region enjoyed the best football had to offer. The Washington Redskins captured their second Super Bowl championship in six years and the Miami Hurricanes won the school's second national football title.

Wherever the action, *they* were there. "They" refers to the men and women who put as much effort into their pursuit of the perfect story or picture as athletes put into their search for excellence. The competition is fierce and the results gratifying. Those who chronicled the 1987 sports world for newspapers and magazines throughout the country continued to move toward the lofty goal of perfection, taking their readers behind the scenes for insight and perspective on the personalities and events that made the year memorable.

The Sporting News is proud to present a small sprinkling of those memories in the 44th edition of *Best Sports Stories*, the anthology that honors the year's top writers and photographers. TSN is editing and publishing its sixth edition of the anthology, which traces its roots to 1944 and the efforts of Irving Marsh and Edward Ehre. The contest to select winners and contributors attracted hundreds of newspaper and magazine entries. It was open to writers and photographers throughout the country and accepted only stories and pictures that were published in 1987. Serving as judges for the sixth straight year was a panel of five professors from the University of Missouri, home of one of the world's most-respected journalism education programs. They are:

Brian Brooks, associate professor of journalism at the University of Missouri and coordinator of the school's editing programs.

George Kennedy, associate dean of the University of Missouri School of Journalism.

Bill Kuykendall, associate professor and director of the University of Missouri photojournalism sequence and director of the international Pictures of the Year competition.

Daryl Moen, professor of journalism and director of the School of Journalism's mid-career programs.

Byron Scott, Meredith professor of journalism and director of the University of Missouri's service journalism program.

Those five judges can attest to the agonizing problems that arise when you sort through hundreds of creative, well-written stories in search of the *four* that deserve special recognition. Likewise, the selection process for *three* pictures. But, after painstakingly considering the merits of each entry, the judges chose the following winners, each of whom receives a $500 prize:

WRITING

Reporting	Norm Clarke	Rocky Mountain News
Feature	Jere Longman	Philadelphia Inquirer
Magazine	Rick Reilly	Sports Illustrated
Commentary	Bob Verdi	The Sporting News

PHOTOGRAPHY

Color	Judy Walgren	Dallas Morning News
B & W Action	Larry Steagall	The Sun (Bremerton, Wash.)
B & W Feature	Louis DeLuca	Dallas Times Herald

It also was difficult to weed the selection list to the choice stories that would appear in this book. By no means are the stories and photos that follow the winning selections losers. They are, rather, a tribute to the sports journalism profession, which seems to get stronger every year. All of the *Best Sports Stories* contributors are providing an entertaining look at the 1987 sports year, as seen through the eyes and lenses of those who were there.

Best Commentary Story

Special Olympics: Something Special

GENERAL

By *BOB VERDI*

From The Sporting News
Copyright © 1987, The Sporting News

These are all athletes who gladly would sign autographs, if they all could.

These are all athletes who would submit to up-close-and-personal interviews, but sometimes their words fail.

These are all athletes who would dearly give back to sports what sports has given them, if only they were agile enough.

These are the 4,717 mentally retarded athletes, ages 8 to 83 from 70 different countries, who graced the University of Notre Dame campus during one magnificent week in August, the occasion being the International Special Olympics. You come here expecting to feel sorrow, and you wind up feeling humbled by the joy that pervades the place. You know that these people have been missing out on a lot of common pleasures since birth and will until death. But you also realize that maybe you've forgotten a few things, too, like what it means to hug someone for finishing eighth out of eight.

You walk into a hotel, and there's a youngster in his track uniform scouring the lobby for any kind of souvenir that says Fighting Irish or Notre Dame on it. And you see the polite lady behind the desk give the youngster a simple postcard, and you see his eyes explode in glee, and although he can't really say thank you, he can't say thank you enough. And you see the lady behind the desk, and you know that she doesn't have tears in her eyes now because she caught a cold.

You run into Bill Hickey, who's the director of food services for the university and who has been serving up thousands of meals daily, and he tells you about the boy he met the other day, the boy from Ireland. Bill tells you that he asked the boy which part of Ireland he was from, north or south? And the boy looked at Bill and said,

"What's the difference? We're all the same." And Bill wondered why they can't understand that back in Ireland where the normal folk shoot at each other in the name of religion.

And then you go out into the sunshine and realize that you've lost a handle out there in the real world, the world of agents who lie, coaches who cheat, college presidents who sanction deceit and athletes who scream when their filet isn't cooked quite right. But these special athletes aren't dumb enough to complain, and they don't hide in a trainer's room after they strike out because, alas, they've spent enough time in trainers' rooms.

They've been sheltered, after all. They haven't learned how to hate, how to be ungrateful or how to practice hypocrisy. And in lieu of drugs, it seems, their narcotics are fresh air, love and companionship.

Mind you, Donna Sue Montgomery, 37, from Kentucky, came to win the 25-meter walk. But when the first-place time was announced as 6.7 seconds and hers was 1 minute, 41 seconds, it didn't seem to matter. She got into her wheelchair with a smile and headed over to receive her medal or ribbon—it didn't matter which. They all earn something, including David Diekow of Alaska, who had to be propped up by a volunteer—on vacation time—to accept his prize for fourth, a red rose, which the youngster held high in a quivering hand.

You see a youngster dribbling a basketball toward the basket, an unmolested layup a sure thing, and then you see him stop short to pick up a fallen opponent from the floor. The two points could wait, but not a helping hand. You see Geary Locke, 23, a local lad, crying because he finished third in his heat, crying because he figured his dad deserved a victory. His dad was Bill Locke, who, perhaps more than anyone else, brought the Games here. But Bill died of a massive hemorrhage three years ago, and Geary wasn't so sure dad would be proud of him now.

"But I know his father is," said June Locke, Geary's mother. She was there when Geary climbed the stairs of the stadium and lit the flame with the torch and said, "Dad, this is for you."

And June Locke was there when Geary stopped crying the other day, when Sargent Shriver, the president of Special Olympics International, presented him that very torch to keep. It was then that June Locke started to cry, because she's a special parent behind a special child. But there are lots of them, too, lots of special parents. You don't hear any of them shouting to kill the umpire, you don't hear any of them browbeating a coach to get their son or daughter into the game and you notice that even the reporters here have developed a rare sense of manners and restraint.

Must be that this isn't reality with all its attendant cynicism and cutthroat mentality. Must be that this is different, a friendlier spot than the Persian Gulf, the Iran-Contra Hearings or even the other Olympics, the ones in which amateurs take steroids to build their muscles and quiet cash to build their trust funds. Must be that this is purer than all the other forms of athletics that call themselves genuine.

"My son Chris is 16," said Sue Coffman, the Area Two Coordinator for the Special Olympics. "Like any mother, I wish that he was born normal, that it didn't take him six years to learn how to tie his shoes. These children, many of them come here not only to compete, but to develop their sense of responsibility, to be able to tell time, to be able to pack their belongings, to be able to live in a dorm or with a strange family.

"Yes, I wish he was born normal, because every parent of a mentally retarded child wonders down deep what will happen to them, who will take care of them when we die? Will they be OK? Will society look down on them, or will society, through events like these, learn to appreciate them? I wish, yes, but also I would not trade my Chris for any child on Earth. He's so good-hearted and so kind, and he was given to me by God for a reason. If it wasn't for Chris, I would never have gotten involved in something so wonderful as this. And besides, you look at these kids smile, and you wonder . . . what is normal?"

Indeed, you wonder exactly who is handicapped here?

Them or us?

Judge's Comments

The distinguishing characteristic of good commentary is that it possesses a point of view, makes an argument, supported by evidence and logically developed. The best commentary makes strong points about important subjects.

Arguably, the most important element in sports and in sportswriting consists of the lessons they offer in human nature, especially the insights they provide into the character of athletes under the stress and in the glory of competition. That element, those insights, run like threads through the top entries in this year's commentary category.

These writers, among the best in contemporary American journalism, explore in a variety of contexts the truth that in lesser hands becomes a cliche—competition reveals character. As Hemingway put it, courage can be defined as grace under pressure. As Bob Verdi puts it in this year's winning column, after watching retarded athletes win and lose with unfailing grace: *"Indeed, you wonder exactly who is handicapped here. Them or us?"*

And, as Tom Boswell puts it, in his eulogy to Dick Howser:

"He will be recalled, and for a long time, as a man who proved the difference between book and cover, between show and substance. With Howser, what you saw was much less than what you finally got."

Those are lines that bring tears to the eyes. But good commentary also can be angry, as in Edwin Pope's outraged demand that professional sports hire black executives. It can even be funny, as in Gene Collier's lament for the *"landmark 200 millionth consecutive losing season"* suffered by Pennsylvania's bears during hunting season.

Subject and tone may differ, but the best commentary lets us know where the writer stands and how he got there. Verdi's work, even more than the others, meets that standard. We can learn from his athletes and from him.

Best Magazine Story

A Ring and a Prayer

WRESTLING

By *RICK REILLY*

From Sports Illustrated
Copyright © 1987, Time, Inc. All Rights Reserved

Easy to say, Matthew, but not so easy to do when Hellface is about to give you a bionic elbow and Krypton is pinning your arms behind your back and the Gravedigger is trying to peel your mask off and the crowd is starting to throw beer. Easy to say, Matthew, when you don't have 86 orphans to feed, a truck acting up and an electricity bill that's a week overdue. Of course, these things never came up in the King James version.

So it is at times like these that Father Sergio Gutierrez, known to Mexican professional wrestling fans as the masked Fray Tormenta (Brother Tempest), must go a bit beyond what they taught him in seminary. Maybe slap a lip grip on his oppressor, followed by a kick-out and a pile drive? Maybe cap it off with some serious rending of clothes and gnashing of teeth?

Unnnngh. Too late. The good and devout padre takes a vicious knee in the solar plexus followed by a whip into the turnbuckle.

"How can you treat a man of God like that?" a woman in the third row is screaming. "You will rot in hell!" Eight rows back, two women are banging on pots with spoons and yelling something about novenas. The crowd in the indoor arena in Mexico City is probably a lot like Mexico in general—about 95 percent Catholic—and when somebody starts wailing and smiting a man of the cloth, they want retribution. Blood would do.

"Kill him, Padre!" hollers one man. "I'll pay for the funeral!"

This is no time to be forgiving anybody's trespasses. This calls for ... the Confessional.

Bounding off the turnbuckle, the good and devout padre leapfrogs Hellface and head-butts the unsuspecting noggin of Krypton.

Spinning on his heels, he takes the Gravedigger and airplanes him out of the ring, then grabs the woozy Krypton and ties him up, public-square style, in the ropes.

This leaves the padre alone, mask-to-mask, with Hellface. Who says they don't write morality plays anymore? Leading with an overhand right (O.K., so the ref didn't see it), the padre sends Hellface to Sominexland with one punch and then—uh-oh, here it comes —locks him up in his south-of-the-border version of the figure-four leg vine, known as the Confessional. And woe be to him who enters it.

Hellface anguishes. The crowd roars. The Confessional is working divinely. Hellface pounds the canvas. *Submission, submission,* the crowd chants. *Repent, sinner.* The Confessional hears all. One, two, three, counts the ref. The good and devout padre emerges gloriously victorious. Cash your check in the back, Padre.

Out of the mouth of babes and sucklings hast thou ordained strength. . . .
—Psalms 8:2

The wrestling priest of Xometla has a toothache. It's 6:10 in the morning, and he's fumbling through the stingy pre-dawn light of his bedroom for the bottle of aspirin, trying not to wake the 16 teen-age boys sleeping on a row of cots that cover most every inch of the cement floor. The bishop may not like it—Catholicism requires a priest to sleep alone in his room—but the bishop hasn't telegrammed lately with any suggestions on how to put 86 orphans to bed at night in a place that is meant to sleep no more than a dozen.

Trying to find the bottle of aspirin, the padre finds a scorpion instead. Unflustered, he mumbles, steps back, slips on the only pair of nonwrestling shoes he owns and stomps the life out ot it. This does not make his toothache any better.

The portly 42-year-old, now unmasked (but never photographed that way) wrestling priest of Xometla routinely strikes fear into no one. He has bushy eyebrows, Coke-bottle glasses with square black rims, hair liberally seasoned with gray and a nose that, having once been broken by a bottle, he can push until it's flush with either side of his chunky face. Still aching from last night's leotard crusade, he stumbles from his room into the courtyard of St. Michael's, the dilapidated 16th-century church that is home for him, 72 boys, 14 girls, three women volunteers, four stray Doberman pinschers, 20 or so pigeons, four kittens and 109,000 flies.

The flies feel particulary at home at St. Michael's because there is only one toilet—and that rarely works—one hole in the cement for the boys to urinate into, no toilet paper (the kids usually use old wrestling newspapers) and a septic system so ancient that it could have been used by Montezuma himself. As an added bonus for the flies, a door with the windows broken out of it leads from the bathroom to the kitchen, less than five feet away. This is one-stop fly shopping at its finest.

The diabetic, overweight, chain-smoking wrestling priest of Xometla doesn't want to be up at this unholy hour, but if he is to keep this orphanage standing—if that's what you call what the crumbling structure is now doing—then he has to keep wrestling. And if he is to keep wrestling he must be in some semblance of shape, and that means getting up before the roosters and running through his tiny farming village of Xometla—about an hour northeast of Mexico City —up the road where the farmers walk their pigs and cows and then, dreadfully, up the mountain.

To force his rotund body up the mountain, he needs inspiration, and such inspiration is now walking out that same bedroom door in the form of 15-year-old Marco Anthony, the padre's *nino* Friday. Marco Anthony rubs the sleep from his black eyes, puts on the same clothes he wore yesterday—and the day before that—sticks his dirty feet into the white espadrilles somebody from the U.S. thought were long past worth keeping (though Marco wears them every day) and lags behind the priest as they make their woeful way to the courtyard gate.

Nobody else is up. Not the 32 little boys who sleep like pretzel sticks in one 11- by 13-foot room and not the 24 bigger ones who are stuffed into a slightly larger room adjacent to it. This scene has the appearance of a college prank. For the two dormitories, there are 56 kids and only one door out. If Xometla had a fire marshal, his star would be revoked.

Of course it used to be worse than this. Not long ago, all the girls had to sleep in with the smaller boys, all those kids in that one room with one exit. But lately the Confessional has been particularly vengeful, so the padre is able to rent two tiny rooms across the street from the church. He puts his 14 girls in there, along with the three women—kind of a permanent slumber party without the popcorn— and one shower to share with 72 boys in the morning. Then again, with only a four-gallon hot-water tank, why bother?

Sleep, *cachorros.* Sleep, young lions, for the padre is going to keep his crummy appointment with the mountain this morning. He will wrestle two matches this week—at about $40 per match—and that means you not only will get three meals a day: he might even be able to buy you some coloring pencils so you can get your homework done. Sleep, for soon enough you will be shuffling half awake through the kitchen into the tiny dining hall, where you will lift your forks carefully to your mouths, trying hard to be sure that your elbow doesn't knock the fork out of the mouth of the one next to you. *Your turn. Now my turn.* Watching over your shoulder will be Jesus, painted splendidly on black velvet but illuminated disrespectfully by one tired light bulb, hanging by its cord as if from a noose, without the benefit of a fixture.

This overworked light can be a literal eyesore when 80 or so kids are jammed into the room, all trying to do their homework by the

60-watt, rust-rimmed bulb. But lousy light comes in handy at meal-time, when it helps the kids forget that what they are having for breakfast today is what they have had for breakfast five days out of the last six—refried beans and tortillas and three fingers of powdered milk.

Still, in a place where the most popular toys—practically the only toys, in fact—are two bald tires; where many of the children shiver in the moonlight, washing their clothes by hand so they have something to put on the next day; where toddlers wear old rags for diapers that are rarely changed in the course of a day; where the stench from the septic tank is sometimes the best cure for a hungry stomach; where, if you are lucky enough to have shoes and you begin to get too big for them, you simply cut out the toes; in a place such as that, the kids seem preposterously, impossibly happy.

And for that, one can thank only the size-XL-hearted wrestling priest of Xometla. So far this year, only three kids have run away from the orphanage—and one, Marco Anthony, came back. They stay, not because they would miss St. Michael's charm but because they think of the padre as their father—and who could ask for better?

"He doesn't beat me or kick me," says one boy. And besides, how many fathers get you to straighten up by giving you the bent-finger cry-uncle pressure grip? (That always brings them to their knees, at which point the padre graciously blesses them.) And how many fathers can show you the finger points of the fake roundhouse punch (a tip: always swing away from the audience) or the Chinese sternum crusher or the nose flattener or the kidney punch or the flying drop-kick? And then hear your confession five minutes later?

And how many priests have sacristy walls where Sly Stallone and Bruce Lee bodyguard the Virgin of Guadalupe? Where Elvis hangs next to the crucifix and where wrestling posters rub elbow pads with the Christmas Mass schedule? "It makes them feel comfortable," says the padre. "They can talk about Bruce Lee and Jesus and Elvis all at once."

The kids stay because he loves them. "We don't have much, but we come by things honestly," he says. "I don't treat them like this is an orphanage. I treat them like it's their own house."

He's right, of course, when he says they don't have much. With no money coming in from an archdiocese that has its own financial problems, and with monthly food costs of $1,200 (clothes are donated), their house is able to stay afloat only by virtue of money the padre gets from baptisms (16,000 pesos apiece or about $7), marriages ($12), special masses ($6), performances of his mariachi band and his electric band (he sings and plays the organ; the kids play bass, guitar and drums), donations and, of course, his moonlighting job as hero in the part-acrobatics, part-mayhem, part-Broadway world of Mexican professional wrestling.

And the wrestling priest of Xometla thanks heaven for that.

*And the Lord said unto Moses, I have seen this people, and behold,
it is a stiff-necked people.*

—Exodus 32:9

To wrestle professionally in Mexico, you must have a good name,
a second job and hair that you're not particularly attached to. Sooner
or later, as a promotional gambit, almost every wrestler in Mexico,
women included, gambles his or her hair on the outcome of a match.
You lose, you have your locks shorn by a barber right there in the
ring afterward.

Considering this, the money is lousy. The biggest wrestling star
in Mexico might make $200 per week, whereas Hulk Hogan proba-
bly grossed more than $2 million this year. No wonder so many Mex-
ican wrestlers wear masks.

The wrestling itself is based on quick feet and agility, as opposed
to American pro wrestling, which is based on quick mouths and good
wardrobe men. Mexican wrestling is at times intricately chore-
ographed, with three-man wrestling teams leaping over and under
one another in long strings of complicated moves, looking as though
they have practiced together for years, which, of course, they have.
Fighting in three-somes allows infinitely more possibilities for anar-
chy and mayhem, even though there are two referees. One ref's job is
primarily to act confused.

The names are different, too. They are less names, really, than
abstract notions: the Fear, the Horror, Man of a Thousand Masks (or
his brother, Man of a Hundred Faces). There are also the standard
demons: the Nazi, Medico Asesino (Dr. Death), Ormuz the Viking
God and the Ghost. These are the *rudos,* the bad guys. The good guys
are the *tecnicos,* and they often wear masks, too.

"The mask gives you an air of mystery," says the padre. The
good guys always prevail over the bad guys, which is not the case in
American pro wrestling, but not before the bad guys win one fall out
of the three and quite nearly win a second.

Fray Tormenta is a good guy even the bad guys like. The other
day, the Spectrum, one of the baddest of the bad guys, brought two
bags of rice to the orphanage. Ormuz, whom the father beat out of his
huge head of hair one night, appears to hold no grudges and, in fact,
came to Xometla the other day to help the father put on an exhibition for his kids, who rarely get to see him wrestle. And in Mexico
City in late November, almost 20,000 people packed Arena Mexico
for a benefit for the padre's children. Everybody came to see the good
father win his match. (You beat the padre on his benefit night and
you can kiss eternal salvation goodbye.) Six million pesos (about
$2,600) was raised. Of course, Father Gutierrez hasn't gotten it yet
and he's not entirely sure he will. In Mexico, nothing is a lock.

If he does, it will be his biggest payday yet and more than he has
made in some years. In 1978, for instance, when he was living and
working in Veracruz, the padre was trying to keep 14 kids fed and

warm. He wasn't doing so well at it. Seven of the kids slept in his car and the other seven with him on the sidewalk.

Things are slightly better these days, but the padre's car at times still serves as sleeping quarters. For an out-of-town match, the promoter sends him plane fare and hotel money. The padre will save the pesos by driving to the match, even if it means a 17-hour haul, one way, as it once did. He'll then wrestle his 20 minutes and drive back, pulling over to sleep when he is tired. "To accept luxury would be taking food out of the mouths of the children," he says.

The padre is nuts about children, any kind of children—runaways, drug addicts, children of prostitutes and abandoned kids. These, of course, are mostly what the padre has already and what he takes in all the time. His crumbling church may be packed to the pigeonholes with hungry children, but the father isn't much good at saying no. He used to have only 45 kids. Thanks to the Mexico City earthquake of two years ago and to new poverty caused by runaway inflation, he keeps adding more. He has taken in eight new ones in the last two months alone, including a three-month-old. And there are plenty more where they came from.

Between 80,000 and 90,000 homeless children walk the streets of Mexico City, according to the padre, all part of a parade of beggars, hawkers, thieves, jugglers, schemers and fire-swallowers trying to scrounge their next meal in the world's most populous metropolitan area. Most of the padre's kids were part of that parade. Anita, 5, was found by the padre's sister lying under a blanket in Mexico City. Alfredo, 14, slept in the subways for two years before he heard about the wrestling priest and begged enough bus fare to come to St. Michael's. Sergio, 15, was a thief. He would steal—"money, cars, whatever," he says—to buy drugs and food.

The padre loves them because he sees himself in them. Growing up in Mexico City, he smoked marijuana and was called "the Crook" by other members of the gang he ran with. He was also the best athlete in the group. He was handy with his fists and was good enough to play soccer professionally for one year, 1961, when he was 16 years old. But his life didn't change for good until the day he went to confession and told the priest he didn't feel worthy of forgiveness. The father convinced him that he could be a fine priest someday.

After being ordained in 1969, he began taking in orphans. One day four years later, he was watching wrestlers on TV when he heard about the "great sums of money" wrestlers made, and he told himself, I could do that. But he couldn't do it because no one would teach him. "Nobody wanted the competition," he says. Finally a wrestler named the Leader agreed to show him a few moves and holds. For a year he learned the ropes until the day came for his first professional match. Against—who else?—the Leader.

"The leader must not have taught me *everything*," the padre says. "I lost."

Since then, he has found his way. Now he is one of Mexico's most popular wrestlers, and he hasn't lost in the last six months. Heaven hath no fury like a priest trying to make a truck payment. The Mexican people eat it up. When someone throws Fray Tormenta out of the ring, mothers and children jump out of their seats, dust him off and give him a boost back through the ropes. Fans often toss money onto the canvas after his matches. Sometimes, as he's walking up the aisles to the changing room, the people's handshakes contain money. Even the photographers help out. They always shoot the padre from the feet up. "To make me look like a giant," he says. He's 5'7" and weighs about 200 pounds.

At his age and size, the father needs all the help he can get. In fact he probably stays alive in wrestling only because the people *will* it to be so. After all, who can really believe his eyes when a man usually twice his opponent's age and half his strength cleans up so consistently? All is forgiven, though, when a man is eye-gouging for the Lord.

Besides, who wants to be the one to tell the padre it's time to hang up his boots? And then tell his kids?

For we wrestle not against flesh and blood, but against . . . the rulers of the darkness of this world.

—Ephesians 6:12

You figure God is in the padre's corner?

"Whoso sheddeth man's blood, by man shall his blood be shed: for in the image of God made he man," says the Bible (Genesis 9:6). It also says (Psalm 37:8), "Cease from anger, and forsake wrath." Ever see a wrestler refrain from either?

Father Gutierrez has suffered broken ribs, twisted shoulders, broken fingers. Could he have wrestled 14 years without anointing others with the same punishment? Wrestling is so bloody in Mexico that it was taken off television for the children's sake. And the padre wrestles *for* his children? In Mexico pro wrestlers have actually been killed. This is not exactly ministering to the sick.

And what of the deceit inherent in pro wrestling? Not every fan knows that the wrestlers play it the way the promoter's script reads. Isn't the priest, then, in the business of lying? Perhaps he wears the mask to hide his face from God?

The padre's superior, Monsignor Magin Torreblanca, the bishop of Texcoco, has never given permission for Father Gutierrez to wrestle professionally. Then again, he has never tried to stop him. He simply looks the other way.

"At first, I didn't approve," says Monsignor Torreblanca. "But since what he does helps the children, then I approve. If he were to change his priorities—say, first came wrestling, then came the church—I would not approve. But he is giving his life for those children."

Says Father Gutierrez, "I think God approves. Otherwise He

would send something to hurt me. And He hasn't done that."

The padre justifies the occasional atomic knee drop as a gift from God to keep his children fed. "The Bible says 'Turn the other cheek,' but when you're in the ring, you sometimes forget you are a priest," says the padre. "And, actually, your opponents forget, too."

He also says, "I want people to see wrestling not as violent but as beautiful, elegant, artistic. I don't think the people who watch me see me as sanguinary. I think they just see me as someone who is trying to fight a good fight."

Jacob wrestled his angel. Jesus got violent in the temple. And the Bible says of the Lord, "his enemies shall lick the dust." What's wrong with trying to make poverty lick the mat?

And besides, Father Gutierrez doesn't totally ignore his vocation when he's in the ring. Once in a while he might lose track of what he's doing and put a sleeper hold on one of the referees, then, seeing his mistake, bless the man. One time he married two wrestlers in a ring —with his mask on. *If anybody should know any reason why these two should not be joined, let him step into the Confessional.*

The ones to worry about, perhaps, are his Catholic opponents. At Arena Mexico, the wrestlers pray to a small shrine of Jesus before walking to the ring. How much guilt, then, does a Catholic wrestler absorb when he gives a poor priest who runs an orphanage the old over-the-knee back buster? "Sometimes it doesn't seem right," says Ormuz the Viking God. "Sometimes I get upset. But then I remember that I am helping the children and it feels good again."

This is one strange soup of life. Take, for instance, the 3 x 5 file card containing his Sunday schedule, which his secretary hands the padre every Saturday night. A typical one reads something like this:

8 a.m.—Mass, St. Miguel's

9—Mass, St. Luca's (in the mountains)

10—Mass, St. Luca's

10:30—Baptism, St. Luca's

11:30—Mass, Maquixco (nine miles away)

1 p.m.—Mass, St. Miguel's

2—Baptism, St. Miguel's

2:30—Special Mass, St. Miguel's

3—Special Mass, St. Miguel's

4—Mass, St. Pedro's (six miles away)

5—Confessions

6—Wrestling match in Acolman (vs. the Leader, best of three falls)

7:30 to 9—Mariachi performance in town festival

"And at nine o'clock," he says with a grin, "I fall in bed like a rock."

For now, though, he dons his bright, multicolored uniform and begins to think of his lines. He's been over this a thousand times. He knows he must project the right image. He prays silently. All eyes will be on him. Soon someone will come for him, and he will walk through a huge door and enter his private stage.

A match against the Gravedigger? Nah. Vespers.

I have fought the good fight, I have finished my course, I have kept the faith.

—1 Timothy 4:7

It will not be the most *feliz* of *navidads* at St. Michael's this year.

All the kids are supposed to bring an ornament to school to help decorate the town during the nine-day *posadas,* the traditional Christmas festivities, but the padre doesn't know where he's going to get the money. He gathers the kids around him in the courtyard.

"Tell your teachers I just cannot afford ornaments this year," he says. "Maybe next year."

The ornaments are just one of the things that won't get crossed off the padre's Christmas list. "Chicken," he says. "The kids would love to have chicken for Christmas dinner. Some have never even tasted chicken. But it's too expensive." So are toys. And decorations. And pinatas. And candy inside the pinatas.

But all that he can live without. The thing the padre really wants for Christmas is his *Cuidad de los Cachorros,* his "city of young lions."

Not more than a five-minute walk from St. Michael's are 10 acres of land the father has purchased to build what he hopes will be a real home, a place with more than one bathroom. It took the padre 10 years to save up the $3,200 it cost to buy the land. It will take another 150 million pesos, about $66,000, to build the home. Right now the padre has 7 million pesos in the bank, plus 6 million (light a candle) coming from the wrestling benefit. Somebody donated an old Renault to the church, and for that he thinks he could get another million pesos ($444). O.K., only 136 million pesos to go. . . .

And, oh, if it ever gets built! "Eight dormitories, big, beautiful dormitories, room enough for all the kids to sleep," he says. "Eight bathrooms, one for every dormitory. It will have a big kitchen, a playground, and a big dining hall with many lights. . . . This is why I fight."

If it ever gets built. Without some divine intervention, it may not. In fact, never mind the new home for a moment. And never mind the ornaments. How much longer can the padre keep food on the table?

"I can wrestle 15 more years," he says, but his body makes you wonder if he can go 15 more days. No problem, he says. He is undergoing a strange medical treatment in which, he says, fluid from a pig's brain is periodically injected into his system. "It will keep my body preserved longer," he says. "Besides, I may be 42, but remember, I'm a priest. I've had no wine, no women, no all-night parties. I've kept in condition."

The padre will probably not make 15 years, but he has got a backup plan. He's training four disciples—three of his boys and a girl—in the beat-up ring behind the church. They all wrestle with masks, and they're all spinoffs of their padre: Tormenta Jr., Tormenta II, etc. The oldest is 15.

But, honestly, without wrestling, can the orphanage even make it?

"No way," says Father Gutierrez. "It's the only way I know to make enough money. I don't know anything else. What would happen to the kids?"

Behold, this dreamer cometh.

—Genesis 37:19

And now, in the midnight blackness, the red-eyed, sore-boned wrestling priest of Xometla comes back to his corner of the sleeping-room-only bedroom at St. Michael's. It has been a long drive home, yet he didn't take his mask off the whole way. You wear the uniform, you stay with the mystery.

He won his match, but a few more victories like this and he'll be broke. The pay was less than $40. And it is not getting any easier to hammer at the devil by day and body-slam *rudos* by night.

He is tired. He longs to be a rock in the bed. He unlaces the mask from the back and pulls it slowly over his head to reveal his weary face.

There's no mystery. If He were here today, trying to keep 86 children warm and fed and out of the streets, would the face of Jesus look very different?

Judge's Comments

Sometime during this primaries-crowded year, a columnist observed that honest emotion seems illegal "in presidential politics and professional wrestling." Rick Reilly's article about the wrestling priest of Xometla shows once again that pundits can be wrong. This is an emotional article; as honest as it is unusual, as interesting as it is readable.

Whether you "believe" in professional wrestling as a legitimate sport or not, you have to believe in Father Sergio Gutierrez (alias Fray Tormenta and Brother Tempest) and his complex little world. Reilly uses the true writer's eye to convince us of this strange reality: scenes, dialogue, little details and subtle commentary. The violent culture of the ring and the impoverished culture of rural Mexico are made to mix nicely for the reader.

Because sports is big news and big industry in this country, many writers concentrate on the events and on the dollars. This is not a story about salary arbitration or about final scores. The rich are nowhere in this yarn. And the final score apparently is being toted by an unseen referee.

Reilly is a consummate story-teller. He hasn't forgotten why we love sports so much: each game or match is a self-contained fairy tale that entertains and distracts. What Reilly adds in this story is the reminder that sport at any level is accomplished by beings with human problems and skills. And a good story-teller compels us to root for those humans even though they have neither agents nor cereal endorsements nor national TV exposure. Readers will find this article entertaining even if they dislike pro wrestling—even if they hate sports.

Best Feature Photo
Jump For Joy

by Louis DeLuca of the Dallas Times Herald. DeLuca caught the
unexpected, joyous reaction of weightlifter Marlan Ingram after
his successful deadlift at the 1987 National Powerlifting Championship. Consistently capturing unexpected, revealing moments
is the signature of great sports photographers. DeLuca certainly
qualifies on that count. This is his third straight Best Sports
Stories winner and he has won in the black-and-white category
four of the last five years. Copyright © 1987, Louis DeLuca, Dallas
Times Herald.

Best Action Photo
Stranglehold

by Larry Steagall of The Sun in Bremerton, Wash. Steagall has captured a remarkable confrontation between Xavier McDaniel of the Seattle SuperSonics and Wes Matthews of the Los Angeles Lakers. McDaniel's stranglehold on Matthews vividly demonstrates the excesses that can occur in high-stress, high-stakes professional athletics. Copyright © 1987, Larry Steagall, The Sun.

Best Feature Story

Chaney Has Held On To His Dream

COLLEGE BASKETBALL

By *JERE LONGMAN*

From the Philadelphia Inquirer
Copyright © 1987, the Philadelphia Inquirer

Above the desk in his crowded rectangle of an office, John Chaney has hung a painting of a little boy sleeping. The boy is wrapped in a rag of a blanket and he sleeps on a bare mattress in a room where plaster has fallen in cakes from the wall. It appears to be a shivery night, but the boy sleeps soundly. He has two things going for him. One is the football tucked next to the blanket. The other is his dreams.

John Chaney looks at that painting and sees his own reflection. A poor young boy facing the rupturing blight of poverty and racism. A boy who worked for dimes in the cafeterias of Jacksonville, Fla., to help support his mother while his stepfather headed up north to find work. A young basketball player who was the Philadelphia Public League player of the year in 1951, but who was overlooked by the local colleges because of his color, not his skill. A young man who faced the same racial barriers with the NBA four years later. A young coach who worked, uncomplainingly, through the junior high and high school ranks, who moved on to Cheyney State and won a Division II national championship in 1978, and who finally, at age 50, got his first shot at a Division I job.

The hard life made John Chaney tough and aggressive and impassioned, but not bitter or resentful. He bided his time, looked both ways at each stop along the way and waited patiently for a shot at the big time. When Temple offered the brass ring four seasons ago, Chaney grabbed. Now he has the Owls roosting high in the wire-service polls, and there is murmured talk of the Final Four. Chaney knew of the possibilities all along. The only thing he ever lacked was an opportunity. He didn't have much when he grew up. But he did have his dreams.

"A lot of me has been without a lot," Chaney said. "We didn't have much, but we did have a good attitude about trying to achieve, of having hope. When you have hope, you tend to do positive, constructive things in life. Once your hopes are destroyed, everything is gone. That's why I'm so aggressively against anyone or anything that would deny a young man an opportunity to get on with his life. Like Proposition 48, which dictates a young man's opportunity based on a test score. Once that opportunity is destroyed hope is destroyed."

★   ★   ★

If you are sitting in your seat at a Temple game, it is a safe bet that John Chaney is not sitting in his. He stalks the sideline, volatile, snarling—barking, he calls it—tie loosened, arms flailing, veins straining in his neck, screaming at his players, harranguing the referees, sometimes even challenging other coaches.

"He's not a drinking man, but he's got that whiskey voice," said Clarence (Bighouse) Gaines, the legendary coach at Winston-Salem who tried to recruit Chaney out of Ben Franklin High. "And he's got those eyes. Gray, cat eyes. Strange-looking eyes."

John Chaney never howls at his players when they are behind. He sits, eyes wide, face transfixed in a death stare. "I'm afraid to say anything when we're behind," he said. "I'm too worried we're going to lose."

It's when Temple is ahead that Chaney does his best Mount St. Helens impersonation. His most infamous explosion took place on February 22, 1984, during halftime of a game Temple won over George Washington, 93-77. To Chaney, it seemed as if the George Washington center, Mike Brown, was throwing left hooks instead of hook shots inside. Chaney brought the point up in a courtious debate with George Washington Coach Gerry Gimelstob and made his point by grabbing Gimelstob around the neck.

As the debate continued, Chaney pointed a finger in Gimelstob's face and said, "I'll knock you out and you know it."

Soon, the fighters were dispatched to neutral corners, and later Gimelstob and Chaney shook hands. "I've had my skirmishes with other coaches," Chaney said after the game. "I've gotten too involved with what's happening out on the court. It's normally been my fault. I've gotten carried away."

Gimelstob is out of coaching now and in real estate. He shrugs off the incident. "Someone once said to me that your greatest strength can also be your greatest weakness," he said. "But I don't see that as a weakness in John. He's emotional. He has to be honest with himself. He can't hide it. As long as your people understand you, it's OK. I have no ax to grind. John's teams always play hard, and they always play under control. In all the time I coached, I don't think we played against a tougher inside player than Granger Hall. I still have dreams of him dunking on my team.

"It was an unfortunate incident. John felt badly. I felt badly. But actually, we get along pretty well. After that, we recruited some of the same players, and that incident was never brought up. There was nothing but straightforward recruiting by two coaches."

Jim O'Brien, now the coach at Boston College, had a heated word or two with Chaney while at St. Bonaventure. He, too, sees nothing malevolent about such heat-of-the-moment exchanges. "The problem with John is that sometimes he points his finger right up in your face, and nobody likes that to happen," O'Brien said. "But if you talk to him about it afterward, he'll probably have no recollection of doing that. He's an intense guy. It's just part of the temperament that makes him a good coach."

Some of the feistier crowds in the Atlantic 10 have laid traps, trying to turn Chaney's emotions against him. At St. Bonaventure, they used to incite him by showering the court with coins. Chaney, O'Brien said, once threatened to go into the stands. O'Brien once tried to have the Bonnies' band placed directly behind the Temple bench, but the Franciscan priests wouldn't allow it.

"Yeah, it used to be a class place," Chaney said, laughing. "They'd throw nickels and dimes, and my players would walk around and gather them up and give them to me. One time they threw quarters. That was really big time. Now, they just throw toilet paper. It's not fair."

West Virginia is a tough crowd, too, but nothing was tougher than Chaney's days at Cheyney State, when his team paid an annual social visit to Gannon College in Erie. "They used to hang up 'Wanted' posters with my picture on 'em," Chaney laughed uproariously. "It was a tough place. We used to have to put on our uniforms before we got there, drive up in the van and play, and rush right out afterward. They used to throw Dynamints, and the police brought dogs when Cheyney came to play. Their athletic director used to say, 'There are only two people who draw in Erie—Frank Sinatra and John Chaney, and not necessarily in that order.' "

Why is Chaney so passionate, so incendiary on the court? Why does he wear his heart and soul on his sleeve the way his players wear numbers on their jerseys?

"That has to come from being poor, and wanting to go farther," said Jay Norman, a former Temple star who is now Chaney's assistant and close friend. "If you don't fight for a piece of the earth, no one's going to give it to you."

"It comes from facing racism his whole life, always being told you can't succeed, doors always closing in your face, and being determined to succeed," said UCLA Coach Walt Hazzard, a Chaney protege.

Dreams. The little kid sleeping with the ball. Hoping. Dreaming.

"I don't think it has anything to do with color, or growing up disadvantaged," Chaney said. "It's just an attitude I developed as a result of being around people who had to make do with a little, or who had to make something from nothing. I've never been able to turn the electric switch to make the lights come on. I always have to rub two sticks together."

Attitude. It's on a billboard alongside the Ben Franklin Bridge. It's on the cover of the media guide. It's always on Chaney's lips. Attitude. Winning is an *attitude.*

"A true athlete, to be truly great, should go out there with the attitude that if somebody sticks a finger in his mouth, he should bite it off, not lick it," Chaney said. "I want my players to take up my value system. Some people say I might be causing my players great damage by yelling at them. Unfortunately, it's the only way I know. I don't have all the psychological means of educational warfare at my disposal.

"Anyway, the kids have an easier job than I do. I have to understand all of them. They only have to stand one of me. I'm a barking guy, but it's like Nixon once said—it's not me people dislike, it's the things I do. When you separate behavior from personality, when the players know you're not getting on them because of their personality, then they understand. They're tough. They can take it."

That's the contradiction about John Chaney. The screaming stops once the game ends. The passion becomes compassion. Last month at Kansas, Nate Blackwell missed two three-point attempts in the final four seconds as Temple lost, 67-64, but instead of walking away in disgust, Chaney searched out Blackwell and embraced him in a hug. On January 24, after witnessing his snowbound team travel for 36 hours, arrive at 7 a.m. for a noon game, and defeat Alabama-Birmingham, 67-60, Chaney cried in the postgame interview.

"I was so proud of their effort, it brought tears to my eyes," he said.

*   *   *

Chaney lived at 17th and Ellsworth when he was a kid, and in some ways, he has never left the old neighborhood. Even now, rather than spend the money on an extravagant pair of new eyeglasses, Chaney borrows his wife Jeanne's. "We have the same vision. We're married, aren't we?"

His close friends remain the same close friends from the old days: Jay Norman, his assistant; Leon Whitley, his backcourt mate at Ben Franklin, who went to Winston-Salem and later lured a kid named Earl Monroe there; Hubert Hemsley, his college roommate at Bethune-Cookman, now a doctor in Compton, Calif.; Victor Harris, who played at West Philly and later coached Chaney in the Narberth Summer League, despite the handicap of polio.

"I couldn't afford car fare, so Victor used to come pick me up and drive me all the way out to Narberth and back," Chaney said. "He perhaps more than any other person, symbolizes that regardless of what happens to you in life, you just keep going and don't complain."

Keep going. Don't complain. At Cheyney State, the cafeteria was closed during the Christmas holidays, so Chaney used to cook for his players. He'd drive 35 miles to the gym early each morning with doughnuts and juice, put a frozen batch of hamburgers or stew on a double-burner stove in the gymnasium, run his players through practice, and serve them lunch at 11. In 1978, a flu epidemic left the campus quarantined after Christmas, and when the food-service people either couldn't or wouldn't open the cafeteria, Chaney cooked for anyone who wanted to eat.

"Served three meals a day," he said. "I'd go to the store and get these big aluminum pans and dozens and dozens of eggs. When you cook in an aluminum pan, it turns the eggs green. The kids would say, "We're not gonna eat these green eggs.' I said, "Shut up and eat.'

"We had a lot of things going on that year, but we still won the championship. I don't know how we did it, but we did it. We didn't complain. It's like looking at a yoke—you either put your head through it and pull, or put your shoulder on it and push."

★   ★   ★

It is 6 a.m. on February 6. The campus is still heavy-lidded, except for McGonigle Hall, which is brightly lit and filled with the sound of John Chaney's voice, like the sound of a subway car screeching to a halt. Eight and a half hours ago, Temple defeated Rhode Island here, 87-75. Now the Owls are back for a morning workout.

"Wakes them up for class," Chaney says.

He is not satisfied this morning. Not with Nate Blackwell's 31 points, or Ramon Rivas' career-high 22, or with an incredible blocked shot that Howard Evans, all of 6-foot-1, pinned on the backboard above the rim. Something else has caught the coach's eye: 11 turnovers.

John Chaney has distilled the game of basketball down to one measurable statistic. Turnovers. To him, that's the heart of the game. Don't turn the ball over. That way you'll get more shots. And if you get more shots than the other guy and play alert defense, you'll be in every game. The Owls average only 9.7 turnovers a game. That's why Temple has, on occasion, shot 37 percent and still won.

"They take care of the ball as well as any team I've seen play," said Boston College's O'Brien.

Not against Rhode Island, they didn't. Not enough to satisfy Chaney, anyway. "I'm going to get T-shirts for each of you, and I'm going to put a big S on the front," he yells at his players. "And we'll get capes. And put a big S on the capes. And you can tell everyone, all the people out there, that it stands for Superman. But you'll know, and I'll know, that it stands for S---head."

Chaney is particularly bothered by a blind pass that was thrown by Evans. The ball was thrown into the corner. To no one. Either someone was supposed to be there, or Evans thought someone was supposed to be there, but no one was. He threw the ball to no one, and it bounced off the wall. Airball.

"My mother wouldn't throw that pass," Chaney barks at Evans. "You still wearin' contacts? Better exchange them for bifocals. Or maybe you need glasses on the side of your head. Or one big lens on the back of your head, like a big Cyclops."

Everyone laughs. No one takes it personally.

Now Chaney is blistering someone else. Blackwell. He remembers a similar pass that Blackwell threw into the corner, threw to no one. Chaney is convinced that it happened a few weeks ago.

"No, Coach, that was against Wyoming," Blackwell says.

Wyoming was two years ago.

That's how much John Chaney hates turnovers.

★   ★   ★

Fifty-four years ago, John Chaney was born into the projects of Jacksonville, Fla. World War II came on, and his stepfather left the family for a year and headed north to find work as a carpenter. "He figured he could avoid the draft, the war if he worked in a defense plant," Chaney said. "So he came to Chester, to work in the shipyards."

His stepfather sent money back to Jacksonville, and eventually he sent for the family. In the meantime, Chaney worked at a cafeteria in Jacksonville, as a busboy, as a waiter, adding piggy-bank money to his mother's meager salary.

"Every day they'd pick 10 or 12 boys to be waiters, 10 or 12 to be busboys," Chaney said. "We'd go there and stand in line in our bowties, red coat, black pants, black shoes, hoping to get picked. If your fingernails were dirty, they sent you home. If your shoes were dirty, they sent you home. If your shirt was dirty, they sent you home. I was good at busing tables, so they let me get in line and wait tables. Somebody might leave a dime tip on the tray, and you'd pick up two trays and there'd be two dimes. I'd bring home $3 a night, $4 a night, to help my mom. She'd work in somebody's house, cleaning up their home. We didn't have a lot, but it was enough to get by on."

When the Chaney family settled in Philadelphia at 17th and Ellsworth, John attended Barrett Junior High. His best friend, Leon Whitley, remembers that the Chaneys didn't have much. They lived over a garage, and Whitley used to joke that it was colder inside the house than outside. What toys Chaney and his friends had, they made for themselves. They fashioned skatemobiles from cardboard boxes, and they made their own movies, pasting the comic strips together with flour, wrapping them around sticks and rolling them through a cigar-box projector.

"All the Milton Bradley stuff, we did on our own," Chaney said. "Our lives were small things and nothing."

The Barrett schoolyard was five or six blocks away, and Chaney spent his time there, playing basketball against other kids for nickels, working on his shooting and ball handling. Basketball wasn't tough. Persuading his stepfather to let him play was tough.

"John wanted to play ball. His father wanted him to work," Whitley said. "His mother let him play. If it was up to John's father, he would have picked up a towel and started washing cars."

His mother won out. Chaney played basketball at Ben Franklin, and in 1951 he was named MVP of the Public League. Tom Gola was MVP of the Catholic League. Gola went to LaSalle. Chaney wanted to stay in Philadelphia, but it didn't work out, because his skin was the wrong color. Blacks were rarely offered scholarships to the local colleges in those days. Jackie Moore was at LaSalle, Sam Sylvester was at Temple. That was it.

"I wanted to play in town, but no one offered me a scholarship," he said.

Bighouse Gaines came to Franklin High one day, looking to sign Chaney up for Winston-Salem. Chaney was absent that day, so he wound up following Hubert Hemsley of West Philly to Bethune-Cookman in Daytona Beach, Fla.

It was at Bethune-Cookman, Chaney said, that he realized that the academic dog wagged the athletic tail, and not the other way around. "My reasons for going were selfish—to play basketball," Chaney said. "My roommate, Hubert Hemsley, made me see how important education was. He was the backbone of my education. He was a pre-med student. He made sure I got out of bed and went to class. He's the reason I got my degree. And on time."

Bethune-Cookman was buzzing with dignitaries in the early '50s. The college president, Mary M. Bethune, served as an adviser in the Franklin Roosevelt and Harry Truman administrations and was the first black woman to head a federal agency. Eleanor Roosevelt visited the campus often, so did Ralph Bunche, undersecretary of the United Nations from 1955 to 1971, as well as sports figures such as Jackie Robinson and Branch Rickey.

"We were exposed to all these world leaders, and the demands put on us were something," Chaney said. "Reading, writing, arithmetic, those were the basics. You had to have them or you didn't graduate. One time I remember a guy, a senior, who walked into the dean's office and said, 'Are the dean in?' And Mrs. Bethune said, 'What did you say?' And he said, 'Are the dean in?' And she said, 'Yes, the dean *are* in, and you *are* staying in school another year.' "

It was also at Bethune-Cookman that Chaney came face-to-face with the festering rawness of racism. The separate drinking facilities for blacks and whites. Going around to the back door of restaurants with his teammates, so they could get food on road trips. Going to New Orleans to play Xavier and sitting in the "colored" section of a movie house with his teammates while whites pelted them with ice cream. Driving slowly through the small towns of Tennessee and Alabama—"almost pushing the van," Chaney said—for fear of being pulled over and hassled by white sheriffs.

"In Daytona, blacks had to have a passport to work in the white areas around the beaches," Hemsley said. "In the four years I was there, I saw the ocean three times. But I think we, John and I, were able to take that anger and fuel it in a more positive direction."

Chaney's outlet was basketball. On the court, he was as feisty a player as he is now a coach. "I had a mean streak," he said.

"Don't try to take the ball off him," Jay Norman said. "You'd get an elbow upside the head."

In the summers, Chaney used to come home and play in the Narberth Summer League. Once a summer, the best of the Philly players would play the best of the New York players. Chaney was at Bethune-Cookman, Wilt Chamberlain was still at Overbrook High. They played on the same Philly all-star team. Chamberlain was the giant, Chaney was in charge.

"One time we were playing, Philly versus New York, and I took a shot from the corner, tried to put it off the backboard, and Wilt just grabbed the ball and put it in," Chaney said. "At that time, there were no basketball people Wilt's size. There were no rules governing goaltending—offensive or defensive. Wilt could just grab one of his teammates' shots and get credit for it, and there were no rules to stop him from covering up the basket at the other end and not letting anything in. So when he grabbed my shot, I called time out. I was the star. I walked up to Wilt and said, "I don't care what you do, but don't you touch *my* shot.' He just looked at me and didn't say anything. I was the boss. He didn't say a word. No siree. And he didn't touch another shot, either."

In 1953, Chaney was named MVP of the NAIA playoffs. He also got a taste of coaching. The coach at Bethune-Cookman, a man named Rudolph "Bunky" Matthews, was, by all accounts, a brilliant orator and riveting motivator, a man who could quote Shakespeare at length, but who supposedly had one small flaw: He liked to bend his elbow. In those days, the coach drove the players from game to game in a van, and a van trip might run 300 miles, and after all that traveling, sometimes a man just needed to quench his thirst.

"Coach had one failing—he liked to booze," Hemsley said. "Once, we were playing Sam Jones' team—it's called North Carolina Central now—and Coach was out of it. John had to coach us through the second half."

Chaney quickly found a style that suited him. "I did a lot of screaming," he said.

After college, the NBA should have followed. It didn't. Once again, race was the barrier. "John had the talent to play in the NBA," said former Temple great Guy Rodgers, who played in the NBA in the '50s and '60s. "But there was an (unwritten) quota about how many blacks could be on a team. A lot of people don't want to admit that. John was truly one of the great ball handlers no one's ever seen. I learned a lot from him."

Chaney tried the Globetrotters for a while, but he didn't like the staged games, the prearranged outcome against teachers and businessmen. So he traveled the Eastern League for 10 years, where he was six times an all-star, and the MVP in 1959-60. He went into coaching at Sayre Junior High and built a 68-9 record. Then he went to Simon Gratz High at the behest of principal Marcus Foster trying to polish Gratz's tarnished image.

"When I first got there, we had a sports banquet, where the athletic department got together and got all these prizes for the kids—gloves, bicycles, jackets," Chaney said. "But the kids doubted themselves so much, had such a low self-esteem, that when we called their names to come on stage and get their prize, many refused to come up."

In one year, Chaney turned a 1-17 team around to 17-1. By the time Chaney left, he had compiled an 84-6 record in 10 years at Cheyney State, he won one Division II national championship, and four times he was named coach of the year in the Pennsylvania State Athletic Conference. The administration gave him a pat on the back, but it wouldn't give him a full professorship in health and physical education. So, when Temple came knocking, he answered the door.

Had he been awarded a full professorship at Cheyney, he said, "I'd still be there."

At Temple, Chaney moved home games from the Palestra onto campus at McGonigle Hall and got big-name teams such as UCLA, Kansas, Virginia and Alabama-Birmingham onto the nonconference schedule. And he set out to win. That he has done 105 times in Temple's last 126 games. Not bad for a guy who grew up with nothing but his dreams.

"No coach in the country's had a tougher road to success than John Chaney," Walt Hazzard said.

It's attitude. Winning is an attitude.

"Talent will only get you so far," Chaney said. "You need one other dimension—attitude. If you wake up with sunshine in your heart even when it's raining outside, you'll get something accomplished."

Judge's Comments

"What's he like?"

It's a question often asked of reporters when people learn that you know someone in the public eye.

Jere Longman of the *Philadelphia Inquirer* answered that question about John Chaney for thousands of readers. This profile examines Chaney from his roots forward. Longman has produced a profile that is tough, honest and frank, just like Chaney.

How does Longman do it?

First, with good reporting. We go back with Chaney to his youth to understand Chaney the adult. We hear Chaney say, *"A lot of me has been without a lot. We didn't have much, but we did have a good attitude about trying to achieve, of having hope."*

Chaney is quotable, and Longman uses quotes as well, but he also provides context and perspective. He has talked to Chaney's opponents and to his friends. What emerges is a well-rounded portrait. As Longman writes, *"The screaming stops once the game ends. The passion becomes compassion."*

What distinguishes this entry from many other excellent ones is that it combines good reporting with equally good story-telling skills. That makes it easy on the reader. It's a long story, but the time passes quickly. And when you are done, you will know what John Chaney is like.

Best Reporting Story

Big Gamble: Betting And Broncomania

PRO FOOTBALL

By *NORM CLARKE*

From the Rocky Mountain News
Copyright © 1987, Denver Publishing Co.

House, Car, Savings Bet in Frenzy
(First of two parts)

Hours before the Super Bowl XXI kickoff, a telephone rang in a Beverly Hills hotel room. Answering it was a gambler, one of Denver's "Dime" bettors. He's called that because he regularly bets $1,000 a game, whether on football, basketball or baseball.

In an unusual role reversal, a Denver bookie was calling to see if the bettor would take some action off his hands.

Broncomaniacs literally were betting the house. And the house payment. And the car. And the savings account—frequently taking their team without the points that were being offered.

It was a crisis for Denver's bookies.

"They were deluged. They wanted to get rid of some of the money," the dime player said. "They were so worried, they weren't taking any more bets."

A well-known Denver bookie confirmed the phenomenon:

"If Denver had won," he said, "every bookie in town would have disappeared. They wouldn't have had the money to cover the action."

It is impossible, of course, to verify how much money was wagered illegally in the Denver area on Super Bowl XXI. But sources on both sides of the law estimate it conservatively at $2 million to $3 million.

Millions more were bet legally by Coloradans who went to Nevada, some representing five-figure betting consortiums.

Whatever the total, the bettors in a state already awash in economic red ink took a bath when the New York Giants turned a close game into a 19-point rout.

A three-month investigation by the *Rocky Mountain News* pieced together a Super Bowl betting frenzy that ran the gamut from small change to six figures, from dollar-a-pop office pools to wagers in excess of $100,000.

"This whole town went crazy," said another big-time Denver bettor.

"Coloradans thought the Broncos were God's chosen team," added a Denver bookie.

At the epicenter was John Elway and The Drive—Keith Bishop's "we-got-'em-just-where-we-want-'em" machismo in the huddle on first-and-98—Elway's great escapes and laserlike passes in the clutch—Rick Karlis' winning overtime kick under a barrage of Clevelanders' dog biscuits.

"There's an unbelievable loyalty level here," said Dick McNamee, agent in charge of the Colorado Bureau of Investigation. "Emotion gets in the way of common sense."

★   ★   ★

Jay Coakley, professor of sociology at the University of Colorado at Colorado Springs and editor of an academic publication called *Sociology of Sports Journal,* offers this analysis of the madness:

"What we've done in society," he said, "is we've created this 'We're No. 1' ideology that creates impossible goals for any one of us as an individual. We've ascribed to that goal and realized it is impossible to achieve individually, so we identify with a group of athletes and hope that we vicariously experience that journey to becoming No. 1.

"I think it explains why people came out of the woodwork and acted so irrationally when Denver went to the Super Bowl. This was finally the chance to be No. 1.

"I had friends who never bet before," Coakley said, "but they ended up betting what I thought were unreasonable amounts of money—$100, $200. It was like a bet constituted a confirmation of our identity with the team."

Acute Broncomania? Dr. Gary May, president of the Colorado Psychiatric Society and a Denver native, believes that's only part of the reason someone would take such a risk.

"Some of the people you cite are pathological gamblers, people that have an illness, a compulsiveness," May said. "Professional gamblers often take advantage of those people because they are basically impaired. They lose all sense of logic: 'The team can absolutely do no wrong.' They are operating on this distorted emotional response."

The betting line opened at 8½ points in Las Vegas, and ranged from 6 to 9½ during Super Bowl week, depending on time and place. It was lower in Denver.

But the spread didn't really matter with Denver bettors. Not since the days of the gold rush and the Orange Crush has such passion swept through the town.

"It was the most unique situation I've seen in 25 years," one of Denver's longtime gamblers told the *News*.

"The bookies were trying to lay off back East. One flew to Vegas with $30,000. They were in a panic, afraid they wouldn't be able to pay. When it gets that lopsided, they become bettors instead of book-makers.

"The game was changed so much they did something I've never seen. If you wanted New York, you had to give 8 points, and if you wanted Denver, you got only 6 points.

"That tells me they were fearful. They tried to discourage good customers from betting on Denver."

Calls to Denver bookies began as soon as the early line was an-nounced, 13 days before the game. A city already bonkers over the Broncos started talking about what was considered a ridiculous spread, and plotting ways to take advantage of it.

At the Rangeview Liquor Store in Northglenn, owner John Cain and a few customers talked about going in together on a modest pot, a little something to bet in Las Vegas.

"We knew the local bookies would hose us (by giving fewer points)," said Cain, "and we knew a guy who was going to Vegas. So we started putting a package together."

Since Cain was merely holding money—not taking a percentage, which is called "vigorish" or a bookmaker's profit margin—he was not breaking a state law. Neither is it illegal to take a "package" to Nevada as long as there is no profit gained by transporting the bet.

Within days, word spread through north Denver and the kitty grew to $3,000. Then $5,000. Then $9,000.

"It got a little bigger than I wanted," said Cain, who kept a list of the bets in his back room.

The final figure was $9,300, he said. A friend insists it was closer to $30,000.

Half of it was bet on the Broncos with 3-1 odds. The other half: Broncos and 9 points.

Package bets from Denver poured into Las Vegas by car and plane.

In one such deal, a Denver-area farmer who raised almost $10,000 flew in, stayed just long enough to lay his bets, then flew back to Colorado.

At Caesars Palace, a Denver man watched incredulously as an-other bettor carrying three attache cases reached the front of the line. He told the clerk he wanted to bet the entire contents on the Broncos.

Within a minute, all betting windows were closed.

"They closed down for about an hour to decide whether to let him bet," said the Denverite, who asked not to be identified. "He wanted to put it in his business account rather than his personal account.

After he bet it, the odds dropped from 9½ to 8½. They say it takes $25,000 to change the odds a quarter of a point."

By midweek, the pilgrimage to Pasadena, Calif., was picking up speed, often with a stopover in Nevada. And for many Broncos fans who couldn't get Super Bowl tickets, the next best thing was a weekend at a Las Vegas casino.

In they streamed, in snazzy sports cars, campers, pickup trucks. Even an orange convertible.

"We had a ton of Denver fans in here, probably because of its proximity," said Mel Exber, director of the Las Vegas Club's sports and race book.

"The most unusual thing I saw was a Bronco fan come in with a handful of credit union checks."

Across town at the Hilton Hotel, Art Manteris watched in amazement as The Orange Shirts queued up at his betting windows.

Manteris is a Vegas whiz kid, 30 years old and already the director of the world's largest sports and race book.

★   ★   ★

Growing up in Pittsburgh during the glory days of Terry Bradshaw and Franco Harris, Manteris experienced what it's like when a town goes crazy over its football team. Even today, he admits, he has his staff at the Hilton decked out in Steelers colors. Still, Broncomania was a remarkable sight.

"Those people bleed orange," he said. "The most amazing thing was they didn't even want to bet Denver with 10 points; they wanted to bet straight up."

Exber saw the same trend that emerged at the Hilton.

"Twice as much money showed on straightup bets for the Broncos," said Exber. A straightup bet involves no odds. "They bet on the Giants to cover the point spread and Denver to win outright. It just didn't make sense.

"It was an unusual pattern of betting," Exber said. "But then, people come out of the woodwork for the Super Bowl. Anybody who would try to figure out why people do certain things would go nuts."

The Broncos' Bishop, for one, appreciates his team's financial followers. When the *News* told him and some teammates recently about the excesses of Broncomania last January, Denver's first Pro Bowl offensive lineman said:

"The only thing I can say about that whole situation is that most of the players I've talked to from other towns, other teams, are envious of us with our situation here and the fans we have.

"You hate to see anybody lose to gambling or any other way," Bishop added. "I'm sorry it happened. But it's like investing in oil or anything else—it's a gamble."

The quarterback for whom Bishop serves as bodyguard understands, too.

"I think the people in Denver are behind us so much—and had so much confidence in us going in," Elway said. "If I was a betting man,

I'd probably have done the same thing, with us getting 9 to 10 points.

"*If* I was a betting man," he emphasized. "I'm not."

Even with the heavy computerization of Nevada's gambling industry, there is no method to accurately determine how much was bet there by Broncos backers. But Manteris knows it was a big number.

He estimates that 60 percent of the $30 million bet—or almost $20 million—was on the Broncos. Manteris is convinced that betting on Super Bowl XXI exceeded all previous single-day sports wagering in Nevada, the only state in the U.S. where betting on team sports is legal.

He said the Hilton had one or two Broncos backers in the six-figure category.

"Our limit is $100,000, but that can go higher for some of our in-house guests and Hilton clients. We had people who went higher on the Broncos."

★   ★   ★

Vic Salerno, director of the sports book operation at Leroy's in Las Vegas, said he's never witnessed such frenzied betting.

At one point, all 15 betting windows at Leroy's had long lines during Super Bowl week, and "We had one guy who worked 10 hours a day and wrote 700 tickets in one shift."

One weekend arrival at Circus Circus on the Las Vegas Strip was a struggling Denver real estate agent.

On Wednesday of Super Bowl Week he found himself with a $2,000 check in hand, his commission from closing a sale.

His house was in foreclosure, and a $1,200 house payment was due in a week. But by Friday he was on the road, with his wife, three kids and a buddy. He had decided to put his money on Denver's favorite horses, even if they were distinct darkhorses.

After checking into his hotel room, the Denver real estate agent wagered $1,500 of the $2,000 on the Broncos. He got 9½ points, considerably more than he could have gotten from a Denver bookie.

"I don't think you could lose with that spread," he said later.

On Sunday, with the Broncos leading 10-9 at halftime, the spread looked even better.

He wasted 10 minutes mulling a new bet. Finally, he jumped in line to bet another $250.

To his chargin, the betting windows closed before he could get down. Later, he shrugged at that bit of luck and dismissed his larger misfortune.

"If you take everything into consideration, they beat us by a fluke," he was saying weeks after the game. "It was on grass and we've got the greatest quarterback in the world."

Losing his house was a very real possibility, but he was not worried.

"I've got 75 days to redeem," he said. "It's not my first time down that chute. I went bankrupt in 1968 and climbed out from underneath that. I know another couple who lost $10,000—blown out!"

For others, the agony of defeat was exceeded by the painful reality of loss.

Hours after New York's 39-20 victory, telephone lines lit up at Life Line of Colorado, a crisis intervention agency.

"We almost doubled our average," said Life Line director Art Ziemann, who handled 15 calls during his midnight-to-8 a.m. shift.

One despondent caller mentioned the Broncos and talked about suicide.

"He said it a couple of times and hung up," said Ziemann.

The next day, an elderly woman entered Cain's liquor store. She stood at the counter and cried.

And at Denver's chapter of Gamblers Anonymous, attendance jumped.

"There was an increase the week after the game and another burst a little after that," said a spokesman for the organization. That spokesman, a member of G.A., wouldn't elaborate on individual cases because G.A. is a confidential organization.

In north Denver, a man who bet the entire equity in his home on the Broncos was unable to cover his loss, said to be $23,000.

The man's bookie, unable to collect the bet in cash, tried to take the house by having the man sign a quit-claim deed.

The bettor's wife, however, threatened to go to the police. Instead of getting the house, the bookie settled for a weekly payoff arrangement. And the bettor stopped talking for fear the bookie would harm him.

"That's gospel," said one of three sources who confirmed the bet.

"We had that guy in here. And another guy who bet his Mustang," said a second source, Don Cianco II, manager of Mr. C's, a popular restaurant and tavern in Thornton.

When the Broncos returned to Denver the day after Super Bowl XXI, they were welcomed by an estimated 100,000 fans at a rousing downtown parade and Civic Center rally. In the crisp, spirited twilight, the city's collective embrace belied the fact that so many in the crowd had gambled on their heroes and lost.

But the players have been reminded of it almost daily during the past few months.

"I've heard nothing but that," Elway said, "people saying, 'I lost all that money in the Super Bowl,' and this and that. I've heard it all winter.

"I say, 'I'm sorry, but we gave everything we've got, everything we had.' "

Pro football players know, of course, that people gamble on their performances. Still, the magnitude of Denver's Super Bowl betting was a shock.

"I knew they supported us every week," said guard Paul Howard. "But I had no idea that people would bet their homes and cars. That's a little bit out of hand."

All-Pro linebacker Karl Mecklenburg agrees.

"It surprises me that people would gamble that much," he said. "I could see if they gambled and had enough to live on, but it doesn't make much sense to gamble away your house."

       ★   ★   ★

Howard, who missed Super Bowl XXI with a knee injury, played in Denver's first Super Bowl. There were bettors then, too, but more modest.

"I remember in 1977, when we came back," he said. "There was a big crowd at the airport, and I heard fans yell, 'You cost me $100. You cost me $50.' I'm thinking, 'That's nothing. I lost a bunch myself.'"

Howard was thinking of a missed pay day; Mecklenburg shares that reaction now.

"Nobody felt worse about losing the game," he said. "We each lost $18,000 (the winner's share) in the process."

Coach Dan Reeves is alarmed by Broncomania's excesses.

"I've coached football and I've watched fans for years and years. And as far as trying to predict a football game, I think it's one of the toughest things to do. That's why they call it gambling.

"I like it that we've got great fans that support us and back us," Reeves said. "But people that bet that kind of money, I feel sorry for them. I feel sad because it's a disease and other people in the family have to suffer."

The suffering, everyone knows, will continue, and possibly grow, as long as the Broncos play football.

Reflecting on his lost house payment, the nearly busted real estate agent was both pragmatist and optimist.

"It's gone," he said. "It's history.

"But I have no regrets. Because I'll win on them again."

Bookmaking Prospers
(Second of two parts)

In 1972, five years before the Broncos' first Super Bowl appearance, bookies were as scarce as NFL victories in Denver.

"It used to be impossible," said a regular Denver bettor who relocated from the South about that time. "I was here 10 years before I could find a bookie."

His solution, he said, was to call home with his bets two or three times a week.

Fifteen years later, by the time the Broncos were playing in their second Super Bowl, placing a bet in Denver is as easy as ordering a pizza.

A three-month investigation by the *Rocky Mountain News* has found that, despite laws passed in 1972 aimed at discouraging illegal sports gambling in Colorado:

• The number of bookies has increased more than tenfold.

• Hundreds of millions of dollars are bet annually with Colorado bookmakers.

• Bookmaking arrests have dwindled as federal, local and state law enforcement priorities changed and funding was reduced.

Commenting on the problem, Sgt. Dan O'Hare, supervisor of organized crime investigations for the Denver Police Department's intelligence bureau, said:

"If you tried to take any effective enforcement action against every bookmaker or person engaged in professional gambling, it would be like chasing the tail of a tornado."

*   *   *

Determining the exact scope is difficult. But interviews with law enforcement agents, gamblers and bookmakers, and an examination of pending court cases, paint a vivid portrait of flourishing illegal activity and alarming consequences.

On Super Bowl XXI alone, the *News* reported yesterday, between $2 million and $3 million was wagered with Denver bookmakers, according to separate estimates from gambling and law enforcement sources. At least one Broncos fan gambled his house, another his house payment, another his car. Others bet their savings.

In addition, the *News* has learned that:

• A bank officer's involvement with bookmakers may have contributed to the failure of an Aurora bank.

• A businessman who was more than $100,000 in debt to his bookie tried to clear the books by giving away one of his national franchises.

"The sad part," said Dick McNamee, agent in charge of the Colorado Bureau of Investigation, "is that the public views this as a victimless crime."

Law enforcement experts claimed in 1972 that organized crime in Colorado was a $50 million-a-year industry, with professional gambling, primarily sports betting, producing most of the take.

"It was a monopoly then," said O'Hare. One group in town had access to the line and you paid for the line. And you joined that organization or you didn't get the line. There were maybe 60 to 70 people involved.

"Now? Take the number of bars in the metro area and multiply by three. There have got to be thousands."

One of Denver's longtime bookies agrees.

"Ten years ago you had 10 bookies and 100 runners. Now you have 1,000 bookies and 10,000 runners." (In bookmaking parlance, a runner is a person hired by a bookmaker to collect and turn in action and, in some cases, take care of payoffs and collections.)

The availability of the betting line makes operating a sport book much easier. The line is published in daily newspapers, carried on cable sports services by telephone.

"You could start a book tomorrow and have it running in no time," O'Hare said. "There's no problem with somebody trying to monopolize because there's not that much competition among bookmakers because there's so much (of a market) out there."

The market is so attractive, O'Hare said, that several years ago one bookmaker sold a portion of his book's client list for $50,000.

O'Hare estimates the amount of money generated by bookmaking and other criminal activity financed by bookmaking approaches $2 billion.

He bases that figure on three factors: the proliferation of bookies, the Denver area's roughly 40 percent population growth in the past 15 years, and the workforce's pay increases during that time.

A bookmaking bust in December 1984 supports his contention.

"They were handling $750,000 a weekend, and they were by no means the biggest," he told the *News*. "In fact, in terms of numbers, they represented a very small circle of people."

O'Hare calls that case, which is scheduled for trial in August, the largest bookmaking bust in Denver history. Evidence from the search warrants was so voluminous that police had to clean out one floor of a building just to store the material.

"And that was just on the major players," said O'Hare.

The operation's clientele illustrates the threat sports gambling presents to the community.

"We had everybody as bettors—stockbrokers, doctors, real estate tycoons, veterinarians and dentists," O'Hare said. A pregnant female police officer who was working on the case found the gynecologist among the bettors, O'Hare said.

Among the 14 men indicted in that bust was Aaron Mosko, a Littleton used-car salesman with a long history of sports gambling arrests.

★   ★   ★

The indictment, which includes charges of operating illegal gambling businesses and tax evasion, alleges that Mosko, 75, accepted about $1 million in illegal bets in November and December 1984.

Another indictment, issued last month by a federal grand jury, implicates Mosko and other gambling figures in the collapse of The Aurora Bank in 1985. No trial date has been set.

In that case, Mosko is accused of laundering $159,808 in gambling proceeds through the bank and with non-payment of a $199,628 loan there. His note was part of $3 million in bad loans to organized crime figures and others that eventually caused the bank to fail, according to a suit filed by the Federal Deposit Insurance Corp.

Mosko's loan, court records show, was arranged through William J. Vanden Eynden of Littleton, a former vice president of the bank who is serving seven years in prison for violating federal banking laws.

Vanden Eynden, in a written statement to the court at the time of his sentencing, said that he gambled regularly, though never through Mosko. He told the court he was introduced to Mosko by a third party who also is a frequent bettor. Vanden Eynden said he told the third party he needed to introduce a friend from Las Vegas to a local bookie.

Vanden Eynden testified that he arranged a loan to Mosko after Mosko agreed to loan him $50,000 to help finance another money-laundering scheme at the bank. Under terms of Mosko's loan to Vanden Eynden, the banker was to repay $100,000—principal plus $50,000 interest—in one month.

After loaning Vanden Eynden $50,000, Mosko executed an unsecured promissory note to The Aurora Bank for $50,000. In the officer's memorandum, Vanden Eynden falsely stated that the purpose of the note was "to purchase automobiles." That loan, never repaid, was rolled over three times—finally totaling $199,628.

"I think people in general do not see the harm in sports gambling," O'Hare said. "They do not recognize the inherent harm.

"The minute you start messing with a bookie, you're thrown into a whole different subculture. Talk about being stuck. How do you report to police that you're involved in some criminal activity that turned sour on you? You don't, you just pay.

"It's a flat dirty business. It's like prostitution. When it increases, all the dirt around it increases. We've seen families fall apart, people lose businesses, an increase in loan sharking, extortion and arsons. There are so many other things connected to it.

"A lot of people don't understand what the term organized crime really means," O'Hare said. "It doesn't really refer to Mafia. There are so many hustlers out there that don't know Mafia, can't spell Mafia. But they're still organized crime."

In 1983, O'Hare recalled, a Denver businessman who owed his bookie $117,000 in gambling debts tried to erase the debts by giving him a business franchise. The bookie refused, insisting instead on a payoff arrangement.

"He let the guy keep firing and the guy had to pay $5,000 a month in interest," said O'Hare.

So how did bookmaking, relatively confined to organized crime families in the '70s, explode from a tightly controlled back-room operation to one of Colorado's fastest growing industries in the '80s?

★   ★   ★

Most experts agree the door was opened to trouble when the state criminal code was revised effective July 1, 1972.

Lawmakers, with input from the judicial and law enforcement communities, drafted a "social gambling" section that identifies a list of activities as gambling—unless they are part of a bona fide social relationship.

"The idea was to decriminalize what you did in your own house, in terms of poker," said Hubert Safran, then a state representative and now a lobbyist for the Colorado Trial Lawyers Association.

But the social gambling section proved to be a huge loophole.

"That's what they (gamblers) always hang their hat on," said O'Hare. "As a result there was reluctance on the part of the district attorney's office to accept cases and fight them in court."

Also in the new law, the penalty for professional gambling was changed to a Class 1 misdemeanor on first offense (six months to two years in jail and $500 to $5,000 fine). It was a Class 5 felony (one to eight years in jail and $1,000 to $100,000 fine) for a second offense within five years.

But that's the rub, say law enforcement officers.

"It takes a long time to convict somebody," said Tony Lombard, chief lobbyist for the Denver Police Department. "And then you're doing all that for a misdemeanor that in a lot of cases the district attorney doesn't want to file."

O'Hare agrees. "There is so little to be gained for filing a misdemeanor charge. You've got to make sure you have a quality violator before you waste your time going after him. And if he's worth your time, you might just as well use the FBI so you can file a federal statute against him so it's a lot heavier fine and penalty."

Safran objects to blaming the new gambling law for an increase in bookmaking.

"I'm sure what the legislature was trying to do was make laws realistic and enforceable," he said. "If they've got a problem, they should change it."

Former state Sen. John Bermingham, prime sponsor of the criminal code bill in 1972 and now an environmental law attorney, agrees.

"If bookmaking has blossomed, then something is wrong with the statute. The district attorneys around the state should do something about it, if it's that blatant."

But Lombard, in his lobbyist role, has tried to do something about it in the legislature. He tried and failed in 1985, 1986 and again last month.

His latest bid was an amendment he slipped in the omnibus crime bill. It would have toughened the penalty for those convicted of professional gambling.

Passage would have bumped the penalty from a Class 1 misdemeanor to Class 5 felony, substantially increasing the fine, probability of imprisonment and length of incarceration.

But it was thrown out.

This time, the reason given was Colorado's budgetary crisis and crowded prisons.

"The department of corrections figures that with the change of law that we would convict and possibly incarcerate 1.5 people a year, and they said the price tag of $23,000 a year was something they didn't feel they could absorb," said Lombard.

* * *

The amendment died a quiet death, Lombard said, because the joint budget committee "felt if it came down to giving a bed to a gambler, maybe a murderer wouldn't get it. So, rather than have the whole bill killed, we took it out."

Lombard said he will try again next year.

Times and attitudes, meanwhile, have changed, too.

"What's really happened, and not just in our state but all over the nation, is everyone has become a lot more tolerant of gambling," O'Hare said. "That alone has increased the number of people who would lay down $100 on a football game by 10 times the numbers in the '70s."

"I hear it all the time," said Broncos quarterback John Elway. " 'Play well because I've got money on you.' It's something you become numb to, like boos."

"The whole state, our whole society," said O'Hare, "has become more tolerant of gambling, just as they did of drugs in the 1960s. They used to put you in prison for five years for doing it, now you get a ticket for $25 and walk off."

Explains one of the state's top gambling agents: "Narcotics is the big thing now. They (public officials) take all resources and put it into that now."

Dick Schussler, press relations officer and legal counsel for the Denver office of the FBI, concurs, noting the agency's gambling caseload is down to "approximately 10 to 15" cases a year.

"Lately we're focusing on traditional crimes and narcotics," Schussler said. "Our big priorities are white-collar crimes—dumping of toxic wastes, HUD and FHA frauds, bank frauds."

That shift is evident in the manpower now assigned to gambling.

"Before 1972," said O'Hare, "there was a unit assigned to the district attorney's office with five to six investigators, and they were out during football season and busting at least a bookmaker a week.

"Now, with our limited resources and manpower, we may bust only three to four a year, and they are only ones we consider worthwhile targets.

"We're not giving up any ground to them voluntarily," he said. "They're taking it. We have to take the limited resources we have and direct them to the area where it's going to have the greatest effect."

"It's a low-priority crime," Lombard agrees. "It's probably one of the lowest-risk, high-profit crimes in the nation."

Broncos Coach Dan Reeves, for one, would like to see the risk increased.

"To me, bookies are just like drug dealers. To me, they're making a living hurting people. And I don't agree with that. A lot of people make a living dealing drugs and they never realize the young people's lives they're ruining. Bookies are doing the same thing, and to me they're almost like leeches. They're sucking blood out of people for a living and I don't agree with that."

Judge's Comments

It's an old cliche that much of America's best writing appears on the sports pages of newspapers and sports magazines. That's probably as true today as it was in the days of Grantland Rice.

What's seldom if ever said is that the best reporting appears in those sections. Why? Take a look at the investigative reporting that appears regularly on the front pages of U.S. newspapers. You'll see little to match it on the sports pages.

That's why it's refreshing to see a sports story that goes beyond the coverage of a big game or match, one that goes beyond the tear-jerking tale of a big-time athlete who has fallen on hard times. In those situations, the story is there and a good writer can grab it and run with it.

Good reporting requires more than interviewing the participants in a big game or match. It requires seeking out those sources that aren't so obvious. It requires digging into the story behind the story. It requires ferreting out the story that isn't so obvious.

That's what Norm Clarke has done in his fascinating investigation of a city gone mad over its football team and the accompanying frenzy in the bookmaking community. Clarke gives readers of the *Rocky Mountain News* a rare glimpse into a side of our society that most of us never see.

In the process, he refutes the myth that illegal betting is a victimless crime.

This thorough examination of a seamy side of sports offers readers of the *Rocky Mountain News* much, much more than the pablum of game coverage served up to the readers of most U.S. sports sections.

With this investigation, Clarke and his newspaper have demonstrated a high level of commitment to quality journalism.

Go Go Girls

by Ralf-Finn Hestoft of the Kankakee Daily Journal. Amy Vaughn, a basketball player for Ford Central High School, gets an artistic welcome from her teammates during introductions at the Illinois state tournament. Copyright © 1987, Kankakee Daily Journal.

12 Straight

by Dale E. Tait of United Press International. Rob Deer and his Milwaukee Brewers teammates were understandably ecstatic April 19 when they captured their season-opening 12th straight victory, thanks in large part to Deer's three-run, game-tying home run in the bottom of the ninth against the Texas Rangers. Copyright © 1987, Dale E. Tait, United Press International.

He Gave His All, Which Was a Lot

BASEBALL

By *THOMAS BOSWELL*

From the Washington Post
Copyright © 1987, Washington Post Co.

Dick Howser's life was much too short. There is nothing he or we could do about that. The reputation and the memories he left behind as his sliver of baseball history are, however, just right. What was within his power, he handled as well as anyone could ask. He will be recalled, and for a long time, as a man who proved the difference between book and cover, between show and substance. With Howser, what you saw was much less than what you finally got.

Howser could not have been given much less in the way of raw material. As they say, he wasn't tall, but he didn't have muscles, either. Yet he played shortstop for eight years in the major leagues and hit .248 which nowadays, probably would have made him a million bucks. Then, it got him a coachship.

Scrubbed and brushed, he was boyish and agreeable; but he couldn't pull off handsome or even mildly impressive. His voice wasn't deep, his glare wouldn't have pierced cream cheese and though he was natively smart, he wasn't brilliant or bookish. He waved home runners and hit fungos for 10 seasons before the New York Yankees promoted him to manager. A boy wonder he wasn't.

In his first season, his team won 103 games and almost made it to the World Series. Then Howser did something that will be remembered much longer. George Steinbrenner told Howser to fire coach Mike Ferraro, one of Howser's friends, as a scapegoat gesture after the playoffs.

Quietly, Howser said, "No."

Steinbrenner screamed, "Yes."

Howser told Steinbrenner to take the most glamorous job in baseball, the job he had worked 22 years to get, and shove it. Fire my friend, fire me.

At a news conference, Steinbrenner tried to gloss over Howser's dismissal, saying Howser had asked to leave and had not been pushed. Howser, a man with no power in his game or personal wealth, quietly and politely told everyone that, though he was sorry he had to point it out, what Steinbrenner had just said was completely untrue and the owner knew it.

Step on Dick Howser and they'd have to get him off you with a wrench.

Within baseball, that incident answered all the questions anybody ever had about Howser. It was a dugout Profile in Courage. You couldn't buy him. You couldn't intimidate him. You couldn't silence him. His loyalty was absolute. No prize baseball could offer could make him lie or betray a friend.

In a world of large, gifted, ambitious, and often belligerent men, Howser quickly became one of the few who was universally respected, admired and warmly liked. One out of three wouldn't be bad. How many others could claim to be all three?

Howser's most remarkable trait was that, when he spoke, people absolutely believed every word. Not that his words were profound or different than those a hundred other managers had said. They weren't. What distinguished Howser was that he said only what he truly thought. In 1985, his Royals trailed California by 7½ games at the All-Star break, but beat the Angels by one game. Then, in the playoffs, they trailed a superior Toronto team, three games to one. Howser called a meeting and said, "I still feel like we can get this thing done."

As second baseman Frank White recalled, "That was about all he said. He didn't yell. But he really believed it. And then we believed it."

No team of mediocre gifts ever did so much against odds so great as those Royals. They beat Toronto, then fell behind the significantly better St. Louis Cardinals, 2-0 and 3-1. They, of course, came back to be world champions, winning six sudden-death postseason games.

The clearest memory from that World Series is of Howser. In Game 2 he had left a struggling starter, Charlie Leibrandt, on the mound and Dan Quisenberry, the most effective relief pitcher of the decade, in the bullpen until too late. Leibrandt lost the game.

The next day in St. Louis, there was no game. Just questions. Thousands of them from hundreds of reporters who were convinced that Howser had blundered badly. The first of several times Howser explained his decision, I still thought he was dead wrong. Then, I noticed my watch. Wave after wave of reporters descended on Howser. Every 20 minutes, the same questions would recur. For two hours, Howser did not move. He knew he would be blasted in every paper, on every radio and TV broadcast from coast to coast. He wasn't going to change the second-guessers' minds.

And he didn't care.

"Second-guessing is part of the game," Howser said. "I do it, too. It's my job to make decisions, then explain them and then take the heat."

So he stood and loaded his own quotes into all the guns aimed at him. The loss of a World Series was going to be laid at his small feet.

When they told Howser last July that he had a malignant brain tumor, he told the Royals to hold his job, please, because he'd be back for spring training.

Some people may think that Dick Howser failed because he could not manage the Royals this year, because he could not beat cancer, because he died Wednesday. Some others think that the day he reported to camp, dozens of pounds underweight and his uniform hanging on him like a sheet, that he won. He stood in his big floppy golf hat with all the fresh scars underneath and answered the questions. He reported for duty. Shoulders back, proud of what was left of himself. Two days later, he retired. Too hot. Too hard.

Howser's private tragedy is simply that he did not live long enough to suit the family he dearly loved. We can't touch that or help it. The public Howser is our province; that part of him got to fulfill most, if not all, of its destiny. In another 20 years of managing he probably would have won more pennants. But he could not have proved anything new about himself. All the best already was on display.

Spar Wars

BOXING

By *FRANZ LIDZ*

From Philadelphia Magazine
Copyright © 1987, Philadelphia Magazine

"Boxers never start out to be sparring partners, any more than actors start out to be understudies."
—A.J. Liebling

Mr. Fuzzy comes in from the rain—big, wet and bearlike. He sheds his windbreaker and he's a little less wet, but he's still big and shaggy in a mud-splattered jogging suit that seems stuck to his body like fresh paint. His red beret is tilted at a sassy angle and festooned with a bright orange button that says DON'T PANIC.

Mr. Fuzzy laughs, a nice laugh of self-deprecation, deep in his throat. "My mother called me Fuzzy because that's the way my hair's always been," he says. "The kids added 'Mister' out of respect."

Marvin Stinson, as Mr. Fuzzy is known to the adult world, is perhaps the last of the great sparring partners. A vagabond band of mostly prizefighters manques, sparring partners drift anonymously from gym to gym, boxer to boxer, working for expenses and bonuses quarried out of their employers' purses. They're like character actors hired for the sole purpose of supporting the star: Some are short, some tall; some indolent, some insolent; some overweight, some undernourished. Most have a lot more cunning than innate fighting ability. Indeed, the greatest gift of all for a professional sparring partner may be a talent for knowing just how hard he can hit his boss and still stay employed.

A handful of sparring mates, like Larry Holmes, Ken Norton and Jersey Joc Walcott, polished their natural skills so highly while sparring that they went on to become headliners. Others, like Jimmy

Young, are ex-top bananas who slipped. But most, in fact nearly all, are like Stinson—courageous and ambitious men who began their careers with the view that they were contenders. Then, due to bad luck or bad advice or a badly inflated idea of their own talent, they wound up boxing their best in another man's training camp.

Stinson, a much-punched heavyweight, was Larry Holmes' steadiest spar mate from 1978 to '83. Then Marvin got too easy to hit and left the ring. He's 33 now, a construction worker. He does a little bricklaying, a little carpentry. He works a seven-day week. In the summer he stands on his front porch selling pretzels, potato chips and Italian water ice, 25 cents a pop. Years of being poked and pummeled by the best heavyweight of his era have left Stinson's face eerily geometric. His lips are stretched half-ovals, his ears are flattened semicircles, his nose is a squashed isosceles triangle. Mr. Fuzzy's a little chunkier around the middle than when he was sparring, but no less tough. He has the look of a combat infantryman who has walked point and survived.

His hand is warm and thick and firm when he takes yours to welcome you to the Warren Street row house he shares with his six kids. It's a neat, tidy place in a rough part of West Philly called The Bottom. Relaxed in an old chair that's come to fit his body, Stinson is surrounded by memorabilia from his boxing career. There's a silver medal he won at the 1974 World Games and the crystal trophy he got two years later as the top heavyweight at the President's Cup in Russia. But the centerpiece is a framed photo inscribed:

TO MARVIN,
BEST WISHES TO MY FRIEND
LARRY HOLMES, THE CHAMP
PEACE '85

Holmes gave Stinson the $20,000 he needed to buy the house. Holmes takes care of his sparring partners financially. He knows the drill. The Easton, Pa., fighter was Muhammad Ali's spar mate for several years, and he had to be talked into becoming the heavyweight champ. Holmes had figured he was doing well when he was getting $500 a week for sparring with Ali; he was earning only $200 for his own fights. He probably helped make Ali a lot better fighter because he was at least as good as most of the opponents Ali fought.

But Holmes is an enigma. He doesn't seem to have drawn any pleasure from his seven-year run as champion. Bitterness spills from his tongue like molten lead. It may be rooted in the knowledge that he has never commanded the respect Ali does, and never will. He hasn't talked to Stinson since September of 1985, when Holmes lost the first of two 15-round decisions to Michael Spinks. Holmes won't answer questions about Stinson, either. "Larry wanted me to spy on Michael and I wouldn't do it," Marvin explains. "They're both my friends." Stinson had been pals with Spinks since the 1976 Olympics.

But Holmes assumed the $15,000 he was paying Stinson would buy more of his friendship.

When Stinson came to him after the bout, Holmes wasn't quite so magnanimous. Stinson's seven-year-old daughter, Nicole, had just been killed in a hit-and-run accident. His wife left him. And he had a lot of bills. He asked Holmes for a couple hundred bucks. "Larry said he didn't have any money," Stinson remembers. A little muscle works in his face each time he says "Larry." "He told me never to call him again, even to say hello."

Stinson is still baffled. "I don't see why Larry treated me the way he did," he says. "I neglected my wife and my family to be with him in camp. I should have worried more about my own career than about getting him ready for fights."

"You can hire any kind of cheap help to get theirself hit. What you got to pay good money for is something that is not going to get hisself hit. By not getting hisself hit, a sparring partner does more good to a fighter because he sets the fighter to studying why he ain't hitting him."

—George Nicholson

Stinson was never a heavy hitter. He had a walk-in style, and was moderately renowned for his willingness to take a punch. "Marvin always gave Larry trouble in the ring," says Sam Solomon, Holmes' former trainer. "That's why Larry kept him." Stinson faced Holmes four times when both were amateurs, losing each bout on points. "When you lose a close decision, you don't feel beaten," says trainer Eddie Futch, who handled Holmes and Spinks. "Marvin was always trying to prove to himself that he was just as good as Larry. A fighter has to actually feel beaten to know the other fellow is superior."

That made Stinson the perfect complement to Holmes. He knew Holmes' moves and countermoves so well he could always stretch him out. He could detect errors, too. "In some ways," says Futch, "Marvin reminded me of George Nicholson."

George Nicholson was an amiable, mannerly slab of a man who worked with Joe Louis for almost 20 years—from the Max Schmeling fights in the 1930s through the final defeat by Rocky Marciano in '53. The Philadelphia native had been set on becoming a lawyer, but switched to boxing when he realized he couldn't speak fast enough. Unfortunately, he couldn't punch fast enough, either. He was never a contender; he seemed to lack the streak of cruelty that makes a champion. But George Nicholson had a limitless fund of common sense that allowed him to speak grand truths about his calling: "Sometimes when I boxing with a fellow that hit me right on the button, and I know he ain't got to hit me on the button, and I boxing with him again and he hit me on the button again, then I going to quit."

Joe Louis was not the kind of fighter to hit a man on the button when he didn't have to. Neither was Holmes nor Ali. These are men who used their sparring partners to extend them but not upend them. For them, sparring was a matter of finesse and intelligence, not a situation in which maximum brutality is brought to bear on a hapless partner.

But there are fighters—well known to all members of the sparring fraternity—who want partners to be nothing so much as flesh-and-blood body bags. They want easy-falling courage-creators. The late Max Schmeling was one, and Gerry Cooney is a current-day member of that group. When a journeyman heavyweight named Phil Brown helped train Cooney in 1979, his employer wore 12-ounce gloves with hard rubber straps wrapped around his knuckles. Brown and the rest were handed bulky 16-ounce training gloves. The day Brown arrived in camp, three sparring partners left. In pain, Brown only agreed to spar after his salary was upped to $1,500 a week. Even then, a week was all he stayed. "It was suicide," he says. "Cooney's in there with 12-ouncers and you've got air bags on your hands. He'd deliberately hurt you just to boost his ego. Even that much money wasn't worth it. Most of it would go towards doctor bills anyway."

This is the way it is for men who spar for a living. Besides the danger of injury, there's also always a demeaning quality to the sparring partner's work—so much so that few like to think of it as a permanent occupation. Typically, a spar mate is treated as part of the gym equipment, scarcely human. Here's how it was last spring for three members of this much-disparaged group during Larry Holmes' training for his rematch with Spinks:

The ring was set up in a smoky lounge of the Konover Hotel in Miami Beach. Three dozen spectators milled around nursing highballs. The ambience was cocktail-party cheery. Holmes climbed through the ropes and paraded around to a smattering of desultory applause. Outside, in a shadowy hallway by the men's room, three heavyweights, their bodies greased for protection, stood like roasters waiting for Frank Perdue.

The ex-champ's new sparring coach was Jody Ballard, who left the ring for good one day when Holmes detached his retina. Ballard wore a white lab coat that said "Jody the Teacher." His colleagues call him Timex because he'd take a lickin' and keep on tickin'. Stinson just calls him The Mouth. They once duked it out in a hotel room, though you won't find the results in "The Ring Record Book."

Holmes' first taker was Donovan (Razor) Ruddock, a quick, muscular, 22-year-old Jamaican built along the lines of Spinks. His record was 12-1 and holding. Holmes was using Ruddock to sharpen his timing.

Ruddock opened with a big burst of jabs a la Spinks and backed Holmes up with a pretty fair right. In the second round, Holmes attacked and pushed the younger fighter around at will. "I'm as good a boxer as Larry is," Ruddock said as he stepped out of the ring. "He's just a little more mature."

Next up was Phil Brown, famed for a strong jab and weak chin. About the only fighter he hasn't worked with is Norman Mailer. Brown was here so Holmes could hone his techniques. Bathed in the disco light, Brown stood still, calm and quiet awaiting Holmes' first punch.

"Stick, stick, stick," Ballard shouted instructions to Brown. "Work your jab up and down like a yo-yo . . ."

Holmes ripped combinations into Brown's stomach. Brown's head sagged. He was throwing punches, but they were not connecting.

"Touch him and get *out* . . ."

Holmes slapped Brown back into a corner. Brown's brow crooked. His eyelids drooped. He was too pinned-in to parry.

"Step around, step around . . ."

Holmes straightened Brown with a left and tagged him with a right cross. Brown answered with weak uppercuts.

"*Flick, flick, flick* . . ."

Holmes doubled up on his hooks. Brown's body slumped, twisted.

"Come on, Phil, this ain't no tappin' contest."

Holmes let loose a big right. Brown's back arched and his knees buckled. The bell sounded. Brown later said, "If Larry's got a clear shot, he'll take it. I've been shooken up and dazed, but it's all part of what he's paying me for."

Last and probably least of the three spar mates was Jerry Williams, a bullet-headed brawler who had a woozy, sleepy look. Holmes was counting on him to build his stamina. They locked shoulders and shuffled heavily for two rounds.

Holmes was sweaty. His manager, Richie Giachetti, doused him with ice water.

"How 'bout giving these boys a hand?" said Holmes to the crowd.

Scattered clapping.

"All right," he said, turning around. "Now how 'bout giving *me* a hand?"

Wild standing ovation.

Somebody told Ruddock to return to the ring and take a bow.

"No," says Ruddock. "It's his show. My time will come. My time will come."

Once in a while, a sparring partner finds that his time has come and he can't stop himself from lashing back. "Every fighter—spar mate or not—is going to wake up some days wondering if he's still got the power," says Eddie Futch. "No matter how well-intentioned he is, he wants to see some results when he throws that punch."

Those results have occasionally caused trouble ever since the days of Spartacus, when cheeky partners literally took the heads off gladiators they were supposed to be tuning up. The most presumptuous sparring partner ever may have been James J. Jeffries, who came to Jim Corbett's camp when he was preparing for an 1897 heavyweight championship fight. Jeffries decked Corbett the first time they sparred, and the champion's morale was so battered that he lost the title. Two years later Jeffries won it.

Of course, if a partner gets too heady he might only earn a bus ticket home—like Jersey Joe Walcott.

Walcott was plucked off a street corner in Merchantville, N.J., one day in 1935 to spar with Joe Louis, who was training for the first Schmeling fight in nearby Pompton Lakes. In the opening round of their training session, Walcott chopped Louis to the canvas with a right to the jaw. Louis's handlers rushed in and refused to let Walcott go another round. They paid him $25 and hustled him out of camp, saying, "You don't have the proper style." The next day, back on the curb in Merchantville, five chums greeted Walcott's return with derisive laughter. "We knew you wouldn't stay there long," they chorused. "He's too much for you."

Eleven years later in Madison Square Garden, Walcott knocked Louis down twice more in a rugged 15-round title match. Louis was headed out of the ring in dejection when he was declared the winner. "I'm sorry, Joe," Louis said after the decision, taking Walcott's hands in his. But Jersey Joe had taken Louis the distance, and lots of folks thought he had won. Which is a lot more than most sparring partners ever get.

"Boxing kept me out of jail. It kept me from being killed. If you crossed me when I was younger, I'd have run you over with my car. I didn't care. I had a no-care attitude. I thought the world owed me something, but the world didn't owe me nothing."

—Marvin Stinson

Born in North Philly, Stinson grew up mostly in Williamstown, N.J., a rural pit stop on the way to Atlantic City. Marion Stinson worked in a spinach cannery; her husband Cal was a pipe cutter who moonlighted as a moonshiner. Marvin used to wash out the 20-gallon barrels and watch the gauges on the still. Cal would get busted every once in a while by revenuers who punched holes in the still and poured kerosene into the mash, but he always rebounded, thereby teaching Marvin a valuable lesson in life: "If you ever find yourself in jail, the first thing to do is bail yourself out."

Cal also bought a new Cadillac every year, which led the Stinson boys to be nicknamed Cadillac. Since Marvin was the youngest of the six, he was called Little Cadillac. At 10, he cruised back to North Philly to live with his grandparents, landing in a street gang called The Valley. "We spoke with sticks, bottles and alley apples," he recalls. Alley apples, he explains, were bricks. "Another gang would jump your friend and kill him and you'd say, 'I'm gonna get me a body.' You couldn't show no fair to nobody because they'd take kindness for weakness."

After beating up a white family he suspected of casting aspersions on his race, Stinson continued his studies at the Yardsville Correctional Center. He was unable to apply his father's axiom, though, and stayed for 11 months. "I was sitting in my cell and I thought to myself, 'Dad didn't raise me to be like this, and I'm not raising my kids to be like this either.' " In prison he decided to become a fighter. "I got a long ways to go," he told his mother upon getting sprung, "and a short time to get there."

He got himself a job and started working out in the gym. Five years later he won the AAU heavyweight championship. Stinson met Michael Spinks as an amateur and hung out with him during the 1976 Olympic trials. A year later they were sparring together when Stinson took a shot to the chops and hit the canvas. As sensitive as a romantic poet, Spinks was reduced to tears at the thought of knocking down his pal with one blow.

"I didn't mean it," Spinks sobbed.

"Hey man," said Stinson. "That's the game." Sparring partners tend to achieve a certain emotional toughness.

Stinson may have stayed in the amateurs too long. He had a hard time getting pro fights. He got calls to work with small-time pugs like Cyclone Hart and Bad Nose Nelson in mean Philadelphia gyms where it's said the fighting is fiercer than in any arena. "I wouldn't take a guy to learn to box in Philadelphia," says Richie Giachetti. "All Philly fighters ever want to do is take your head off." Stinson found that all he could make was chump change, the nickle-and-dime wages dispensed in gyms above North Philly strip joints.

He got occasional fights of his own and built a respectable 12-3-3 pro record by filling in undercards on short notice. His biggest purse, $7,500, was earned losing to Jimmy Young. He supplemented his income by working construction and stuffing shopping bags with peaches from nearby orchards. He'd sell them for a buck out of the trunk of *his* Caddie.

Leon Spinks hired Stinson as a spar mate for his first seven pro bouts, which culminated in his celebrated upset of Ali. "I used to try to keep Leon out of trouble," says Stinson, "but it got to be too much for me." He still tries. "I say, 'Get it together, Leon.' And he says, 'Uh-huh.' "

In 1978 Stinson went to Holmes' camp to spar. He was joined by two others: Leroy Diggs, who was recruited out of a New Jersey gas station, and Wendell Bailey, a would-be stand-up comic with a sharp left hand. Bailey got in the habit of appearing at camp between happy hours and baiting Holmes.

"What's Bailey been doing?" Holmes would bark at his trainer, Sam Solomon.

"Out late, drinkin'."

"Then I *want* him."

But Holmes never got him. "As much as Larry tried to put Wendell away," says Solomon, "he couldn't do nothin' with him."

A couple of months later Bailey's wife put him away. Permanently. She stuck a knife in him and he died running away.

Stinson became a regular in Holmes' training camp pretty much by default. He made $500 a week sparring two three-minute rounds a day. When Holmes fought Ali and Cooney, Marvin got a $1,000 bonus after both fights. But Stinson never collected the $10,000 Holmes promised to the first sparring partner who knocked him down. A good spar mate needs to operate with discretion. "I never tried to really hurt Larry," Stinson says. "He was my payday. I always have to think about where I'm gonna get paid after tomorrow."

"It ain't how much power you got, it's how much smarts. If you take five punches to get one in, it'll rattle your brain. I had over 200 fights and you ain't see me rattlin'."

—Marvin Stinson

Stinson's heir apparent is Oscar Holman, a 200-pound cruiser-weight who makes a living sparring with 240-pound heavyweights. Holman, 27, has been the one regular in Gerry Cooney's camp of day trippers. He's a quick, cagey counter-puncher who has stayed around as long as he has on wits and endurance.

Holman got into boxing as a teenager in North Philly, joining a street gang called Mack and Butler. But the main artery in his left forearm got razored, and he entered the Army, where the mayhem was more organized and perhaps less dangerous. He boxed on the team at Fort Collins. When his four and a half years were up, he turned pro.

Holman's four-year record is 13-6, but he lost his most recent fight on a 10th-round TKO. "The ref shouldn't have stopped it," he insists. "I wasn't hurt. I didn't even get hit with nothin'. Now I have to go back to my drawing board."

Even though Holman makes $500 a week for sparring with Cooney, he thinks of himself as a professional boxer, not just a professional spar mate. "In my mind, I'm being paid for gettin' in shape," he says. "Full-time sparring is for retired boxers." In five years, he figures, he'll have saved enough to quit the ring and invest in real estate. "Someday I'll build my own junior mansion from scratch," he says. "I'll have me swimming pools. I'll have me a gym. A maid. A butler. A cook. A chauffeur. That's all I need right there." Until then he's living in his mother's row house.

Last May, Holman showed up at the Lancaster hotel where Cooney was training for his comeback bout with Eddie Gregg. For days, Cooney's manager, Dennis Rappaport, had been frantically calling around for sparring partners. Cooney's reputation as a spar mate-basher was widely known. Rappaport was beginning to feel like a recruiting sergeant at a pacifists' convention. He got the decidedly unformidable Jimmy Clark to come in, but Clark got floored one day and left without bothering to pick up his paycheck.

"I wish I had a hair for every sparring partner Gerry's knocked out," said the balding Rappaport. "Or every one who took off in the middle of the night. Or who had a sister who just got killed in a car accident. We must have had 20 relatives die."

Rappaport boasted that Cooney had gone through as many as three sparring partners in a round and 20 in a week. "We never ask them to hold back," he said. "Just throw punches. If they ease up on Gerry, he can't get a workout." Which was why Rappaport was somewhat reluctant to call in Holman, who was usually too busy protecting himself to throw punches.

"I don't want to get my head knocked off," Holman explained. "You can't get careless with Gerry. If you do, he'll send you soul-searching with a left hook."

But he agreed to come to Lancaster to take Cooney's kind of punishment, as did a sinewy, young, unknown Floridian named Ken Davis. Except for a week in Mike Tyson's camp, the 6-foot-3-inch, 214-pound Davis hadn't fought in nine months. He'd been racking balls at George's Pool Room in Fort Myers.

"Can he punch?" Rappaport had asked Davis's trainer.

"Sure he can punch," came the reply.

"Is he in shape?"

"Sure he's in shape."

Actually, the only recent fight Davis had was outside a 7-Eleven, where he decked a woman in an argument. Her head hit the sidewalk, and two days later she died. Davis was charged with manslaughter. He says it was merely a boxer's reflex after the woman came up behind him and smacked him with her purse.

Holman advised Davis to approach his work in the ring with Cooney cautiously. Davis hadn't thrown even a semblance of a punch before Cooney had knocked Davis's mouthpiece out. Davis's moves were mostly backward. Cooney popped him over the left eye. He popped him again and again. Davis bounced back and forth off the ropes like he'd rather be rasslin'. At the end of the three rounds his eyes were as swollen as blueberry popovers. He left the ring heaving and looking vacant.

Holman fared much better. He bobbed, he weaved, he peeka-booed. He played hit-and-run. At dinner, Holman ordered a couple of steaks, but Davis didn't have much of an appetite. "I just wanted to get the feel of how hard Cooney hits," Davis alibied while poking at the flounder on his plate. "He was catching me, but he wasn't putting nothing in his punches. To be honest, I was looking forward to him beating me up more. Tomorrow I'll go get him."

Holman nodded in commiseration and said, "Lemme see a piece of that fish, man."

Davis spent the evening in bed nursing his wounds. He and Holman stayed up for a western called *My Name Is Nobody*. "That's me," joked Holman. "Just another hired gun."

Davis said he needed the $350 a week to support his wife and four kids and help pay his legal fees in the manslaughter charge. "That dead woman is on my mind every night," he mumbled. "Sometimes I wish I'd never gotten into boxing. If I hadn't been a boxer, this never would have happened." He began boxing seven years ago because all his friends were. "Every week I'd see their names in the papers," he recalled. "I wanted *my* name in the papers." He taught himself to box and won his first five pro bouts. "Then I got overmatched and lost my next five," he said. "It sounds kinda weird, but in Florida, guys are afraid to fight me, even though I'm out of shape." He was about to give up on boxing when Rappaport called. But Davis didn't want to make sparring a career. "There ain't no glory for me," he explained. "You never get heard about, and when your time comes, you're all punched out."

The following afternoon Davis watched warily as Holman feint-ed, covered and back-pedaled for two rounds. "The harder you come at Cooney," Holman advised Davis, "the more messed up you get."

Davis entered the ring and started his first round so far away from Cooney that he couldn't even hit his gloves. He dropped his guard. Cooney hooked him with a big left and followed with a right. Davis collapsed like he'd been hit by a wrecking ball. He was out cold for nearly a minute.

When Davis was revived, he was told to finish out the round so he wouldn't lose his courage forever. He sank in a chair after the bell rang and his voice faded into a low rumble. "Cooney hit me with a devastating hook," he told Holman. "At least I *thought* it was a hook."

Davis had pretty much made up his mind to go home. "I told my friends I'd be here for five weeks, and I only last two days," he said, slowing turning his head from side to side. "I know I'm no match for Cooney, even in a workout. When he loads up on me, I can't help him. I don't even feel like they have to pay me."

Holman asked Davis if he planned to give up sparring. No, no, no, Davis laughed, not at all. "I've got a pretty good jab myself," he said. "And everyone's not like Cooney."

A week later Holman returned home, too. One of Gentleman Gerry's lethal lefts had broken his jaw.

"When I find myself getting punch-drunk I'm going to quit. I'm going to look me up a profitable business somewhere that's a profit in it."

—George Nicholson

It's Sunday noon and Mr. Fuzzy is making apple pie. Rain last night canceled his construction job for the day. So he bought a bushel of Winesaps. He pares the apples and heaps them into a big boiling pot. After they have softened, he ladles a small mountain of them into a pie crust and dusts it with sugar, vanilla and cinnamon. Then he carefully places slabs of butter along the sides and covers it all with dough. "Making corn liquor was never this easy," he says.

In another corner of the kitchen, Stinson's sons Tank and Melvin plunge the quarters they earn packing groceries into a Space Invader game their dad bought during better times. On the tape deck, Aretha Franklin wails "Amazing Grace." Stinson listens and watches the oven. His eyes grow dark.

"My wife, Redbone, made a pretty good apple pie," he muses. "She left me because she was tired of this life." Redbone went to live in New York with three of their children, Tank, John and Tomeka. But their new life wasn't any better than the old. The kids called Marvin every night, asking him to bring them back. Marvin sent them bus tickets.

"It was rough living without your upside-down pineapple cakes," John says.

"Was that all you missed?" asks Stinson.

"No, sir," says Tank slyly. "We missed your applesauce, too."

Mr. Fuzzy smiles. He might still be boxing if he hadn't been stopped three years ago in the ninth round of a bout with the forgettable Eddie Gregg. Stinson still believes he was ahead on the cards, but he had suffered a cut over his left eye that was big enough to drop a sympathy card in. "I can run for the last three rounds," he pleaded with the ref. "I'm smart enough. I can hold him if I have to." The ref remained unconvinced and Gregg won on a TKO. Stinson wept in the ring.

Barely two months later, Stinson's sparring career ended, too. Eddie Futch took him aside and told him, "You're getting hit more often with solid shots. Give it up." Today Futch says of Stinson, "He has such a big heart that he continued to go ahead full steam. It was just too much for a human body to absorb. I told him it was time to retire while he was still physically and mentally OK. A lot of fighters can't deal with it and hate you." Stinson hated to quit, but he took Futch's advice.

"I'm just trying to put food on my kids' table and take care of them," Stinson says. "Times are hard, but I'd never beg for my job back. I've got a patio to pour and a chimney to fix. I'm glad Larry made it. I know I couldn't have done it sparring much longer. I'd never recommend that to nobody. It's like when they finish you up, they throw you away and go get another dummy. God left me with all my senses. Let's keep it at that."

Young's Views Never Shaded

GENERAL

By *RON RAPOPORT*

From the Chicago Sun-Times
Copyright © 1987, the Chicago Sun-Times

The last time I was in New York, Dick Young wasn't. Not that it made any difference, you understand. Even from his semi-retirement home in Nevada, he had the whole town in an uproar.

"STAND UP AND BOO" the headline over his column in the *New York Post* commanded. Dwight Gooden was returning from drug rehab to pitch for the Mets and Young was outraged.

Outrage was Young's normal public condition, one from which he never retreated during his 40-year writing career. He was an angry young man, an angry middle-aged man and well on his way to becoming an angry old man when he died Monday at 69.

Toward the end, Young was something of a caricature of himself, a man whose politics were somewhere to the right of Attila the Hun and whose world was constantly under siege from liberal politicians, ingrate athletes and young sportswriters who saw things differently than he did.

Yet even at the end, he was compelling and inescapable. He was the best-read sportswriter of his time—of all time, probably—and extremely influential even on the members of his trade who ran at the sight of him.

Young was, I thought, almost insane in his unforgiving attitude toward those who strayed from his narrow definition of righteous behavior. And once you incurred his wrath, you could never escape from his clutches. You were good or you were bad—no shades of gray ever clouded his vision—and if you were bad the drumbeat on your head would keep pounding for years.

"My America" is what Young called his view of the world and in the end he admitted he used the phrase almost facetiously just because it bugged people. Ross Wetzsteon, who wrote a swell article entitled "Dick Young's America" two years ago, defined that country as "a land of afternoon ballgames, hardworking newspapermen, respect for mom—and electric chairs."

Yet it was on those rare occasions when you found yourself agreeing with him that you realized just what kind of hold Young had on his readers. For when he did stumble across the truth, you could only wince in your appreciation of his insight.

Why don't you like Muhammad Ali? somebody once wrote him. Because I tend to like the people who like me, Young answered. Has anybody ever defined the nature of friendship more simply or better than that? I wondered. In expressing his contempt for the younger breed of sportswriters, who he thought were more concerned with style than substance, Young said, "If you've got a story you report it, if you don't you write it." I don't know how many of us would admit it in public, but that was a bull's-eye to the heart.

Young often was given credit for livening up sportswriting by taking it into the locker room. Although nobody did it better than he did—his column in the *New York Daily News* and then the *Post* was called "Clubhouse Confidential"—I'm not sure this was his greatest accomplishment. With the coming of television, we'd have been down there rooting around for quotes soon enough anyway.

Where Young really made his mark, I believe, was in his insistence that sportswriters be given some access, some breathing room, some respect. In short, that they be allowed to do their jobs in the face of ever more crowded press boxes, ever later starting times and ever earlier deadlines.

Nobody ever railed against a closed locker room more than Young did. Nobody ever screamed at an aggressive television cameraman louder. And nobody—political reactionary or bleeding-heart liberal—ever defended the rights of women sportswriters more forthrightly against shameful harassment.

During the World Series last year, in a room behind the press box in Fenway Park, Young gave what amounted to his farewell address. It was a rabble-rousing, to-the-barricades, don't-let-the-bastards-grind-you-down speech that only he could have made. We were laughing and cheering at the same time and even those who hated him knew that as he was leaving New York, we were losing something important.

I never knew what Young's religious convictions were, but if it includes a heaven my money says he's walking up to God right now and saying, "Listen, Gooden's pitching tonight and I want you to stand up and boo."

Something Special

by Billy Weeks of the Chattanooga Times. Two special athletes await their turn to compete in the Special Swim Olympics at Orange Grove School in Chattanooga, Tenn. Copyright © 1987, Billy Weeks, Chattanooga Times.

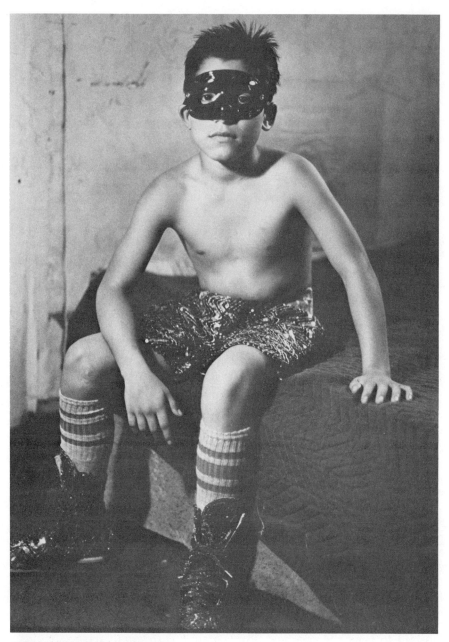

Machine Gun

by Arlene Schulman of The Village Voice. Hamilton Verano is an 11-year-old fighter, better known in New Jersey as "Machine Gun." This masked man is already being billed as a future champion. Copyright © 1987, Arlene Schulman, The Village Voice.

The Secret Life Of Jerry Smith

PRO FOOTBALL

By *PERRY DEANE YOUNG* & *RANDY RIELAND*

From The Washingtonian
Copyright © 1987, The Washingtonian

As the family, friends, and Redskin teammates of Jerry Smith stood in awkward conversation beside his sealed casket, their talk kept coming back to the poem.

"The Man in the Glass" was a corny expression of what Polonius tells his departing son in Shakespeare's *Hamlet:* "To thine own self be true." Everyone at the Rinaldi Funeral Home in Silver Spring that day remembered it as Jerry's poem. No one knew where it had come from. All they knew was that every time he made a speech—and as a Redskin, Jerry Smith had made hundreds of speeches—he never failed to recite it.

It seemed only fitting that it be read during funeral services at St. John the Baptist Church the following morning. Joe Riley (not his real name) swore that one way or another, he'd find it. When he got home, Riley, an ex-seminarian who had been a frequent housemate of Smith's during his years in Washington, called a congressional aide he knew and asked him to make an emergency request to the Library of Congress.

A library staffer called back in record time with the poem. Coincidentally, they had just processed another request for it. Someone wanted to read the poem at Tip O'Neill's retirement party. It was also a favorite of his.

So the next morning, as he came to the end of his eulogy, former Redskin chaplain Tom Skinner closed with "The Man in the Glass." And just as they had grinned and shuddered in the past whenever Jerry recited it—with that odd mixture of pride and embarrassment they had often felt for him—Smith's teammates and family sat there, thinking, "Here it comes again, the poem, one final time."

When you get what you want in your struggle for pelf
And the world makes you king for a day,
Just go to the mirror and look at yourself
And see what the man has to say.

It isn't your father or mother or wife
Whose judgment upon you must pass
The one whose verdict counts most in your life
Is the one staring back in the glass.

He's the one you must satisfy beyond all the rest,
For he's with you right up to the end;
And you have passed your most difficult test
If the man in the glass is your friend!

The poem's irony was not lost on those seated in the church. Jerry had often said that honesty and integrity were the most important qualities a man could have, and yet for the past 20 years he had been leading a double life. Publicly, he was a football hero, the greatest Redskin tight end ever, a man who had won the respect of Vince Lombardi and George Allen, two of the most demanding, hard-nosed coaches the game has known. He was devoted to his family, a warm, open, oversized boy who was generous to a fault.

Privately, he was a man who wrestled with his bisexuality, but one whose gridiron fame helped him gain entree to an exclusive gay culture—parties at Fire Island and Acapulco, Mardi Gras dinners with Roy Cohn. It was only as he lay dying of AIDS in a Silver Spring hospital room that his secret became public knowledge.

One could only wonder how many Jerry Smiths looked back from the glass.

★   ★   ★

By the time he was drafted in 1965 by the Redskins in the ninth round, Jerry Smith was an athlete with impressive college statistics and a reputation as a tireless worker. In his younger days, however, it was hard to imagine a more unlikely football star.

He was born July 19, 1943, in Eugene, Ore., the second of three children of Bill and Laverne Smith, but he spent most of his childhood in San Lorenzo, a suburb of Oakland, Calif.

Bill Smith was a big man, 6-foot-3 and 240 pounds, a manager for Western Electric for 43 years. Jerry's older brother, Ed, says his father was "very work-oriented." Bill Smith had two families to support, including children from his first marriage. When he took as his second wife Laverne Maillard, who was 16 and had been raised in a strict Catholic household, her family was scandalized. For the next 50 years, they shunned her, with the exception of one brother who met with her secretly. Laverne brought up her children as the best friends and siblings she had lost through marriage. To them, she was always Laverne, not Mom.

Jerry was a scrawny boy and closer to his mother than to his older brother, Ed. Both were teenagers by the time their sister, Bonnie, was born.

Ed was a good kid, easygoing and cautious. Jerry always seemed to be taking risks and occasionally getting into trouble. Yet his mother was always there when he needed her as a child, and she would be there 40 years later as he lay dying. She lived in the hospital with Jerry during his last two months.

In his youth, Jerry was neither a good student nor a star athlete. "He was a tall skinny kid, and he was not fast," recalls one of his coaches. With little playing experience, he started his senior year as a 140-pound, left-handed quarterback but was shifted to tight end. "Even my father laughed at me," he told an interviewer. "No college wanted me."

But Smith impressed his coaches with his dedication. "If Jerry's nose was bleeding," his high school coach remembers, "he went after it more. He loved football. He loved contact." It was a quality that would sustain Smith throughout his career, that would win over teammates and coaches. "I'd like to have a whole team of Jerry Smiths," Vince Lombardi would say.

★   ★   ★

There was another side of Jerry Smith: the risk-taker, the part of him that liked to walk along the edge.

He was fired from a job in a doughnut shop because he was taking more doughnuts for his family than he was selling. He got into trouble at another job when he and an older woman were accused of stealing credit cards. Laverne had to get him out of that mess.

And there was his first bisexual experience.

As Jerry would explain it in an anonymous interview published in the *Washington Star* almost 15 years later, he was a high school senior involved with a 19-year-old woman. She had her own apartment, and they often went there to make love. But one night she asked an old boyfriend of hers to join in her lovemaking with Jerry. The scene was repeated over the summer.

"It was exciting, for the moment," he said. But then came the flood of guilt. "I thought, 'My God, I'm a freak.' I couldn't understand. I wanted to run away and shoot myself."

For a teenager who had grown up in a working-class Catholic family, it was a terrible sin. Jerry was ashamed and confused and scared that someone would find out. If that happened, his life might as well be over.

It was a fear that would shape his life from then on. He would push himself to become an overachiever on the football field; there, all that mattered was how he played the game. Besides, if he proved himself a man on the field, nobody would ever call him a sissy.

Perhaps there were other motivations, but clearly "something happened" to Jerry about the time he finished high school, his brother Ed remembers, and his family still marvels at the transformation.

The skinny kid with no ambition suddenly became a fanatically dedicated athlete. He seemed obsessed in mind and spirit. Time and again he had to go into a hospital with injuries after he had pushed his body too far.

In his personal life, he found other ways to handle his insecurities. "I went out and tried to make every girl in the world, to prove I was not a freak," he would later tell *Star* reporter Lynn Rosellini. And throughout his college career, he said, he suppressed any feelings he had for men.

★   ★   ★

No one who saw Smith practice and play during college could have doubted his manliness. First at tiny Eastern Arizona Junior College, then at Arizona State University, he established himself as a rugged, aggressive tight end. At junior college he caught more than 50 passes his freshman year and more than 80 the next year.

Those statistics talked, and suddenly the big schools were interested. Smith turned down Notre Dame and Southern California and instead chose Arizona State, primarily because of Jack Stovall, an assistant coach there. Stovall had shown up at the junior college to take a look at the team's quarterback, but he was much more impressed with its tight end. He took Smith to the town's only cafe, and over hamburgers and malts Jerry sealed his commitment to ASU with a handshake.

The school was no intellectual haven, but its sports teams, particularly in football and baseball, were at the top college level. Once again Smith was up to the challenge. In 1964, his senior year, he set a school record with 42 catches and was a big factor in the team's 8-2 record. He was named an All-America.

Smith made a lasting impression on then-ASU Coach Frank Kush, who was a legendary disciplinarian.

"He was a gangly kid, unsure of himself when he first showed up. He had limited skills, especially in blocking," Kush would later tell a reporter. "He was a 99-to-1 shot who exemplified what dedication can overcome. He probably got more out of the talent he had than any player I ever coached."

The Washington Redskins, who had drafted his former teammate Charley Taylor the previous year, were similarly impressed. When the team signed Smith, they gave him a $19,000 bonus, which he promptly sent home. Take the family to Hawaii, he told his parents, who took him up on the offer. "Typical of Jerry," Ed Smith says.

★   ★   ★

Smith entered pro football a shy and self-conscious kid, even for a rookie. Along with the other new players, he was introduced at a Redskin alumni banquet, but when the spotlight fell on him, he bowed his head all the way down to the table and kept it there until the light passed.

To try to bring the young receiver out of his shell, Otto Graham, then the Redskin coach, urged him to do some public speaking. Smith was reluctant at first, but he became one of the team's most prolific speakers, sometimes giving two or three speeches a night. Mostly he spoke to groups of young people. Smith hit it off with kids, partly because they didn't expect him to be clever or polished, partly because he never talked down to them, even after he became a local hero.

And stardom was not long in coming.

He started the last five games of his rookie year after wide receiver Preston Carpenter was injured. The next season he was moved back to tight end, and that's when he blossomed—even though, at 210 pounds, he was light for his position. He became—along with Sonny Jurgensen, Charley Taylor, and Bobby Mitchell—part of the league's most feared passing attack and by the end of the season led all NFL tight ends with 54 receptions. The next season he scored 12 touchdowns and caught 67 passes, an NFL record for tight ends at the time. Not particularly fast and 30 pounds lighter than most of the players he had to block, Smith still became the standard against which all the league's other tight ends were measured.

★   ★   ★

Smith was one of the bright spots on a marginally successful team when Vince Lombardi arrived in 1969. Lombardi had been lured out of Green Bay with the then-astronomical salary of $100,000 and the challenge of making a winner out of a team that had not been one since 1955.

Lombardi hadn't mellowed a bit. He was as demanding as ever, expecting total commitment from his players, both physically and emotionally. Jerry Smith, he would later say, was his kind of player.

And Lombardi was Jerry Smith's kind of coach—intense, forthright, uncompromising, someone for whom football was an uncomplicated, brutal game and excellence was achieved only through determination, discipline, and practice.

"I keep saying, 'What am I doing here? Me, Jerry Smith, playing for Vince Lombardi! My God, am I dreaming?' " he told a reporter.

Lombardi would coach the Redskins for only one season, but it was one of Smith's best—54 receptions and nine touchdowns—and he was rewarded with the Redskins' Outstanding Player Award. By training camp the next season, Lombardi was in Georgetown University Hospital, dying of cancer. The last two players to visit him in the hospital were Smith and Brig Owens, Smith's best friend on the team.

★   ★   ★

The late '60s would be a pivotal time in Smith's personal life. The California boy who had come to the Redskins with a Marine-style crewcut let his hair grow into what would become his trademark blond mop. And with his ever-present sandals, he started wearing mod outfits.

"I enjoy life, and clothes are a definite part of that good life," he said in an interview. "I don't wear the high fashions to impress anyone. I just enjoy wearing them. The same goes for my long hair. I wore it short for 22 years, and now I wear it long just for a change.

"And being a bachelor, I might add that girls appreciate a cool-looking guy."

Smith looked the part, so the media cultivated his image as a free-spirited, fun-loving California playboy. A 1968 *Washington Star* story on Smith, who was then sharing an apartment with quarterback Harry Theofiledes, was headlined "Smith Swings from Right to Left." The story said that Smith's philosophy was "to enjoy life and live it to the fullest. He does."

In fact, Smith had been involved in a serious relationship with a woman, a schoolteacher from Ohio, and the papers said they were engaged to be married. But suddenly he broke off the relationship. He would explain why years later in his confessional *Star* interview.

"I thought I was quite normal. I was going to get married. I thought I could handle it. One week I was camping with some friends in the Midwest during the off-season, just minding my own business, playing a little volleyball and trying to get some rays. I realized that I was attracting someone."

That someone was a male college student who later invited Smith to a party.

"We went out three or four nights in a row," he said. "Nothing happened. On the fifth night he suggested it." And they made love for the first time.

He told his girlfriend. "I didn't want to deceive her. She accepted it. But I couldn't. It became more and more evident to me that I couldn't maintain a lasting relationship. And what if we had a family? Who would suffer?"

There would be other male lovers during his Redskin years, including a college baseball player to whom Smith was introduced by a secretly gay priest. The priest was the person who gave Smith a copy of "The Man in the Glass."

The poem's message, which Smith clearly took to heart, might seem at odds with his secret lifestyle. But it could be interpreted another way, particularly one verse:

You may fool the whole world down your pathway of years,
And get pats on the back as you pass;
But your final reward will be heartaches and tears
If you've cheated the man in the glass!

By acting on his homosexual feelings, Smith was being honest with himself, and in spite of his growing celebrity, he felt he had no obligation to talk about his sex life with anybody.

Besides, it was only one hidden corner of his life, one that had nothing to do with how he played football or his relationships with his family and old friends.

★   ★   ★

In the fall of 1968 Smith met a young woman who was as effervescent and down-to-earth as he was.

Dee Radovich was a University of Maryland freshman and a big Redskin fan. When she saw Jerry Smith eating dinner at Duke Zeibert's one Sunday night, she couldn't help asking for his autograph.

All she had for him to sign was a homecoming-game ticket stub, but Smith obliged, then grabbed another piece of paper and scribbled a note. He held it out to Dee but wouldn't let go until she looked him in the eyes. "I mean it," he told her.

"If you want tickets to any of the games, call me at this number," the note read. Dee was thrilled, but it was a few weeks before she was able to hook up with Smith and arrange to pick up tickets at the Silver Spring house where he was living. He invited her back to the house for a post-game party of "nuns and priests and cookies and milk."

That's exactly what she found when she got there. But by the time the party ended, "Jerry had them all doing the funky chicken," remembers Dee. She didn't have much time with Smith, who was busy as host and social director, but she hit it off with Don Meyers, his old friend who was visiting from California. For the next several nights, it was Meyers she was paired off with.

But Meyers went back to California, and one night when Smith brought her a letter from his friend, he and Dee ended up going out to dinner. That was the beginning. From that night on, Dee was Jerry's girl, attending all the home games and some out-of-town games as his date. She would sit with the Redskins' wives during the game and then wait in the wives' lounge for Jerry. He was usually the last one out.

She was a college student, and he was a Redskin star with a lot of obligations, including his nightly speeches, but they managed to build a social life. Sometimes they went out dancing; other times they went to Clyde's in Georgetown. Most often, they hung out with his friends on the team—players like Mike Bragg, Brig Owens, Pat Fischer, Walt Rock, and Harry Theofiledes.

That's one of the things Dee loved about him. Here was this football hero, this guy the papers described as a wild and free spirit, and what he liked most was sitting around with a few friends, telling stories and laughing or speeding along in his car with Dee, singing "Under the Boardwalk" or "Silhouettes on the Shade" together as loudly as they could.

Once Dee and her sister were doubledating with Jerry and a guitar player from a rock band. Someone started playing around with a camera, and the next thing Dee knew Jerry had grabbed her and stuffed her into the trunk of his car. He piled in next to her, and they squeezed together for a giddy snapshot. It was a guileless moment that typified their relationship. Dee still carries the photo.

★   ★   ★

They dated for almost eight years. "He was just so lovable, like a big teddy bear," says Dee. "He was a very giving, compassionate man."

They talked of marriage occassionally, and Jerry even gave Dee a diamond ring. But Dee was still in her early 20s and, having witnessed several divorces, was afraid of marriage. She also knew that although she thought Jerry would be a good husband and a great father, football would be his life as long as he could play it.

"I felt I'd lost touch with my friends, that I'd lost my identity. We didn't see my friends that often because they'd always end up talking football with Jerry or asking him for his autograph," she says. "I told him that when he was through with football, we could talk about marriage, but it seemed at the time that he'd be playing forever." Slowly but amicably, they drifted apart.

There had been another shadow on their relationship, one that Dee says she never knew about—Jerry's gay lovers. Dee had heard the rumors about Jerry before she went out with him, but dismissed them as gossip. Their sex life, she says, was normal, and although Jerry often went on long vacations by himself in the off-season and would go out without her, she had no reason to suspect that he was bisexual.

The only clue came during a moment when Jerry confessed to having "an inner turmoil." He spoke in vague terms, but Dee knew him well enough to suspect he was troubled by his sexuality.

At his request, they went to see a therapist. While Jerry talked to the therapist, Dee sat in the next room, but when she realized she could overhear him, she walked away. This was a private conversation, she thought; if he wanted her to hear it, he would have said so.

Later he asked her if she had heard what he'd said. He said he had talked loudly because there were things he wanted her to hear, things he couldn't tell her to her face. But the moment had passed, and he would never again bring up the subject with Dee. Even with those who loved him, it was a secret he couldn't share.

★   ★   ★

One of the players who joined the Redskins during the short Lombardi era was David Kopay, a feisty running back who had played for the San Francisco 49ers and Detroit Lions.

Kopay's time in Washington was pivotal because it was here that he met Jerry Smith. And it was Smith who unwittingly prompted Kopay to become the first gay pro-football player to go public.

When they first met in the Redskins' training camp during the summer of 1969, Kopay and Smith had a lot in common, not all of it readily apparent. They were both California-tanned blonds, and both had grown up in strict Catholic working-class families. Both were also unsuited to play their positions but made up in intensity what they lacked in size and speed.

Their other common bond would reveal itself more slowly. Kopay had had only one prior homosexual experience, with a college fraternity brother. He had tried to dismiss it as an isolated drunken episode, and later when a woman friend who possibly sensed Kopay's homosexuality took him to a gay bar in Detroit, he fled in fearful confusion.

Gradually, as they got to know each other, Kopay and Smith sensed that they shared a secret. There was no confrontation or heart-wrenching confession; they simply began dropping clues to each other and after a while, says Kopay, were able to talk fairly openly about it.

★   ★   ★

One night Kopay went with Smith to a dark gay bar on the outskirts of Baltimore. Nothing happened that night, but it was the first time Kopay had gone out purposely looking for a gay situation. In time the two would venture into gay bars in Washington, such as the downstairs Hideaway across from where the FBI Building now stands, or the old Plus One bar on Capitol Hill. It was an underworld into which they thought they could disappear, but as two muscular bronzed athletes, they hardly went unnoticed.

That's one reason the Pier 9 was their favorite place. Located in DC's warehouse district, it was the city's first gay disco but from the beginning attracted almost as many straights as gays. So it was acceptable for Smith and Kopay to be seen there, although several black Redskins whose girlfriends had spotted them in the club kidded them about it. But it was good-humored teasing, and if the other players suspected anything, they didn't act put off by it.

It was also during this period that Smith gave Kopay a peek into his secret life. He would sometimes fly to Fort Lauderdale, Acapulco, Santa Monica, or Cleveland, where he would take on an assumed name. His favorite was Lance, although he dropped that one when the Dallas Cowboys' Lance Rentzel was arrested for exposing himself to young girls. In Cleveland Smith was known as Buster, a college football scout. In other places, he might be a lumberjack from Oregon or a swimming coach from Alabama. It was as if whatever he did in this forbidden speakeasy world didn't count or didn't have to be real.

One night after a game in 1969, Kopay and Smith got very drunk at the Pier 9 and ended up at a friend's house in Silver Spring. As Kopay tells the story, he fell asleep but woke up in the middle of the night when Smith crawled into bed with him. What followed was an awkward bit of fumbling, but they ended up making love. To Kopay it was all his dreams of a physical mate come true. To Smith, apparently, it was just another roll in the hay.

Smith wanted no part of sex with Kopay again, and while he didn't go out of his way to exclude him from his circle of friends, neither did he try to include him. Meanwhile, Kopay was following Smith's example in all kinds of ways. He let his hair grow long and began to build his own stylish and flamboyant wardrobe. And following tips on gay bars he had picked up from Smith, Kopay made trips to Fort Lauderdale and Acapulco.

The dalliance with Kopay was out of the ordinary for Smith; he generally tried to keep football and his private life separate. But his two lives would cross again the next season, compounding his confusion.

★   ★   ★

Like many of the Redskins, Smith was taken with a rookie defensive back who joined the club in 1970. Jon Jaqua was not only a dedicated athlete; he was also outgoing and handsome, with classic, chiseled features. He had grown up on a ranch in a highly educated household, and had an unusual combination of strength and refinement that few of his teammates would ever know.

But Jaqua was anxious about his lack of experience and doubted his football abilities. Smith made him a special project. Long after practices had ended, he could be seen working with Jaqua, going over pass patterns and coverages. He found Jaqua an apartment not far from where he lived in Georgetown.

One night after a pre-season game on the road, Kopay and Smith went out to a gay disco, where they both got drunk. When they returned to the team's hotel, Kopay went to sleep and assumed Smith had done the same.

But the next morning in the hotel coffee shop, Kopay was approached by a nervous Jaqua, who asked if he could speak to him alone in the lobby. There he told Kopay that the night before Smith had come to his room and asked if he could sleep there because he had been locked out of his own.

Jaqua obliged, but after they had lain down Smith put his arms around him and tried to make love to him. Jaqua was shocked and said he dragged Smith into the bathroom so they wouldn't wake his roommate. With the bathroom light in his eyes, Smith crossed himself and sobbed, "God, forgive me; I don't know what I was doing. I must be crazy."

"Dave, that is crazy, isn't it?" Jaqua asked Kopay, who fumbled for an answer that wouldn't reveal his and Smith's secret. He suggested that Smith had just been very drunk and hadn't known what he was doing.

And that's the way it would be left, a drunken episode that was never discussed again. For years Smith and Jaqua remained close friends. Kopay, meanwhile, would eventually confess to Jaqua that he was a homosexual. Jaqua muttered, "That's really something," and from that point on he and Kopay never had a serious conversation.

★   ★   ★

During the times they discussed their predicament, Smith and Kopay agreed that somebody should write a book on the subject. But neither felt he had the courage to go public.

In late 1975, the issue was forced when *Washington Star* reporter Lynn Rosellini requested, through the Redskins, an interview with Smith. Rosellini was working on her first major assignment at the *Star,* a series on homosexuals in sports, and several sportswriters had suggested she talk to Smith. She wasn't optimistic. So far she had met with a lot of resistance. Billie Jean King, for one, had slammed down the phone when Rosellini mentioned the subject of her series.

Without revealing the nature of her story, she arranged to meet Smith at the Key Bridge Marriott. He was sitting by the window when Rosellini walked in. Shyly, she introduced herself, then sat down and blurted out her purpose: "I'm writing a series about homosexuals in sports, and several people said I should talk to you." The warm smile on Smith's face vanished, and he bowed his head. For several long minutes he sat staring at his hands.

Rosellini would always remember the hands—"The massive, scarred hands," as she later described them. She was sure he wouldn't go through with it.

Suddenly, he looked up at her. He would talk, he said, but only if he was not identified by name, position, team, or the city where he played.

"I was staggered," Rosellini remembers, and her questions were almost as nervous as his responses. When was his first experience? How old was he? What did he think afterward?

"I remember being mortified at myself asking these questions," she says. "I remember him being very concerned about his business. He just had so much to lose. He was very halting and stumbling, and it was difficult for him to answer some of the questions."

But when the long-dreaded confrontation finally came, Smith answered the questions with the kind of honesty he'd always talked about when he recited "The Man in the Glass." For the first time, he was able to talk about the fears and pain of leading a double life.

"Who can you talk to? Who can you explain it to?" Smith asked. "I really can't discuss it with many people. I don't think people can understand the pressure of my profession, how important it is to be discreet." He went on, venting anxiety and anger that had been building for years.

"It's because of this All-American image. What's an All-American image today? Is it apple pie and gee whiz? Or is it honesty and integrity? If I enjoy being with somebody, male or female, and I'm not intruding on anyone else, I consider it normal. I'm not trying to wave a flag and say that this is what you should do. I'm saying what a person does is his own business. That people don't see you as an object. Christ, we're not objects!"

The interview lasted more than two hours, and Rosellini still regards it as the most moving experience of her writing career. Now with *U.S. News & World Report*, she says she'll never forget Smith's hands or the look on his face as he poured out his heart. "I just admired the guy's guts so much—and I still do."

Aside from vague references to a few gay friends, Smith never discussed the interview with anyone. One reason neither he nor the story came under closer scrutiny is that it was upstaged overnight.

David Kopay, no longer in football, was living in Washington and looking for a new career. He picked up the *Star* one December afternoon and was shocked to see a headline promoting a story inside on homosexuals in sports. He was even more stunned when he read the story and recognized the player as Jerry Smith. Kopay frantically tried to get in touch with Smith, but never did. He did locate Rosellini and told her that he, too, had a story to tell—and that she could use his name.

Kopay felt he had nothing left to lose. Besides, his competitive instincts made him want to go one better than his friend. The resulting story caused a sensation. It led to a book co-written with Kopay that became a best-seller.

Smith was upset by the book, friends say, and for a long time he avoided Kopay. Once when they met, Kopay remembers, Smith just grinned and said, "You're really something, Kopay, really something," the same thing Lombardi would say to players without letting them know if he was praising them or making fun of them.

*   *   *

By the time of the Rosellini interview in 1975, Smith was nearing the end of his football career. He would never top the 1969 season under Lombardi, when he was chosen to play in the Pro Bowl for the second time.

Under George Allen, brought in as coach in 1971, Smith's role had been diminished. Allen preferred a conservative, run-oriented offense to the wide-open attack in which Smith had flourished. Allen also liked his tight ends big—250 pounds or so—because he chose to use them as blockers.

But Smith, the consummate team player, adjusted. He concentrated on improving his blocking. "I remember we'd be going in to look at game films," says former Redskin punter Mike Bragg, "and Jerry would always ask me to watch his blocking and tell him how he looked."

Although his numbers as a receiver dropped, Smith still managed to be a key figure in the Redskins' first Super Bowl season in 1972. He caught only 21 passes that year, but seven receptions were for touchdowns. "Jerry loved scoring touchdowns," says Bragg. "When he was running off the field after scoring a touchdown and all the guys would come over and slap hands, that's when Jerry was the happiest."

Allen most remembers Smith for a play that season that had nothing to do with scoring touchdowns. "The biggest play Jerry ever made wasn't a reception, and it received little notice," Allen wrote in the *Los Angeles Herald Examiner* after Smith's death. "During the 1972 NFC title game with the Cowboys, we were leading 3-0 in the second quarter when a fumble occurred on the Redskins' 20-yard line. The ball was bouncing around with the Cowboys in hot pursuit, but when the players unpiled, a Redskin had recovered. His name was Jerry Smith.

"In 30 years of NFL games, I can't remember a tight end retreating 15 yards in his own backfield to recover a fumble. That fumble recovery allowed us to go on and win the NFC championship 26-3. If Dallas had recovered inside the Redskins' 10, it might have been a different game. That one play describes the way in which Jerry lived. He was always doing something important and spectacular for his team."

The Redskins lost to Miami in the Super Bowl, 14-7, but only bad luck prevented Smith from being a hero. He was open in the end zone on one play, and quarterback Billy Kilmer spotted him. But Kilmer's pass bounced off the cross bar. After the season, the league's owners voted to move the goal posts to the back of the end zone.

★   ★   ★

For much of the rest of his career, Smith was plagued by injures. He missed most of one season with a groin injury, another with four broken vertebrae. When he could, he tried to hide his injuries from the trainer. Only his close friends on the team knew how much pain he felt every time he got hit on the field. "He was always hurting," says Brig Owens, Smith's team roommate. "I don't know how many times I had to help him get out of bed and into a hot shower before he could get moving."

Smith also had to contend with a string of competitors brought in by Allen, large tight ends such as Alvin Reed and Jean Fugett, who were better suited to the Allen style of play. Characteristically, Smith responded to the challenge with grace, working after practice with the men who were trying to take his job.

At the start of the 1976 season, Fugett won the starting job that had been held by Smith for almost a decade. Fugett told reporters that Smith deserved the credit. "I told Jerry that if I stay in the game long enough and a young kid comes along and beats me out, well, I just hope I can be the type of man he's been. It goes against everything you would think. He's been helping me with my assignments, my techniques. These are things he doesn't have to do, but he does. That's just Jerry."

For a player as competitive as Smith was, the demotion had to be demoralizing. But no one recalls hearing him complain, not even in private to his family. He had the same reaction for everyone: "It's the best thing for the team."

★   ★   ★

His self-effacing personality made Smith one of the most popular Redskins, both with fans and with his teammates. But he was close to only a handful of Redskins. He became increasingly protective of his private life; one sportswriter described him as the Greta Garbo of the Redskins. Often his only social contact with many teammates was at the ritual team meals before and after games.

His best friend on the team was Brig Owens, the star defensive back who came to the Redskins in 1966, a year after Smith. Both were soft-spoken men from affectionate families, and they ended up as roommates.

What made the pairing unusual at the time was that Smith was white and Owens black, but it proved not to be a barrier. "They really were like brothers," says Dee Radovich. "Before I met Jerry, I really was prejudiced. But he taught me not to categorize or label people."

Like most football roommates, Smith and Owens developed their own rituals. They both participated in the team's Bible-study classes. The night before every road game they would order hot-fudge sundaes from room service and Smith would sign Owens's name on the check. On game day, they made sure that they hit each other's pads first when they went out on the field. And during the game they made a point of watching each other and giving each other advice.

Sometimes, during practice, they would have fistfights. But they knew that came with their competitive instincts, and they would laugh about it later. "Jerry would say, 'You were feeling pretty feisty out there, weren't ya?'" Owens says.

The friendship stretched into the off-season. Smith and Owens set up a camp for youngsters that lasted three years. They helped organize a program to train young sportsmen through the National Guard, which still exists.

They also came to know each other's family well. Smith became "Uncle Jerry" to Owens' two daughters, Robin and Tracy, and every Christmas he would show up at the Owens house loaded with gifts. When the story about Smith's fatal illness broke, it was Owens who protected Smith's family by handling all media inquiries.

How much Owens knew of Smith's secret lifestyle is unclear because it's a subject he refuses to discuss. Smith's homosexuality was long rumored in the bars around Washington, and it's likely that at least some of his teammates were aware of it. But they chose not to make an issue of it. "Jerry had so much class," says Mike Bragg, "that nobody would give a damn."

No one could question Smith's commitment to either football or the Redskins, and that's all that mattered to his teammates. The kinds of bonds forged on football teams are based on shared moments of exhilaration and anguish on the field. Former Redskin lineman Ray Schoenke told a reporter after Smith died, "We knew how to survive (in the NFL) together. But we didn't have a chance to know one another."

★   ★   ★

Smith's last game as a Redskin was in December 1977. He had been used sparingly that year, catching only one pass. Both he and Owens had been cut by George Allen just before the season opener, only to be called back 10 days later.

Smith ended his 13-year Redskin career as one of the team's top receivers. He still ranks third among Redskin receivers in receptions (421) and touchdown catches (60), which means he scored a touchdown for every seven catches. His teammates nicknamed him

"Home Run."

"He was a perfectionist," says Owens. "He thought he should catch every ball he touched. The funny thing is that he never knew how great he was, not until the end of his career. I remember one time he said to me, 'You know, I match up pretty well against the rest of these guys.' "

But Smith wasn't one to bask in his football glory, and by the time he retired he had a second career in full bloom. In 1972 he had begun working for real estate broker Jack Foley, eventually becoming one of the firm's best salesmen. By 1975 he was ready to get into the home-building business and convinced his brother, Ed, and his old friend Don Meyers to move here from California. Together with Foley, the four of them formed Smith Brothers Builders.

It was part of Jerry's plan to bring his whole family east. Because of commitments in Washington, he was spending less and less of his off-season time in California. At the same time, his brother's construction business was feeling the effects of a slow market. Washington had a much stronger housing market, he told Ed. Besides, Laverne was alone now—Bill Smith had died in 1971—and Bonnie was just finishing junior college. The timing was right for a fresh start. He would take care of everything, Jerry said.

And he did. He found a house for Ed in Rockville and one for Laverne and Bonnie in Germantown. He found a place to board Bonnie's two horses and arranged to ship them cross-country. He applied to the University of Maryland for Bonnie without her knowing it. She says she found out when a letter came from Maryland, telling her she'd been accepted.

So the Smiths sold everything except their clothes, Ed's tools, and a stereo, and with Meyers drove cross-country in a truck and the family Volkswagen.

★   ★   ★

Within a year both households had moved to townhouses a few blocks apart in Gaithersburg. A year or so later, the whole family was living together in an old farmhouse on 60 acres in Damascus. The plan was to turn the property into a sort of family compound with several homes, built not within sight of each other but within easy walking distance. In the meantime, everyone, including Jerry, lived in the farmhouse, which Ed was remodeling.

It was an unusual living arrangement, but the Smiths were an unusually close family. Back in California they had all lived together in a large house Ed had built on a lot big enough to include a swimming pool and some pastureland for Bonnie's horses. Laverne, Bonnie, Ed, and Ed's first wife lived downstairs; upstairs Jerry had a big apartment with a separate entrance, which he shared with Chuck, his lover at the time. The apartment had only one bedroom and one bed, but Jerry was otherwise very discreet about the relationship in front of his family.

"He didn't volunteer anything. We didn't ask anything," says

Bonnie. "There were times when it went through our minds. But it was his life."

Whatever his private life, Jerry's family didn't seem to care. To them, he was the affectionate and perpetually upbeat son and brother. He was always kidding around, phoning home and pretending he was someone else or introducing himself as "The Peach from Long Beach." He was the family patriarch after his father's death, the one who took care of business matters and handled the major responsibilities. But he also managed to hang on to his boyish charm and never seemed much interested in settling down. He was too impulsive, Ed says, and elusive.

"Jerry was always looking at his watch," he says. "He always had somewhere else to go."

★   ★   ★

That was the pattern of Smith's life. He was constantly moving, rarely living in one place for more than a year. And when he didn't have a full schedule of public appearances, he was traveling, once taking a trip around the world.

Smith also remained a frequent visitor to the gay spots of Fire Island, Provincetown, and Fort Lauderdale. In Fort Lauderdale, he bought the family house of a young law student he had met at Georgetown University. In troubled times later on, the man would buy back half, and then all of the house. But for years it remained an escape for Smith, up to the time of his fatal illness.

It was at Fire Island that Smith met lawyer Roy Cohn. Although he lived a flamboyant homosexual life, Cohn denied he was gay until his death last year, and his associates attempted to cover up the fact that he had died of AIDS. He and Smith didn't have a lot in common, aside from the need to be discreet, but Jerry, according to his friend Joe Riley, found Cohn a witty and entertaining dinner companion, and when Smith and Riley were in Provincetown, N.Y., or at the Mardi Gras in New Orleans, Cohn would often have them to dinner.

Smith also continued to make the circuit of Washington's gay clubs, places like the Lost and Found in southeast DC. When he drank too much, a darker, violent side of his personality would emerge. One club banned him from its huge anniversary party— which he had attended five previous years—because of several scenes, according to Riley.

Riley says he was with Smith no fewer than a dozen times when Smith was stopped for speeding or drunken driving. The police officers would look at Smith, then at his license, and invariably shake hands with the football star and forget about the traffic ticket.

Gay friends remember violent incidents involving Smith and a man he was involved with in the early '80s. One night Smith and his lover were out hitting the bars when they ran into a friend, whom they invited back to the house Jerry built for himself on the property in Damascus. But before they headed out to Maryland, Smith stopped at one more bar, the Lost and Found. Smith darted inside, and the friend waited in the car with the lover, who had passed out in the back seat. The lover woke up, and when he saw Smith had gone inside he jumped behind the wheel and started the engine. Smith came running out of the bar and lunged at his lover through the open window. The friend excused himself and left the two in a mad tangle in the middle of the street.

The relationship soured so much that Smith moved out of the house in Damascus where the two had been living together and moved back in with Riley, who had a townhouse on Capitol Hill.

As troubled as his personal life had become, Smith's post-football business career had turned almost as stressful. Smith Brothers had built three subdivisions in Montgomery County, but none of the four partners had made much money. So in late 1979 Smith and Don Meyers split off and formed Burlingame Builders.

They received contracts for several projects, one of which was a new home for Sugar Ray Leonard in Prince George's County. (Leonard has since moved to Potomac.) But interest rates started climbing, the housing market softened, and Smith was soon overextended on his loans.

Smith became depressed about the business and told Riley that he felt nothing in his life had worked out. Then in 1982, Riley took a chance phone call that would turn Smith's life in a completely different direction.

★   ★   ★

Dan Cain had called Joe Riley because he wanted to find Dave Kopay. Cain, the former owner of Tex's Colorado Street Bar, a popular gay club in Austin, Texas, planned to open a new gay disco and wanted a celebrity involved with it. He thought Kopay would be ideal, but Riley said he didn't know how to reach him. "How about Jerry Smith?" Riley asked, adding that Smith happened to be staying with him.

Smith got on the phone. He liked Cain's proposal and a few days later flew to Austin to work out the terms. No cash was required up front from Smith, but he would make monthly payments to pay off a note.

Smith made no attempt to hide his affiliation with the bar, known as the Boathouse. In a story about its opening in the local gay paper, *This Week in Texas,* Smith was listed as owner, and his past connection with the Redskins was duly noted. For the first time, says Cain, "Jerry had no other life." He lived as an openly gay businessman, but the straight press took no notice that the once-famous football player was running a gay bar in Austin.

For a few months the bar did very well. Eventually Smith managed to raise a lump-sum payment to buy out Cain, and the Boathouse was his.

Cain later ended up buying back Tex's across the street and going into direct competition with Smith. But he had little contact with his former partner, and the last time he saw Smith was a glimpse of him going into the Boathouse. He remembers that Jerry looked thin.

By then, the Boathouse's popularity had peaked, and business was falling. Smith admitted as much to his old friend Jack Foley during a Christmas visit here in 1984. Foley didn't hesitate. He asked Smith to come back to Washington to work with him at the First Washington Mortgage Corporation, a firm Foley had joined in 1982. When he followed up his pitch with a long letter to Smith telling him what a good mortgage-loan salesman he would be, Jerry was sold.

In March 1985 he came back to Washington for the last time.

★   ★   ★

He moved in with Joe Blair, the former Redskin public-relations man, then working for the University of Maryland. Blair lived alone in Silver Springs, and for years his house had been open to any Redskin who needed a place to stay. Smith had lived there before, back in the days when he first started dating Dee Radovich.

He and Dee hadn't had much contact since his move to Texas, but their paths crossed again that fall. Dee was working with real estate settlements herself, and one day she noticed a case on her desk that had been signed by a Gerald T. Smith. She called the number and asked if this was *the* Jerry Smith, the famous football player.

He sounded flustered, then answered, "Yes."

"It's Dee," she laughed. They talked for a while, catching up on each other and their families. Jerry mentioned that he needed to get something from her firm and said he'd stop by.

He showed up late one afternoon, wandered back to Dee's office, and knocked on the door. When Dee looked up she was shocked. Gone was his boyish mop of hair; instead he had it slicked back. Even more noticeable was how thin and drawn his face had become.

"You look great," he said, noticing her reaction. "I look old. I'm really aging badly." They talked about having dinner sometime. They would never see each other again.

★   ★   ★

In late December of 1985, Radovich read in the newspaper that Smith had been hospitalized with pneumonia. She called the hospital and they talked for a long time and agreed that once he got better, they would get together. But Smith would never get better.

Smith had gone into the hospital just before Christmas. He hadn't been looking well, and when he developed a nagging cough Joe Blair became concerned. Blair told Smith to see a doctor, but he put off making an appointment.

Smith was now working for the Fairway Mortgage Corporation —which Foley and a partner had formed the month before—and although he made an appearance at the office Christmas party, he couldn't stop coughing.

That was on a Friday. By Sunday he was so weak he called his mother. Laverne rushed over to Blair's house, then took her son to the emergency room of Holy Cross Hospital. After an examination, the emergency-room intern sent him home with strong cough syrup.

The next morning Jerry, who had spent the night at his sister's house, could barely stand up. His sister called Dr. Jay Weiner, who had treated Smith in the past. He diagnosed the illness as pneumonia and admitted him to Holy Cross Hospital.

Christmas came while Smith was waiting for test results. He seemed to be feeling better, thanks to heavy doses of antibiotics, and was able to sit up to open his gifts: slacks and a golf shirt from Bonnie, slippers and gloves from Laverne, a briefcase from Ed.

A few days later Bonnie was visiting Jerry when Dr. Weiner walked into the room. He asked her to leave, and she knew it wasn't good news.

For an interminably long 15 minutes, the doctor talked to Jerry alone. Finally, he told Bonnie she could come back in the room. "Tell her what you told me," Jerry said.

Weiner went into a detailed, clinical explanation of the test results, but his conclusion was clear and chilling: Jerry had AIDS.

★　　★　　★

By mid-January of 1986, Smith had regained enough strength to go home to the family house in Damascus. By February, his weight back up to 195, he was able to move in with Blair and work half-days at Fairway Mortgage. He kept his illness a secret. It was like "playing hurt" again, only this time he was doing it in real life.

As late as April he played nine holes of golf. The family told him and each other that he played well, looked fine, but they all knew it wasn't true. Jerry was slipping a little more every day. In July he came down with a cytomegalovirus and checked back into Holy Cross.

The doctors there transferred him to George Washington University Hospital, where he could undergo an experimental treatment that was comparable to chemotherapy.

The treatment, Bonnie says, had three pages of side effects—hair loss, vomiting, liver damage—and was an exhausting two-weeks-on, two-weeks-off program. Jerry seemed to be throwing up the entire time he was there and didn't appear to be getting better. He finally insisted on being taken home.

Bonnie and her husband, Steve Gilchrist, rented a hospital bed and brought Jerry home with them. They were no longer living in the renovated farmhouse—that had been sold. Instead they, along with their two small sons and Laverne, were staying in a small Gaithersburg apartment, waiting for their new home to be built in Sandy Spring. But they made room.

Jerry tried to stay positive. He would start sentences with "Now, I'm not thinking negative, but . . ." and go on to talk about his will and other final arrangements.

"It was real tough to watch," says Ed Smith. "He was so strong and so positive. He'd say, 'I'm slipping some more,' but he never pitied himself." Within a few weeks, Jerry was back in Holy Cross, and everyone in the family knew he wouldn't be coming home.

*   *   *

The news began to spread. Smith's closest friends, Brig Owens and Jack Foley, confirmed their fears with the family, and soon other friends and former Redskins found out, too.

Those who went to visit him in the hospital were devastated by what they saw. "He had always kept himself in such super physical shape. But this disease had taken his body down to nothing," says Mike Bragg. "He had no color. He looked so old."

It was a matter of time before someone in the media broke the story. A local television crew, acting on a tip, had tried to sneak into George Washington Hospital when Jerry was there. Joe Blair suggested that the family give the story to a reporter they knew and trusted; it was the only way to make sure the subject would be handled with sensitivity. They selected George Solomon, sports editor at the *Washington Post* and a family friend. He agreed not to discuss Jerry's "lifestyle" and to let the family read over the story before it was printed.

The story, on page one on August 26, 1986, told how Smith's weight had dropped 150 pounds, how he hadn't eaten solid food in three months. "I'm trying hard to fight this," Jerry said, "but I don't have many good days." In fact, he was already drifting in and out of consciousness; it had taken two visits for Solomon to get enough quotes.

The day the story appeared, Jerry and the rest of the family gathered in his room to watch the evening news. They switched channels and were pleased to see that all of the reports seemed positive. Almost immediately, telegrams began arriving at the hospital, all of them wishing Jerry well or thanking him for all he had done as a Redskin.

Ultimately, the family received hundreds of cards and letters, many of them from young men who still had the autographs they had asked Jerry to sign for them as kids.

*   *   *

The response was a comfort to Jerry. Earlier in the summer he had received a letter notifying him that he would be inducted into the Washington Hall of Stars at RFK Stadium in the fall.

Laverne worried that members of the selection committee might change their minds when they heard Jerry had AIDS. Jerry tried to reassure her that they would understand, just as his old teammates and fans would. But in truth, he didn't know how they would react.

"He kept himself going until the article came out," Ed Smith says. "It was like he had done this final thing and it was positive, and then he just seemed to give up." Two weeks later he was so feeble he could only scrawl a shaky "X" on his will.

By then, his protective wall of Brig Owens, Jack Foley, and Joe Blair was, at Jerry's request, turning away all other visitors. Dee Radovich called and Joe Riley actually showed up at the hospital, but both were turned away. They were told Jerry didn't want anyone to see him in his condition.

Dave Kopay sent Jerry a letter and a copy of a speech about why it was so important for people to be honest about their homosexuality. In part, his note read, "Without you I would never have done any of this." By the time the letter arrived, Jerry was under such heavy sedation that he wasn't aware of it.

Toward the end, when his body had shriveled to almost 100 pounds, Jerry seemed to be alert only when Bonnie's young sons, Tim and Matt, were in the room. The family would notice a trace of a smile on his face when he heard the boys' voices, and sometimes he would try to wave good-bye when they said they were leaving.

Through late summer and early fall, Laverne rarely left the hospital. He had made his peace with God, he told her.

On Wednesday, October 15, the family stopped at the hospital for a visit before going out to dinner. When they walked into Jerry's room, they realized that sometime in the past few minutes he had died. He was 43.

★   ★   ★

Two weeks after the funeral, at which two dozen former teammates had served as honorary pallbearers, Jerry Smith was to be inducted posthumously into the Redskins' Hall of Stars at RFK Stadium. It was a home game, and the stands were filled. Jack Foley waited anxiously for the half-time ceremony, nervous about how the fans would react.

"Maybe 2,000 of the people in the stands knew Jerry and knew all he had done, and there were 50,000 that didn't even know him. All they knew was that he died of AIDS," he remembers thinking. "I figured somebody'd shout 'c - - - sucker' or 'fag' or something."

But as Laverne Smith walked out to the center of the field to accept the award for her son, Foley looked around and all he could hear was applause. "Everybody, I mean everybody, in that whole stadium was clapping."

In his anonymous interview with the *Washington Star,* Jerry said he could not deal with his homosexuality in public, but that he had accepted it privately. The story concluded: "Someday, he says, he hopes others will accept it, too."

Now the fans knew about him and his secret life, and they, too, finally accepted it. But Jerry Smith would never know.

A Day of Little Challenges

BASEBALL

By *SCOTT OSTLER*

From the Los Angeles Times
Copyright © 1987, the Los Angeles Times

It was the morning of the day her husband would integrate baseball, 40 years ago today, but as she stood on a street corner in midtown Manhattan, Rachel Robinson's more immediate concern was integrating a taxicab.

She was holding her 5-month-old son Jackie Jr. He was dressed in his California baby clothes and she was trying to keep him warm against the chilly New York morning. Rachel carried a bag filled with the standard baby gear, diapers and bottles. She tried to hail a cab.

Several stopped, but quickly sped away when Mrs. Robinson told them she had to go to Ebbets Field, across the river. Rachel was new to New York and wasn't sure whether it was her skin color or the inconvenient destination the cabbies objected to.

She finally got a cab and arrived at the ballpark on time, but there were other little concerns. Where does a young mother warm a bottle of formula at Ebbets Field? Answer: At the hot dog stand, of course.

"Looking back, I think our worrying about the little problems— where to eat, how to get around—was our way of defending against being overwhelmed by the larger anxieties," Rachel Robinson says.

The little things. For Jackie, things like what to wear. What is the proper go-to-work attire for the young man on his first day of integrating the national pastime? Robinson owned one suit, navy blue, but this was no time to overdress, to call attention to himself. It was just another ballgame. He was just another rookie. He wore sports clothes.

Little things, like how to act around teammates, some of whom a month earlier had circulated a petition denouncing team owner Branch Rickey's plan to let a black man play on their team.

Little concerns, like what if Jackie is on base when Dixie Walker, or one of the other Southern-born Dodgers, hits a home run? Should Robinson stop at home plate, wait for his teammate and shake his hand, as dictated by baseball tradition and etiquette: Many of the Dodgers had never shaken a black hand, and to force them to do so in public might cause them acute humiliation.

Jackie and Rachel had plenty of little things to occupy their minds that opening day.

Only five days earlier, Jackie had learned that he would be playing in Brooklyn, not with the Dodgers' minor league club in Montreal. The Robinsons, reunited after spring training, had no friends or relatives in New York, and not much money.

They took a small room at the McAlpin Hotel on 34th St., just off Broadway. It was cozy. Just Jackie, Rachel, Jackie Jr. and dozens of newspaper writers who streamed in and out of the room in those first few days to interview the man who would change baseball.

In the months and years to come, greater New York City would bow at the Robinsons' feet. They would be respected and admired. Eventually they would live in style and comfort, and at the finest restaurants they would be whisked past long lines and given the best tables. But now they took turns eating in a cafeteria downstairs, and their tiny bathroom was a jungle of hanging diapers.

Fortunately, they were not unsuited to challenges. In fact, had Branch Rickey conducted a nation-wide search for a young couple to withstand hardship and to present a favorable image, regardless of race, it's doubtful he could have done better than the Robinsons.

They were college educated, bright and articulate, not to mention attractive. Jackie was a handsome, powerfully built man who carried himself proudly, was religious, and didn't drink or smoke. In a time when blacks customarily wore dark clothing so as not to accentuate their skin color, Jackie, who was very dark-skinned, always wore white shirts.

"He was very unambivalent about his racial identification," Rachel Robinson says. "He was proud to be black, he had no feelings of inferiority."

Rachel was simply a knockout, a pretty and poised young woman. In terms of pride, confidence and inner strength, she was easily her husband's match.

Jackie and Rachel were very much a team. Their honeymoon had been an expenses-paid trip to sunny Florida for 1946 minor league spring training. En route, they were bumped off two airline flights for unspecified reasons, and when they finally boarded a bus in Florida, the driver ordered them to the rear.

Through many such indignities, they quietly endured together. Jackie would play 10 seasons for the Dodgers and Rachel would never miss a home game.

Opening Day, 1947, was marked by an absence of fanfare for Robinson's historic debut. A less-than-capacity crowd of 25,623 turned out at Ebbets Field, although it is significant that at least half the fans were black.

Rickey took great pains that Robinson not become an instant one-man social crusade. The Dodgers owner feared a white backlash against Robinson. A couple of months earlier Rickey had addressed a group of black community leaders in Brooklyn, urging them not to use Robinson as a symbol, not to wave him like a racial banner.

"The biggest threat to his success is the Negro people themselves," Rickey told the audience.

Also threatening his success were the Dodger players themselves. In spring training, before Jackie's Montreal club opened a seven-game exhibition series with the Dodgers, Rickey told Robinson, "I want you to be a whirling demon."

Rickey wanted Robinson to make such an impression on the Dodgers that the players would demand his promotion to the big leagues. It didn't work out that way, although Robinson hit .625 in that series.

In one game, he beat out a bunt to second baseman Eddie Stanky. Stanky called time out and, in frustration and anger, hurled the ball over the grandstand.

No Dodger demanded Robinson's promotion, but Rickey made the move anyway, as quietly as he could, and Jackie was the Dodgers' starting first baseman 40 years ago today.

Robinson wasn't sure that day what level of acceptance he might receive from his new teammates, but he wasn't expecting much. He knew he would live apart from the others, at home and on the road, and that there would be no immediate camaraderie.

It was enough that he was getting a chance to play. He hadn't always had that. As an officer in the Army during World War II, he had gone to the baseball field and asked to try out for the camp team. The officer in charge told Robinson, "You have to play with the colored team." That was the officer's little joke. There was no colored team.

But now Jackie was getting his shot. He didn't want to blow it. Opportunities didn't exactly abound. His older brother Mack, a college graduate and an Olympic track hero, was working as a janitor.

Robinson had to make a big impact, but he had to do it quietly. Rickey not only made Robinson vow to refrain from any physical or verbal retaliation for three seasons, but also insisted that Robinson do no radio interviews that first season, sign no endorsement contracts and write no magazine articles. Rickey even counseled Robinson to avoid playing cards with teammates on train rides, fearing touchy situations.

Many doubted that Robinson would be able to control his temper, which was legendary. He was not a man to suffer racial insults quietly. Now he would have to.

"We can't fight our way through this," Rickey had told Robinson. "We've got no army."

Those were the kinds of little things on Jackie's mind on opening day, besides the usual rookie anxiety and the challenge of playing a position he had never played until that spring.

The Dodgers were facing the Boston Braves, who had Johnny Sain on the mound. Robinson batted second in the order, behind Stanky. In the bottom of the first inning, Robinson grounded out to third.

He flied to left his next time at bat, then bounced sharply into a double play. He came to bat in the bottom of the seventh, the Dodgers trailing, 3-2.

The fans wanted action. Soon they would come to know Jackie as the most arrogant, exciting and intimidating baserunner in the game. Reading eyewitness accounts of his exploits, you picture Robinson dancing off third base, breathing fire.

For years to come, the most popular playground game in Brooklyn would be "pickle," simple rundowns with the kid in the middle always playing the part of Jackie Robinson.

But for now, all the fans knew were rumors of greatness. With a runner on first, Robinson pushed a bunt toward first baseman Earl Torgeson. Torgeson knew of Robinson's speed and his hurried throw to first hit Jackie on the shoulder blade. The ball caromed into right field and the Dodgers had runners on second and third.

Pete Reiser followed with a double, Robinson scored the go-ahead run and the Dodgers won, 5-3.

"The debut of Jackie Robinson was quite uneventful," wrote Arthur Daley in the next day's *New York Times*. "The muscular Negro minds his own business and shrewdly makes no effort to push himself. He speaks quietly and intelligently when spoken to, and already has made a strong impression."

In the *Los Angeles Times*, the game rated two paragraphs and a box score. Robinson wasn't mentioned until the second paragraph of the news-service story:

"Although he did not get a hit in three official times at bat, Jackie Robinson, first Negro to play in modern big league ball, signalized his official debut as a Dodger by sprinting home with the deciding run on Reiser's smash and playing perfect ball at first base."

It *was* a relatively uneventful day, considering what would unfold the rest of that season, and the nine to follow. The vicious racial taunts from opposing dugouts, the threatened player boycotts, would not start for another week or so. The regular death, rape and kidnap threats against the Robinson family hadn't yet begun.

The Dodgers would win the pennant that season, and Robinson would be named rookie of the year. He would eventually be inducted into the Hall of Fame.

But that was all in the future. So was much of the battle to integrate the sport. Jackie Robinson didn't exactly open the floodgates.

By the end of the 1953 season, only six of the 16 major league teams had a black player.

Still, the first step had been taken. That would seem to have called for a celebration in the Robinson household. But to celebrate would have been to admit the enormousness of what Jackie and Rachel had done and of what was ahead. It served them better to worry about the small things.

Tough Luck

by Dave Kraus of the Tulsa Tribune. High school swimmer Tracy Stevenson from Jenks, Okla., is comforted by teammates after giving out on the last lap and failing to finish a race in a 500-yard freestyle event. Copyright © 1987, The Tulsa Tribune.

The Yawner

by John F. Rhodes of the Dallas Morning News. Dallas Cowboys Coach Tom Landry wasn't about to let the tension of the NFL players' strike get to him as he watched his team warm up before the Cowboys' first replacement game. Copyright © 1987, John F. Rhodes, Dallas Morning News.

Steroids: Deadly Deception

GENERAL

By *BILL UTTERBACK*

From the Pittsburgh Press
Copyright © 1987, the Pittsburgh Press

Check out America's heroes: Hulk Hogan. Superman. Rocky. Rambo. Arnold Schwartzenegger. Mike Tyson.

They have something in common.

Large muscles.

"Our culture is enamored with the bodybuilder's physique. That's in style now," said Dr. Terry Todd, a former steroids-using power-lifter and fitness author from the University of Texas.

"Twenty years ago it would have been laughable to see guys like Arnold Schwartzenegger and Sylvester Stallone in the movies. They would have been freaks, monsters. Now they're romantic leads in movies that make billions of dollars."

There are three ways to obtain a bodybuilder's physique: Genetically; years of dedication to training and diet; anabolic steroids.

Since few people are born with Superman's genes and many lack the patience and drive of top athletes and performers, drug use has become fashionable in gymnasiums and fitness clubs.

"People are infatuated with muscle," Todd said, "and anabolic steroids give you muscle."

★   ★   ★

Anabolic steroids are physically and psychologically dangerous. Often they are obtained illegally. They are banned by the National Football League, the National Collegiate Athletic Association and the International Olympic Committee.

Still, hundreds of thousands—perhaps millions—use the drugs.

"It is an epidemic," said Dr. William Taylor, a member of the U.S. Olympic Committee's Drug Control Program.

"It is a national health problem, a very dangerous situation," said Dr. Robert Goldman of Chicago, chairman of the Amateur Athletic Union Sportsmedicine Committee and author of the anti-steroids book, "Death in the Locker Room."

Steroids can lead to a variety of life-threatening side effects. Doctors have discovered links between steroids use and heart disease, liver disease, cancer, sexual dysfunction, psychosis and addiction.

"Steroids are more dangerous than cocaine," said Dr. Ronald Lawrence of the U.S. Olympic Committee.

But nobody—or too few—listens.

The Food and Drug Administration estimates as many as 2 million people are injecting and ingesting steroids every day.

Professional and college athletes such as football players, shot putters, powerlifters and bodybuilders represent part of the problem.

However, steroids also are used in great numbers by hundreds of thousands of non-athletes in fitness clubs and gymnasiums.

"Steroids use has gone way beyond the small groups of top athletes who used them 10 years ago. It has exploded into the heart of society," Taylor said.

"Everybody, every age group, is using them. Everybody wants to look like a bodybuilder. It's not a sports problem anymore. It's a social problem. People are taking these drugs just to look good at the beach."

The growing demand for steroids has fueled a huge black market. Illegal dealers, many of whom smuggle drugs from Central America and Europe, do more than $100 million of business annually, according to the FDA.

The American Medical Association estimates that fewer than 25 percent of the nation's steroids users have prescriptions for their drugs.

The steroids explosion inspires several questions:

• What are steroids?
• Why are they so popular?
• Why are doctors alarmed?
• How has the black market flourished?
• What can be done?

★ ★ ★

What are steroids?

They are prescription drugs synthetically derived from testosterone, a male hormone. They can be taken orally or by injection. They were not designed for athletic enhancement, although some doctors will prescribe them for athletes.

Dr. Gene A. Riley, professor of pharmacology at Duquesne University, said steroids are prescribed for a variety of problems in men caused by genetics, disease, injury or age.

Anabolic steroids are different from corticosteroids, which are prescribed for allergies, tissue rejection in transplant patients and as an antiinflammatory agent in conditions such as arthritis.

"People using corticosteroids hear steroids in the news and think they're using the same drugs the athletes are getting in trouble for. They're not the same. The drugs are diametrically opposite," Riley said.

Anabolic steroids are derivatives of chemical compounds produced naturally in the male testes. Corticosteroids are derivatives of chemicals produced in the adrenal cortex.

★   ★   ★

Why are steroids so popular?

Because they work. They develop muscles faster and further than conventional diet and training methods. They make you bigger and stronger.

Scott Genslinger, 30, of North Hills jumped from 140 pounds to 250 in two years.

Ben Lawrence, a former football player at Indiana U. (Pa.) who went to training camp with the Steelers, jumped from 250 to 298. His bench press improved from 400 to "almost 600."

"If we keep telling people that steroids won't help them grow, they'll just laugh at us," said Dr. Carol Proudfit, senior scientist of the AMA. "They know better."

★   ★   ★

Who uses steroids?

Athletes use them to increase size, strength and endurance.

"Steroids are the most abused drug in football, college and the NFL," Bill Fralic of Pitt and the Atlanta Falcons said.

"It would have been impossible to become a professional—to make a living—without using drugs," said Dave Hawks of Shaler, who is considered to be one of the top five bodybuilders in the world.

"You can't compete on an international level without them," said Larry Pacifico, nine-time world powerlifting champion.

Runners and swimmers also use them. Steroids strengthen endurance muscles as well as power muscles, prevent injuries from overuses and allow athletes to bounce back quicker after difficult workouts.

Non-athletes have different reasons for supplementing their workouts with steroids. The drugs make you bigger, and bigger is more attractive.

"Everybody has an ego. . . . When you are big and strong, people notice you, they envy you," Genslinger said.

Genslinger has witnessed widespread steroids use in Pittsburgh.

"I know of 14- and 15-year-old kids who use them. I know of 50-year-old men. It's not just athletes. It is everybody."

"We have reports of children as young as 12 using steroids," Goldman said. "We know that steroids are commonly used at the high school level."

★   ★   ★

Why are doctors alarmed?

The medical world is concerned because steroids are being misused—often in megadoses, often two or four drugs simultaneously—and many steroids users have developed painful, sometimes life-threatening side effects.

"Athletes are using themselves as human guinea pigs," said Don Leggett of the FDA.

But they continue to take steroids at least partially because the link between drugs and disease is thin. It is impossible to conduct definitive tests. You can't give 100 men large doses of drugs and wait to see how many die of cancer.

"There are no studies that prove steroids cause cancer or heart disease, but there is strong anecdotal evidence," said Proudfit of the AMA.

Dr. Richard Strauss, who has done extensive steroids research at Ohio State University, has observed the following side effects among steroids-using athletes: Sterility, impotency, acne, baldness, breast development in males, muscle and tendon damage, irritability and aggressive behavior, increased blood pressure, heart attack, liver tumors, liver cancer and kidney tumors.

Women develop additional side effects: Lower voice, increased facial hair, enlarged clitoris, menstruation diminished or stopped, increased libido, breast decrease, increase in body hair and loss of scalp hair.

Is there a definitive link between anabolic steroids and cancer?

"The answer is not clear," Strauss said, "but there is sufficient evidence to cause concern."

Is there a definitive link between anabolic steroids and heart disease? Yes, Taylor said.

"Your arteries become slowly clotted by the drugs. Then you fall over with a heart attack. No warning.

"If you have the genetic potential for heart disease, it (steroids use) is one of the highest risk factors that we know of. If your father or uncle had a heart attack in his 50s or 60s, you could move your heart attack up into your late 20s or early 30s."

Strauss said problems with the reproductive system may be the most common side effect.

"It may be that the sterility and impotency end when an athlete quits taking the drug, but we're not entirely sure of that. We've seen a number of unnatural sperm for a long period of time after athletes quit taking the drug."

Lawrence, a Los Angeles psychiatrist/neurosurgeon, said the psychological side effects of the drug may be the most serious.

"There are two psychological problems that develop: psychosis and habituation.

"Athletes can become paranoid and they respond to the paranoia with aggression, sometimes violent aggression. They can become hostile."

Habituation is a psychological dependence on the drug.

"They feel they can't live without the drugs. They're terrified of shrinking, of losing their strength."

Bill Lumas, a sales representative from California who had a steroids-induced liver tumor, experienced dependency. After his liver surgery, he spent a week in a hospital psychiatric unit battling withdrawal.

"I was afraid to go one day without my drugs. I was hooked on the stuff. I was afraid I was going to lose all the weight I had gained."

Rocky Rauch, a bodybuilding champion from Lake Geneva, Wis., experienced paranoia that led to rage.

"I would get so mad it was unreal. I felt like if anybody looked at me wrong, I should break their neck."

After Lumas used steroids, his wife Patti became the victim of his rage. He would grab her, push her, shake her, throw things at her and abuse her verbally. He became reclusive.

"It's really quite a shock to live with someone who is hooked on steroids," she said. "It was like living in a war zone."

There are other dangers linked to steroids use.

Doctors at a hospital in Long Island, N.Y., recently treated an acquired immune deficiency syndrome (AIDS) patient who contracted the disease through a hypodermic needle he shared with other athletes, all of whom injected anabolic steroids.

Adolescent males are subject to additional risk, Strauss said.

"If a boy has not reached his full height, he may stunt his growth. Anabolic steroids tend to close the growth plates at the ends of bones sooner than normal, permanently decreasing further growth."

Taylor said it is difficult to determine why and when steroids lead to health problems.

"We can't predict what is a safe dosage and what is a dangerous dosage. Taken in low amounts, the drugs are probably safe. But in low amounts, you don't get bulk. So nobody's taking these drugs in low amounts. They're taking them in huge amounts."

Despite the risks, athletes take steroids without fear. The horror stories are frightening, but they are not common.

"There is no real hard-core evidence that steroids are more dangerous than cigarettes, but they still sell cigarettes and people still smoke," Genslinger said.

"Everybody makes choices. Everybody takes risks."

Strauss said Genslinger's ideas are similar to most athletes.

"To the athletes, the chance of incurring serious problems from steroids are very remote. And they're right. They are remote, but they're also very real.

★   ★   ★

Why has the black market flourished?

Because steroids are difficult to obtain legally. Few doctors will write prescriptions for steroids, although the ones who do might not be operating unethically. If doctors believe steroids in small, monitored doses are safe, they may prescribe them for athletic enhancement.

"I don't think that you could prove it is unethical," Proudfit said. "Ethics is a very difficult point to interpret.

"There are many cases where drugs are prescribed for conditions other than the ones printed on the FDA-approved label. That happens commonly. That practice is not considered illegal or unethical."

Yet the doctors who prescribe steroids for athletes are careful to conceal the practice. Of the many doctors interviewed for this series, not one would speak on the record about prescribing steroids and not one would allow his name to be used. Of the many athletes interviewed who obtain steroids legally—dozens of athletes—not one would reveal the name of his doctor.

The illegal method of obtaining steroids can be easy or difficult, Genslinger said.

"Sometimes it seemed like everybody and his brother were selling steroids and sometimes nobody had the stuff."

Some who sold steroids had legitimate wholesale drug licenses. Charles Radler was one of those.

Radler, who was operating out of Penn Hills, was the biggest steroids dealer in the nation in 1983, according to District Attorney Robert Colville of Allegheny County. He could buy drugs from American manufacturers and sell them to hospitals, pharmacies and doctors. However, he broke the law. He sold to athletes and other individuals. He pleaded guilty to 18 counts of illegal distribution and served a year in prison.

Some dealers, like Radler, get their drugs from legitimate manufacturers. Among the FDA's most recent arrests were pharmacists in Texas, Illinois and New Jersey. Most of the illegal steroids, however, apparently come to America from abroad.

In May, the FDA and Justice Department dismantled a $70 million syndicate that operated from an underground laboratory in Tijuana, Mexico, and serviced a market from San Diego to Minnesota to Florida.

"There has been considerable steroid traffic across the Mexican border," said the FDA's Leggett, "but Mexico is just one example of a country where drugs are easily available to people who want to smuggle them into this country."

Assistant District Attorney Greg Nescott of Allegheny County said there are two steroids investigations ongoing in Pittsburgh. But steroids do not receive much attention from police.

"Steroids are not a very high priority drug right now," Nescott said. "Most drug investigations concentrate on the more dangerous, more addictive drugs like cocaine and heroin. Nobody is looking to bust users of steroids. No one is going into the gyms and arresting people."

Illegal steroids pose a major problem for users, Genslinger said. You can get the drugs, but you can't get any medical advice with them.

"There are situations where people who sell steroids have never used them. They don't know the difference between drugs. They tell you that $20 bottles are better than $5 bottles because they can make more money. They tell you that 10 tablets a day are better than five because you'll have to buy more. They don't know what they're doing to your body. They only know what makes them the most money."

★   ★   ★

How do you eliminate the steroids problem?

Three choices: Enforcement, drug testing, education.

The FDA and the Justice Department have accelerated their investigations into the black market. They are making arrests.

Taylor of the U.S. Olympic Committee said the process would be easier if steroids were reclassified as controlled substances, just like cocaine, heroin and amphetamines. Reclassification would mean the powerful Drug Enforcement Agency—with additional money and manpower—would join the hunt.

The International Olympic Committee and the National Collegiate Athletic Association have been testing for steroids. The Pan American Sports Organization, which tested medal winners, disqualified U.S. hammer thrower Bill Green and two Venezuelan weightlifters two weeks ago for steroids use. The National Football League tested every player this month.

The easiest and most obvious solution to the steroids problem is education. Few users, especially teenagers, are fully aware of the dangers.

"I've talked to too many kids who are full of misconceptions about steroids," Pitt football strength coach Buddy Morris said.

"Not enough schools are teaching it. It should be emphasized in the classroom and in the textbooks," Goldman said.

A few Pennsylvania educators are addressing the subject.

Woodland Hills held a mandatory steroids assembly. Central Catholic health teacher Bill Morton clips articles from journals and gives them to his classes. Bill Elder, head football coach at Mount Pleasant, annually brings a doctor to an August football practice to discuss the dangers of steroids, alcohol and other drugs.

The University of Pittsburgh offered athletes a new class, Drugs in Sports, on an elective basis during the winter term. In the fall it will be mandatory for all freshmen athletes.

Education will not eliminate the problem of steroids in sports, but it may diminish it.

"Anybody with a brain will quit using steroids when they learn of all the potential dangers," Goldman said, "but there are some athletes out there without a brain and no amount of education will reach them."

The Power and the Kingdom of Joe Paterno

COLLEGE FOOTBALL

By *JAY SEARCY*

From Philadelphia Inquirer Magazine
Copyright © 1987, the Philadelphia Inquirer

Edna Thompson is playing a game of spades at her dining room table with two of her children and a friend on a cold February Sunday night in Knoxville, Tenn., when newspaper and television reporters begin calling every few minutes.

"Is Joe Paterno at your house?" they ask. "Has he been there? Is he coming?"

"Nah," Mrs. Thompson says, "ain't no Joe Paterno at my house." And no, she says, she hasn't heard from him, isn't expecting him and has no idea where he might be. She doesn't even know the man. She goes back to her card game and wonders aloud why all the commotion about Joe Paterno. A lot of college coaches have visited her house in the last few weeks, but none has attracted this kind of attention.

"He's the legend, Mama," explains her son, Sorrell. "The living legend."

At that moment, Joseph Vincent Paterno, head football coach at Pennsylvania State University, is at the Knoxville airport waiting for the arrival of USAir Flight 324 from Pittsburgh. Leroy Thompson, Edna's youngest son and perhaps the No. 1 high school football prospect in the nation, sought by more than 100 schools, is aboard that flight. Leroy has spent the weekend at Penn State, the last school on his list of five permitted visits. The athlete voted Mr. Tennessee Football, everybody's All-America, and probably the greatest running back Knoxville has ever produced, will be making his choice of colleges soon now.

Someone spots Paterno at the airport, then someone else recognizes him, and before long, Knoxville's three television stations and two newspaper offices are abuzz with a rumor: Joe Paterno's in town. He must be after Leroy.

Other big-time college recruiters have been wooing this 17-year-old superstar, but no other coach has caused this kind of concern, posed such a threat to take away Tennessee's prize son. This is Joe Paterno, dean of the major-college football coaches, architect of six undefeated seasons, a man who has never had a losing season in his 37 years of coaching.

With his never-ending crusade for higher academic standards, with his players' 85 percent graduation rate, and with his whistle-clean, no-cheat image, Paterno has long been finding a crest of popularity. But he really hit the top of the popularity charts in January when his wholesome, clean-cut, Penn State football team upset a brazen, cock-sure University of Miami for the national collegiate championship in the Fiesta Bowl, the school's second national crown in five years. That dramatic game was as much a clash of philosophies and lifestyles as it was a contest of two massive collegiate football powers: Coat-and-tie vs. the T-shirt, Yes-sir vs. Uh-huh, Straight vs. Cool. Indeed, it convinced just about every football parent and player in America—who wasn't convinced already—that Joe Paterno is much more than a great and gifted football coach. He is right up there with Mother Teresa—a saint, the god of football. At a time when stories of blatant player payoffs and academic abuses of athletes are shocking the country, here is a man of his word. Or words. Joe Paterno has many of them, including these top 10, life-long favorites: God, family, country, valor, work, education, discipline, loyalty, integrity and excellence.

Of course, he believes them. But he also makes very conscious use of them in a college football empire created for and controlled by Joe Paterno. Almost no one says no to this man. His massive web of influence includes his recruits, their families, his coaches, their wives, his family, the media and anyone else who happens to stray too near the edge of Penn State football. It is a widely held supposition that it was the issue of control, or the lack of it, that caused him in 1973 to turn down a million-dollar coaching opportunity in the National Football League.

In his 21 years as head coach at Penn State, Paterno has become a master manipulator, knowing just when to show emotion—and which—when to discipline, when to be soft, when to joke, when to play on valor, when to be the scholar or when to roll out the morality. He has created an image so perfect that he sometimes finds it difficult to live with, and cynics find it difficult to believe. His football world is a series of acts, and sometimes when he moves from scene to scene, he seems to be writing the dialogue as he goes. But Joe Paterno is also producer, director and star. Always it is Joe Paterno in control. Now, let's watch and see how he does it. Leroy Thompson and his family offer a rare view of a consummate actor at work.

Paterno talked to Leroy only briefly on campus but promised to see him again in Knoxville, so he meets him at the airport. They ride to Leroy's home together, along with Penn State assistant coach Jim Caldwell, and a little after 10 p.m. there is a knock on Mrs. Thompson's door. Once more she interrupts the card game, walks to the door and pulls it open. She sees two men, but her eyes fix on the bespectacled one in front wearing the big fuzzy coat.

"Hi, I'm Joe Paterno," he says. "And of course you've met Coach Caldwell here. I think I'm returning a package of yours."

And with that, Leroy steps into view, wearing a mischievous grin above a Penn State jersey. Enter Joe Paterno, laughing. Just a friendly guy.

There is a flurry of introductions and hand-shaking, and Mrs. Thompson's friend makes a frantic dash to the store to buy film for the family camera.

"Well, first, see," Mrs. Thompson remembers about that visit, "he was sitting over there (on the couch) and he made a couple of jokes. He looked real serious and said he had something to tell us but that it was off the record." She covers her mouth and laughs at the thought of it. Paterno, she says, told a story of how he received a call from Johnny Majors, the University of Tennessee football coach. "He said, Coach Majors called me and said, 'Joe, I've got this kid down here named Leroy Thompson who is a great athlete, and I need somebody to come down here and take him off my hands. Would you mind coming down to Knoxville and sign him?'

"Everybody just laughed," Mrs. Thompson recalls, "and that broke the ice, you know."

Then Paterno dances closer to the subject that he knows is on the mother's mind. "He said if Leroy goes to Penn State and makes an A, he gets to sleep in a bed. If he makes a B, he sleeps on the floor. And if he makes a C, he sleeps outside or someplace. That was just a joke, but I prefer that he be serious about that one.

"You know, he was just so *eeeeasy.*"

That's because the situation calls for easy. It is not time to play the preacher, it is not time to pump up the disciplinarian. Here is a willing, eager audience, and Paterno, well-briefed by his assistant coaches, plays them gently.

This is Act One, Scene One of one of the most successful, longest-playing shows in major college football. Paterno, 60, the lawyer's son from Brooklyn, the English lit major, can act it out with his eyes closed, for it is a role he has played for almost four decades—from State College, Pa., to the shores of the Atlantic, from Pennsauken to L.A.—and he plays it with confidence and great flair. He plays it so well because he believes every word to be the absolute truth. The names and the location change, but the story line seldom varies: Paterno moves quietly into enemy recruiting territory, subtly casts a spell on his subject, warms Mama's heart, charms Daddy, excites the neighborhood, then waits patiently for the magic result. *Voila!* Another of America's prize athletic talents rides off to Happy Valley,

U.S.A., home of Joe Paterno's no-frills, no-nonsense finishing school for football players. Guaranteed 99.44 percent pure. Approved by Good Housekeeping, the U.S. Food and Drug Administration, and President Reagan.

What Paterno says now, what he does in the next few minutes, will be crucial to Leroy's recruitment. It has been in settings such as this, Paterno knows, that he has won his 199 games, here in the living rooms and dining rooms and kitchens of America. And he'll use whatever props he's given for the role. "If mama makes cookies, you eat the cookies," he says. He will gain 14 pounds before the recruiting season ends.

"You have to be a bit of an actor," he has said many times. Today the father figure, tonight the preacher, tomorrow the shouting agitator. Nobody can be all those things, say the cynics. So they call him a fraud. Pompous, they say. A hypocrite.

Nobody can dispute his results, since he has averaged nine victories a year for 21 years, since his team has a current regular-season winning streak of 22 games, since his teams have played on national TV 75 times, been to 18 bowls and have had 15 Top 10 finishes in the national polls, and since he has been named coach of the year four times. So when his detractors call him The Legend, or Joe "No-Deal" Paterno, or Saint Joe, they do it with at least a little respect.

Many say that Paterno's longtime crusade has at last made an impact, helping to turn the corner in the battle to cleanup cheating in big-time college athletics. Pressure from parents and educators has increased. Penalties have stiffened. Public awareness of unethical practices is at an all-time high. Joe Paterno's voice in the wilderness is now echoing across America: Reform! Quit the cheating! Save our children! Save our schools! Raise our standards! Return to discipline!

The national championship has once again put the spotlight on his football program. It has created a new curiosity about the man and his methods—and it has created new jealousies. Some people say Paterno's proselytizing is just an attempt to extend the boundaries of his control to a national arena.

★   ★   ★

"He didn't come here acting like no big shot," Edna Thompson continues. "It was like he was just one of us. I told him, I said, 'I lost my money betting against Penn State in that Miami game,' and he said, 'You bet against me?' and we laughed.

"But Coach Paterno didn't come in here talking football. He talked about academics, and he talked to the children just so easy. Sissy (Leroy's sister) was still sitting at the table and he said, 'What you playing?' and she said 'spades,' and so he wanted to know how to play. Sissy showed him and he sat down and played her hand for her. He won with it, too. . . .

"Everybody else came in here talking football, football, football and making all kinds of promises about what they were going to do for Leroy. But Coach Paterno kept stressing academics. You know, what Penn State's record for graduating athletes. Like 88 percent or something. Higher than the regular students. I looked it up, and it was higher than what he said.

"Other coaches talked about academics, too, you know. Like they said Leroy would have a four-year scholarship, and if he got hurt he would still go to school. But nobody put academics first like Paterno."

Throughout the visit, Leroy hardly says a word. He studies the stranger, listening intently. "If you come to Penn State," the coach tells Leroy, "I'm going to work you. This person you see sitting here isn't going to be the same person you'll see out there on that practice field."

It is Honest Joe Paterno now, consciously letting Leroy see a bit of back stage. But "I can't see it," Leroy says later. "I can't imagine him on the coaching side. This little bitty skinny dude. . . . I want to see him. I can't picture it." And he laughs at the thought.

It is almost midnight when Paterno says good night to the Thompson family and returns to his hotel. Every other time he had been to Knoxville, he tells them, he has stayed at the home of his friend Johnny Majors. "This time," he says, "I didn't get an invitation." Exit Joe Paterno, laughing.

The Thompson family is too excited to sleep. They talk about the visit far into the night.

"So that's The Legend," says Mrs. Thompson. "I don't know Joe Paterno the coach. The person I saw was Joe Paterno the man, and I like him."

★   ★   ★

The following Tuesday, Paterno returns unexpectedly to Knoxville to watch Leroy play a basketball game. Act One, Scene Two, the message of which is clear: You're important.

Then on Friday, Paterno makes a third trip down, so alarming that it is the lead story on the 11 o'clock news. TV cameramen camp in front of the Thompson home. Neighbors gawk out windows and mill around the hallway. Two Tennessee assistant coaches park down the street at a pay phone, waiting for a chance to call Leroy. And when Paterno and Leroy ride somewhere to talk in private, a local radio station interrupts a show to report: "Leroy Thompson and Penn State coach Joe Paterno have just left the Thompson apartment in Leroy's 1979 Mustang. They turned north on Dandridge Avenue and. . . ."

"You know, Leroy," the coach tells the athlete, "it would be wrong for me to make a lot of promises to you and say you're going to start, or do this or that. I've got to be loyal to the other players I have. I could tell you that, and then when I go back to them, what do I say?"

He tells Leroy that he will get an education, that he will be tested for drugs ("not because I think you have a problem, but because I don't want you to get one"), that he will get an opportunity like everyone else.

Leroy signs with Penn State the next day, ending the most celebrated recruiting campaign in Knoxville history.

★   ★   ★

When the writer of this article returns from Knoxville, after interviewing the Thompson family, his phone rings. It is the Penn
State sports information director, acting on orders from Paterno.
"You know how Coach Paterno feels about publicizing his recruits,"
he says. "He's upset. I'm calling to protest."

Act Two: Paterno has clearly dropped the role of friendly adviser. Now he is the dictator.

Any other college coach would be bragging about signing an athlete of Leroy's abilities. Not Paterno. It's an example of his attempt
at total control. He has never allowed any of his five children to be
interviewed, and two of them are grown and living independently.
To a degree, he controls what his players wear, how they speak and
to whom, what they say, where they go, when they go to bed, whom
they hang out with. He even assigns roommates. He forces the media
to meet him on his terms. Practice sessions are closed. Player interviews are by permission only.

The control over his coaches is almost as great. Before he hires a
coach, he insists on talking to the coach's wife. He wants assurance
that the wife understands and can cope with the 16-hour days, the
seven-day weeks, the hotel Christmases. He looks not for a particular coaching skill, but for a particular personality ("I can *teach* him
how we coach," Paterno says). He wants a variety of personalities so
that staff meetings are stimulating and challenging. He wants an
agitator, a doubter, a peacemaker, a gambler, a firebrand, youth,
age. He once dismissed an assistant, not because he wasn't a good
football coach, but because he was the wrong personality for the
proper blend.

Sometimes the shouting from staff meetings can be heard in the
lobby outside the coaches offices—an indication that all is healthy.
Business as usual. But despite all the healthy arguments, in the end,
it's Joe Paterno's way. "Sometimes I could kick myself," Paterno
says. "Somebody will bring up an idea that maybe we tried 35 years
ago, and I'll say, 'No, we've tried that and it didn't work.' I should let
them try it, find out for themselves."

Over the next few days, the reporter tries to reach Mrs. Thompson for additional information. She is no longer available for comment.

"He's so serious," says Paterno's sister, Florence, "he was born
with a frown on his face."

Paterno lives his private life as intensely as his public one. He
helps countless charities. He speaks frequently, often for free, and
sends hand-written messages and makes telephone calls to sick or
troubled friends. He lives in an unpretentious home in a workaday
neighborhood a mile off campus. His phone number is in the book. He

often walks home from practice and spends what spare time he has listening to opera and reading. (His summer reading list includes Joseph Priestly's "History of Western Civilization," Gore Vidal's "Empire," Virgil's "Aenead," Richard Nixon's "Leaders"—his copy a gift from Nixon himself—and Allan Bloom's "The Closing of the American Mind.")

He is reported to make well over $100,000 a year, barely in the top 20 among America's top-paid coaches. He could double or triple that easily if he wanted to sell his name, as many coaches do. But except for a few commercial ventures, he has given his image to Penn State for marketing (lifesize cardboard Joe Paterno photo cutouts called Standup Joes at $24.95 each, or a table model for $8.95, posters for $10, JoePa golf balls, T-shirts, glasses and, on the list for consideration this year, a Joe Paterno bronze bust). He actively solicits donations and is responsible for millions of dollars in gifts to the university every year. He is now serving as vice chairman for a five-year, $200 million fund-raising campaign, to which he personally donated $150,000, $50,000 for minority scholarships and $100,000 for the library.

Perhaps no one understands Joe Paterno more than his brother, George, who played in the streets of Brooklyn with him, lined up beside him in the backfield at Brown in the late '40s and has, for 12 years, been the radio analyst for Penn State games. George, 57, is the assistant athletic director at the U.S. Merchant Marine Academy.

"I want to preface this by saying that I don't believe in this sainthood and genius business," he says, "but never, when it came to morality or his beliefs, do I recall Joe giving in. If he ever bent, it was so he could accomplish something for the greater good.

"We went to a Jesuit school (Brooklyn Prep), and both of us were very close to the Jesuits. They get you at a time when they temper you and formulate you. I think my father was what I call a pragmatic idealist, so you get a kid who genetically already has that running through his system and then you go through an idealistic education with very bright Jesuit teachers. (Joe) took it very seriously.

"I remember one Christmas we wanted bicycles, and my father hid the bicycles in the storage room. I was the guy who was always suspicious and got in trouble all the time. I knew they were there, so I got one of my cousins to come over with a screwdriver, and I took the bicycles out before Christmas and pedaled them around the cellar. Joe thought it was awful that I would do such a thing.

"We were in the same class at Brown (George the fullback, Joe the quarterback), and that was more or less the beginning of what you see now in him. He had been called into the service at the end of World War II, and when he came out he was really mature. For a while we were roommates, but he was always telling me what to do and so that didn't work. I used to fool around, play a little cards. He was trying to make me stay in and study every night. He was very dedicated to excelling in sports and studies."

Joe Paterno concedes now that he was abrasive and demanding when he was a young assistant coach. He even acknowledges that he probably would have been fired at most schools. "I was downright rude at times when I couldn't get my way, like a little bad kid," he says. "I thought I was right all the time."

★   ★   ★

Act three. The Penn State practice field. Paterno's costume is khaki pants, rolled up a turn at the bottom, white socks, black shoes and a gray sweatshirt. Notes flap around in a hip pocket, and he walks from drill to drill with a frown on his face, looking at nothing in particular and seeing everything.

The 100 or so players wear color-coded jerseys—light blue for the first offense, dark blue for the first defense; green for the second offense, red for the second defense. Injured players wear a red cross on a white apron. On the jerseys there are no numbers, no names. Since practices are closed to the public, the media (this day, the first of spring practice, is an exception), the students, the professors, the girlfriends, even the parents, who is he hiding the players' identities from? Does he think there are spies in the sky?

In their white helmets, the players look like multicolored mushrooms in formation. Everyone is busy. The pace is double time. If you are not working, you have no place here. The practice field is Joe Paterno's classroom. There will be no distractions.

The only sounds are the popping of pads, the grunting players, and the whistles and shouts of the assistant coaches:

"HURRY! GET BACK! LET'S GO, LET'S GO!"

"WAKE UP, BOB! WAKE UP!"

"NO! NO! NO! LET'S DO IT AGAIN!"

"NOW THAT'S A TACKLE, MIKE! EVERYBODY SEE THAT!"

Practice is so intense, the assistant coaches often rush to the site of a tackle shouting instructions even before the players can untangle.

"WHAT DID I SAY? DON'T LET HIM GET OUTSIDE ON YOU!"

"YOU GONNA LET HIM PUSH YOU AROUND LIKE THAT?"

Four drills are going at once, nonstop action, and Paterno stands with his hands on his hips. Sometimes he says something casually to an assistant or to a player, but sometimes he explodes into a blind, red-faced rage, runs up into the face of a player and screeches, eyeball to eyeball: "THAT'S 15 YARDS! YOU CAN'T GRAB HIM LIKE THAT! USE YOUR HEAD!"

The player remembers those eyes, that scream, for a lifetime.

Bob White, a standout senior defensive tackle on last season's national championship team, was once the target of Paterno's outrage. "I had a slight knee injury and I had been off a few weeks," he remembers, "and the first day back at practice I was favoring it a little more than I should. So for the first couple of series, I didn't do so hot. Suddenly he ran up to me and screamed in my face, 'YOU STINK! YOU'RE LOUSY! THAT'S AWFUL!' I still remember how I felt after that.

"It's amazing how much better the knee got."

Trey Bauer, a senior linebacker on last year's team, objected to Paterno's heavy hand at the beginning. "He told you when to practice, when to get treatment, when to go to class," Bauer says. "He took away your individuality. But it was just a matter of me maturing. Now I recognize if you want to win, you have to do it the way one person says. Sometimes I really think he's not far from being a saint."

It's Paterno's motivator role. He knows it. His philosophy is to make practice tougher than any game will ever be and to play every down as if the team is behind. "We do everything faster at practice than it happens in a game, work harder and longer," says Bauer. "He's always pushing us to think. He won't let you get careless. So when we go into a game, we think we're better prepared, better conditioned, that nobody could work as hard as we did, that we're ready for whatever someone throws at us. You start thinking that way, and your confidence builds."

"When we finish up practice," says quarterback coach Bob Phillips, "we'll have two foreign team offenses running against one defense at an extremely fast pace, faster than what's going to be in a game. And we'll give the defense all kinds of problems and shifts, trying to frustrate them so that they know what can happen on Saturday in front of 85,000 (fans). If there's one thing (Paterno) does best, it's that he teaches our kids not to make big mistakes in key situations and that if you make a bad play, it can't affect the next one or the next two. That's when you lose football games."

Three times a week he talks to the squad before practice. He may read something from a newspaper on the dangers of drugs or alcohol, issue a warning about agents or strangers, read a letter from a fan, quote a philosopher, tell a joke. "Write your mother," he says from time to time. "Go to church. Wear socks. Cut your hair."

Paterno gives each assistant coach responsibility for six or eight players, to advise and help and to keep an eye on. If classes are cut, or grades begin to slip or if the language is strong, a player soon finds himself in Paterno's office. And then Paterno becomes the father talking to the son.

"Sometimes maybe I'll see a kid at church, and maybe he doesn't look like I think our kid ought to look going to church," Paterno explains, "and I'll call him in and say, 'Hey, when you go to church, don't go looking like that. Why don't you put on a nice shirt and put a pair of socks on?' Once in a while I'll call in a kid and say, 'You know, you're getting carried away with the language. You know, you wouldn't want to use that kind of language in front of your mother.'"

He has disciplined his children in much the same way. Including some screaming. "If I've got a problem with somebody, whether it's with the team or at home, I want to get it right on the table," he says. ". . I say, 'Now don't give me any baloney. I want to know what you're thinking. And I'm not going to be angry as long as you're honest with me.' Now I may blow my stack, then I'll calm down and say, 'OK, let's be honest about this thing. Do you think you're giving me 100 percent? Do you think you're practicing as hard as you can?' Most of these kids have never been pushed. They don't know how good they are, how good they can be, unless somebody makes them do it.

"Or maybe I sit my kid down because I'm not comfortable about some of the people he's hanging around with, maybe getting involved with something I don't know about. I'll say, 'Hey, you fooling around with drugs?' You know, just, 'Hey, don't give me any baloney. Are the guys you're hanging around with using drugs? Do you think you can handle it?' Now, I don't know how effective I am. I've still got two young guys. I have the same concern as every other parent.

"Kids have to know you're interested. If I chew a kid out, I may go to the locker room afterwards and call him in the office and say, 'Do you understand why I'm up and down your back? Do you realize that I think you can be awfully good, but you're not paying attention to details? You're sloppy. You don't seem involved. You're not approaching the practice field with the right attitude.' And I'll say, 'I'm going to chew you up and down until I get you where you're good.' I get a kick out of people who think you can win without being a tough guy in this league. You can't. To get results, you've got to be on top of people."

Not at games, though. Unlike at practices, during a game, Paterno plays it quiet. Now is the time to guide, to reassure. An image of smooth control is what's called for. In 1981 Penn State was losing 14-0 to rival Pitt. Pitt was about to score again, and it was still the first quarter. "Don't panic," said Joe Paterno. "Stick to your game plan."

So the offense got together on the sideline and said, "Enough's enough," and Penn State went back out and won, 48-14. After the game, Paterno walked in the locker room for his usual post-game talk. He quieted the celebration. "Look," he said. "I don't want you to remember how you feel right now. You're feeling pretty good. But I want you to remember how you felt when you were down 14-0 in a national television game, and you were about to get your face put in the mud and have somebody rub your nose in it.

"Remember how you kept your poise and held hands and pulled it out. Those are the things to remember, because you're going to be down 14-0 a lot of times in your life."

★　　　★　　　★

That's how it works when it works. And in 21 years Paterno has made it work very well. But what happens, some people wonder, the year he has his first losing season? Or a second? What if the recruits won't respond to his siren call? Would his act continue to play? Would Paterno lose control?

Nobody knows for sure. But there have been small hints, tiny clues. In 1983, Paterno lost badly two weeks in a row, to Notre Dame and Pitt. The team was hurting and embarrassed—and cost him a prestigious bowl game. Everybody around Paterno suffered. He was a tyrant, impossible to live with, awful to be around. At such times, some people feel, the script seems to have changed. The actor loses his place. Maybe his audience is actually seeing some of the offstage reality.

"There was one time," says Bob White, the defensive tackle, "when he came into the locker room at halftime and we were playing lousy and he just came in and threw a couple chairs up against the wall, kicked some chairs and said something real quick, like 'I hope you get your heads out of your rear ends.' Then he just walked out."

Another time, a final question in an interview last spring seemed to unsettle Paterno. It concerned the issue of player recruitment and eligibility violations—cheating. Paterno is proud of his record and of Penn State's clean image, but, strangely, it is a subject that seems to make him uncomfortable.

Dapper in a tweed jacket and tie, he sails through the interview, answering questions he's heard a hundred times before. In the lobby outside his office, he is asked to talk about cheating. Bear Bryant, in his later days, admitted that he cheated when he was a young coach. When you were a young coach at Penn State, did you ever cheat?

"We've never cheated," he says emphatically. Then he pauses. "Now, the rules were different back in the old days when you could give a kid a job," he goes on, "and we had a job program and what have you. I don't . . . you know . . . you shouldn't say I've never cheated, because in 37 years you're not sure that's true."

A rare side of Joe Paterno begins to show—an uneasy, uncertain side. He begins to stumble. The words come hard and haltingly. He's not a cheat and the image is important to him, but maybe, somewhere, a long time ago. . . ? He can hardly bring himself to say aloud that, perhaps, he has ever been less than perfect.

He looks the reporter directly in the eye, but he is groping for his lines. "But I don't remember . . . I remember. . . . It was never a pattern to cheat around here. If there was some cheating done, oh, I'm trying to think. . . . I really don't. . . . Well, you know we may have . . . you know. . . . We had a kid one time who was married and had a baby and we went around and dug up furniture to furnish his apartment so he could make it. That may have been illegal at the time. I'm really not sure whether it was or wasn't and I really didn't care. Because it was . . . it might have been . . . so I don't know.

"It is not my nature to cheat. I know at some time, I'm sure, someplace in my life I've done some thing I'm not particularly proud of, you know, maybe a lie when I got in a jam when I was a kid or something like that. But unfortunately, to a degree, I have almost literally been brainwashed because of the people I've been around. Put yourself in Don Quixote's frame of mind, literally. I've been almost groomed to be a realist and a romantic."

Suddenly Joe Paterno's dilemma becomes apparent: If he says he's never cheated, he'll be lying, and if he tells the truth, he must admit he was a cheat.

"That doesn't mean that, with my aggressiveness, that I have not somewhere down the line, I'm sure, done something that could be considered cheating. I mean, I could not have been as aggressive as I have been—recruiting as an assistant coach, I was aggressive as I could be—you know, whether I could have done something, said something that misled somebody. I think I would be dishonest if I told you that, that I had not done something like that. . . . And I think that's what Bryant was referring to. There was a point when he had gone to Texas A&M, and he was aggressive because he had to get it done, and it wasn't even in your own mind thinking that it was cheating. It had to be done, and I'm sure I've probably done some of that. Now that's rationalization, of course, on my part. That's cheating."

There. He said it. Now everybody can relax. He's one of us, after all. No saint. No magician. It's good old Joe "Human Being" Paterno from Brooklyn. Ninety-nine and forty-four hundredths percent pure.

The Rise and Gall Of Walters and Bloom

COLLEGE ATHLETICS

By *BILL BRUBAKER*

From the Washington Post
Copyright © 1987, the Washington Post

They stormed into the sports agency business with an open checkbook and a hidden agenda—and the sports agency business never has been the same. From college town to college town they traveled, huddling in cramped hotel rooms with star athletes, signing them to secret contracts that jeopardized their eligibility under NCAA rules.

NCAA rules? Norby Walters and Lloyd Bloom cared not a whit about NCAA rules. "Excuse me, I don't belong to their organization," Walters said. "The NCAA, I'm not going to let them tell me how to run my business," Bloom agreed.

So when Texas running back Edwin Simmons seemed interested in hiring an agent before his senior season last summer, Walters and Bloom loaned him $4,000 to seal the deal. And when Purdue All-America cornerback Rod Woodson—another preseason recruit—wanted to take his girlfriend and parents to the Hula Bowl in Hawaii, arrangements were made. "I paid their hotel bills, plane fares and gave Rod's mother over $1,000 to go shopping," Bloom said. "I gave them the time of their lives."

By January of this year, Walters and Bloom had become the hottest secret agents since 007, having signed some 30 college athletes, eight of whom would be selected in the first round of the NFL draft. "We were the talk of the sports world," Walters boasted. "We did our jobs so good that we rocked the entire damn sports community."

Then, suddenly, the empire they called World Sports & Entertainment Inc. began to collapse.

First, no fewer than 20 of Walters' and Bloom's clients defected to other agencies. Then came published allegations that Walters and

Bloom had threatened former clients with bodily harm. And, in April, a federal grand jury investigating alleged use of drugs, fraud, violence and prostitution in the sports business began asking questions about them.

Today, Walters and Bloom are well on their way to becoming the most investigated agents in the history of sport—and an intriguing picture of their once-secretive business practices has begun to emerge.

For their part, Walters and Bloom—who say they have not violated any civil or criminal laws—cannot understand what all the fuss is all about.

"I mean, Gary Hart's thing—he runs for president of the United States—is already forgiven," said Bloom, 28, a former nightclub promoter and collections agent who lives in suburban Los Angeles. "But this crap is in the paper every day. Who the hell am I to be in the papers every day? I'm meaningless."

"I've never even been picked up for a speeding ticket," said Walters, 55, a New York City-based booking agent for black entertainers, including Patti LaBelle and Kool and the Gang. "I'm so damn stupidly legitimate, it's incredible."

Suffice it to say: Norby Walters and Lloyd Bloom are no longer rocking the sports agency profession. Today, it is they who are being rocked:

• Already dozens of athletes have been subpoenaed to testify before the grand jury empaneled in the Federal Building in Chicago. According to sources familiar with the investigation, the grand jury is looking into allegations of extortion, racketeering, wire fraud and mail fraud in connection with their signing of—and loaning money to—college athletes. Some athletes also could face charges of fraud, for knowingly violating the terms of their scholarships, and tax evasion, for failing to report monies received from WSE.

Martin Rauch, a lawyer who represents former Iowa running back Ronnie Harmon, was asked by a U.S. attorney if he had any information about the 1986 Iowa-UCLA Rose Bowl being fixed. Harmon, a former WSE client who now plays for the Buffalo Bills, had four fumbles in the game, won by UCLA. Rauch said he told the federal prosecutor: "I don't know anything about a fix." Rauch has instructed Harmon not to talk to the news media.

Asked recently where he thought the grand jury investigation was going, Walters said: "To hell, I hope."

• At NCAA headquarters, enforcement director David Berst said he "would not be surprised" if a dozen or more college athletes are declared ineligible for having signed with—or taken money from—Walters and Bloom. According to Bloom, WSE has loaned several hundred thousand dollars to college athletes over the last two years. WSE has filed suit against six athletes, charging them with breach of contract and failure to repay loans or expenses. "We have some information about certain players (who have eligibility remaining),"

Berst said. "We're going to try to develop further information this summer."

Already, Alabama basketball star Derrick McKey has been declared ineligible for his senior year because he signed with WSE. Last week, Pittsburgh football players Charles Gladman and Teryl Austin reportedly were suspended from their team following a university investigation into their alleged association with WSE. Austin reportedly said he accepted money from Walters. Gladman has denied the allegation.

• In Washington, the NFL Players Association's agent certification committee is investigating allegations that Bloom and Walters threatened former WSE clients with physical harm. The investigation could lead to Bloom's decertification as a registered agent. (Walters never applied for NFLPA certification.) Bloom said an NFLPA official notified him that two athletes—neither of whom was identified by the union—complained of being threatened by Bloom. Bloom said of the allegation: "I could never harm anyone. Ask my wife. She'll tell you that I'm afraid to even kill a bug."

In March, the *Atlanta Constitution* reported that two former WSE clients had informed the NFLPA that they had been threatened by Walters. "Both players' stories were almost identical," the *Constitution* quoted an NFLPA source. "They said Walters called them and told them, 'I'm going to talk to my people in Las Vegas and get them to break your legs.' " Walters said of the allegation: "The NFLPA is totally, completely full of crap."

Throughout these investigations, Walters and Bloom have been objects of intense scrutiny by news media. Bloom complained that a reporter phoned a former high school teacher "looking for dirt about me" and that he was stalked by a photographer at Los Angeles International Airport. "I tried to hide my face from the camera," Bloom recalled. "I felt like a criminal."

Walters had been questioned by reporters about his association some two decades ago with John (Sonny) Franzese, a reputed captain in the Colombo crime family. Walters explained in an interview with the *Washington Post*: "I'm an agent now for 20 years. But 15 years before that I was a restaurant owner in New York. I owned 21 different places. When you're in the restaurant business you really meet a lot of people. I mean, you *really* meet a lot of people. . . . I knew (Franzese). You know, he was just a kind of a person that you know."

Walters said he had no business relationship with Franzese, who in 1967 was sentenced to 50 years in prison for conspiring to rob banks. Franzese was paroled after serving 10 years, but later was recommitted to a federal prison for violating the terms of his parole.

How did Bloom and Walters get in this mess?

Bloom allowed the faintest of smiles.

"Good question," he said.

In the spring of 1984, Bloom was working for his father's credit and collections business in Westchester County, N.Y., and promoting "theme nights" at glitzy Manhattan discos. The work was fine, but Bloom, 24 years old, was itching for a change. "I wanted to become a sports agent," he said. Why? "Because I felt agents weren't doing right by the athletes. They were really ripping them off."

Bloom could not afford to bankroll his own business, so he called on Walters, whom he had met six years earlier at a Gloria Gaynor/ Village People concert.

"I said, 'Norby, you're No. 1 in black music. Your company is a very legit company. Very big. Why not expand it to sports?' " Bloom recalled. "Norby liked the idea. He said, 'Great.' I said, 'I'll do the legwork and you fund the business.' He said, 'Fine.' "

Their first client was Tracy Henderson, a wide receiver from Iowa State who, according to Bloom, signed with WSE after the completion of his eligibility. Henderson was selected by the New York Giants in the fifth round of the 1985 draft.

In the midst of contract negotiations, Walters invited Giants General Manager George Young to his office on Broadway.

"A nice man," Walters said of Young. "When he came to my office, he looked around and said, 'There's no question in my mind that in 24 months you'll be the biggest agent in sports. You can't be this (a successful entertainment agent) and not be that (a successful sports agent).' "

Walters later invited Young to a party at Visage, a Manhattan disco. "There were 2,000 people wall-to-wall, just everybody in show business," Walters recalled. "And these were only my closest and dearest friends. George couldn't believe that a businessman would throw a party for 2,000 people and be surrounded by stars all over the place."

For a while, WSE had only one client—Henderson. "I told Norby that most of the college athletes had already signed with other agents," Bloom remembered. "Norby said, 'Ah ha! That's the game! If they've all signed early, then the only way is to join them and beat them doubly at their game.' "

Walters and Bloom, who are white, decided they would recruit only black athletes. "We stick to blacks," Bloom said. "That's what we know best. We're plugged into the black market."

Would they even attempt to recruit a white athlete?

Bloom shook his head.

"If I go to a black concert, an R & B show, everybody's dressed up, everybody's moving in a good groove," he explained. "You go to a white rock 'n' roll concert, like the Rolling Stones or Bruce Springsteen, everybody looks like a mass murderer, like they're capable of going to McDonald's and blowing up the whole joint. It's just a different type of group. I've never recruited a white athlete."

WSE's first undergraduate client was Ronnie Harmon, who was signed in the spring of 1985, as a junior. Over a one-year period, Harmon accepted $54,172 in loans from Walters and Bloom, according to a lawsuit filed by WSE. In his answer to that suit, Harmon admitted signing with WSE during his junior season but denied receiving that amount of money.

The other afternoon, at the townhouse in Sherman Oaks, Calif., that he shares with his wife, actress Donna Denton (former co-star of "Mickey Spillane's Mike Hammer"), Bloom described the system he has used to recruit and sign clients:

"First," he said, "I'd get the player's phone number. . . . You know, call the football office (at a university) . . . you know, use whatever I can to get a phone number."

Once he contacted the athlete, he would make his best pitch: "Patti LaBelle—one woman alone—makes more than four first-rounders. So if we're capable of handling her career, we sure can handle you." And if that didn't work: "What are you going to do? Go with some local, broken-down attorney?"

If the athlete seemed interested, Bloom said he would warn him about the risks of violating NCAA rules: "If this gets out, you can lose your eligibility. But we're the only ones who know about it. So it shouldn't get out unless you brag. Because we're not going to brag about it.' "

As an inducement to sign, Bloom said, he would offer to loan the athlete some money, which would not have to be repaid, he said, if the athlete did not sign a pro contract. "So I was the one who was gambling," Bloom said. "Instead of going to Atlantic City or Las Vegas, I was gambling that a kid's going to be a thoroughbred."

Finally, Bloom said, the athlete's contract with WSE would be postdated (presumably so it could not be used as evidence that the athlete had violated NCAA rules). "We postdated the contracts to protect the kids," Bloom said. "And to make everything easy, understandable."

In the spring of '86, Walters and Bloom really got rolling.

In Austin, they signed Simmons, the junior running back at Texas. "He got a total of $4,000 to sign," Bloom said. "Then he even brought his teammates and friends. He said, 'If you bring me $1,000 a player I can bring you a lot of stars.' "

Bloom said he agreed to pay Simmons a $1,000-per-player finder's fee. "Edwin said, 'Don't go anywhere. I'll be right back. I'm going to find my other teammates,' " Bloom recalled.

Two hours later, according to Bloom, Simmons returned with William Harris, a 6-foot-5, 235-pound tight end who would later transfer to Bishop College in Dallas.

"William Harris says, 'Oh, man, this is unreal. Look at this: You're representing Patti LaBelle. You're representing stars,' " Bloom said. "He told me he couldn't sleep for two nights after he signed with us, he was so excited. He was with the agent of the stars."

A week later, Bloom said he returned to Austin to sign Everett Gay, a junior receiver for the Longhorns.

"I got so excited that I signed three in one shot from one school, I was having palpitations," Bloom said. "I thought I was going to have to check in for an electrocardiogram."

Simmons' lawyer, Willie Anderson, confirmed that his client signed with—and accepted money from—WSE before his senior season. Anderson said he did not know if Simmons requested or received any finder's fees. Simmons was not available for an interview last week. Gay has admitted signing with WSE before his senior season. Harris declined to comment on his alleged relationship with WSE.

Bloom and Walters said they did not hesitate in giving athletes a chance to break NCAA rules because they believed many had already accepted under-the-table payments from coaches and boosters.

"If the universities are breaking the NCAA rules, why blame the agents?" Bloom said.

So they pushed on:

● To Dallas, where, according to Bloom, they signed four SMU juniors: Jerry Ball, Ronald Morris, Jeff Atkins and Terence Mann. "Then I returned to Dallas to watch them play in their spring game," Bloom recalled. "I felt like I was in the clouds. I mean, it was really great." Ball confirmed that he signed with WSE as a junior. Steve Endicott, an agent representing Morris, Atkins and Mann, has instructed his clients not to make any public comments.

● To Pennsylvania, where they signed Pittsburgh defensive lineman Tony Woods, who was later invited by his new agents to a premiere party in New York for "The Golden Child," a movie starring Eddie Murphy. "I introduced Tony Woods to Sylvester Stallone and Eddie Murphy," Bloom said. "He met Patti LaBelle and hung out with Patti LaBelle all night. I mean, he was going crazy. Tony said, 'Man, this is the greatest!' "

● To Alabama, where they signed Auburn running back Brent Fullwood. "We signed him before his senior season," Bloom said. "We told him, 'You know, it's against NCAA rules.' He says, 'No problem.' " Fullwood, a first-round draft pick of the Green Bay Packers, admitted through his agent, George Kickliter, that he signed with WSE before his senior season but denied that Bloom had warned him about NCAA rules.

No fewer than half of WSE's 30 recruits last year were signed before their senior seasons, according to Bloom. The secret to WSE's success? "I think it was just that we had the power of a major music company," Bloom said. "And that music is America."

As this year's NFL draft approached, some 20 WSE clients, including Atkins, Morris and Simmons, decided that Walters and Bloom were no longer playing their tune.

"They got scared," Bloom said. "Other agents were talking bad about us."

During one three-week period, Walters and Bloom's names were mentioned frequently in unfavorable contexts.

On March 6, a man was shot and killed in Dallas while driving a

Datsun 300ZX owned by Atkins. Police did not rule out the possibility that Atkins was the target of the shooting. Walters' and Bloom's names were mentioned in news reports about the shooting. Police found no evidence that Walters and Bloom were in any way involved in the incident. Walters said recently: "I'm an agent. What do I know about people getting shot in cars?"

On March 12, Walters was quoted in the *Constitution* as saying he signed and loaned money to players before their completion of their eligibility.

Four days later, Kathe Clements, an associate of Skokie, Ill., sports agent Steve Zucker, was stabbed and beaten unconscious by a man who entered her office wearing a ski mask and black gloves. Again, there was speculation in the media that Walters and Bloom could have been involved, because of a dispute they had had with Zucker over a client. But, again, police found no evidence that they were involved. Walters and Bloom said they were not involved in any way. Walters said he told two FBI agents, who questioned him about the incident: "Listen, I don't even know where the hell Skokie, Illinois, is. I never heard of the damn place."

Then, on March 28, the *New York Times* reported that the FBI office in Dallas was in possession of a recording of a phone conversation between Bloom and former SMU player Morris during which Bloom threatened to have Morris' hands broken if he signed with another agent.

Bloom said in an interview with the *Post* that he was indeed angry that Morris had fired WSE. Of a phone conversation with Morris, Bloom recalled: "I could have said something and got angry and yelled . . . saying, 'Your stupidity! How can you want to leave? I mean, why? What did we do wrong by you?' Raising my voice and yelling like I would yell at my wife or something." But he added: "I would never threaten anybody."

Howard Pearl, the Harvard-educated assistant U.S. attorney who is spearheading the grand jury investigation, seems intent on exploring every dark alley in this ever-darkening scandal. According to sources familiar with the investigation, athletes are being asked if Walters, Bloom or any WSE employee offered them drugs or prostitutes.

"Drugs? Let me put it to you this way," Walters said. "If right now you asked me where to find a marijuana cigarette, I wouldn't know where to find one."

Prostitutes? "Right now," Walters said, "if somebody in this show-business life—the fast lane—asked me, 'Do you know a prostitute?' I would have to find out, 'Does somebody know one somewhere?' "

Walters called the investigation a "witchhunt" and charged that the 33-year-old Pearl is interested primarily in "getting his name in the papers so he can get himself a good job with a major law firm in Chicago." Pearl declined to respond to Walters' allegation or to discuss any aspect of the investigation.

Norby Walters and Lloyd Bloom say they will continue to do business as usual. They still have 10 clients, they say, and the 1987-88 recruiting season is upon them.

"In the football business there are so many sleazy bums—broken down valises, I call them—who don't have two quarters to rub together," Bloom said. "So I'll be back. I'll be darned if I'm going to let the other agents defeat me. I'm going to come back stronger than ever."

Straight Pool: Rack 'Em Up

BILLIARDS

By *LEW FREEDMAN*

From the Anchorage Daily News
Copyright © 1987, the Anchorage Daily News

"*At the end of the game, you count up the money and that's how you know who's best.*"—George C. Scott in "The Hustler."

Pool hall life is in black and white. There are no clocks, no seasons. You can dress them up, disguise them, decorate them, but underneath it all they are still black and white.

They are bus stop people with nowhere to go, homes for people with houses, but nobody in them, havens for men who wield cue sticks like swords.

Pool halls are shelters for the city's wanderers, who care nothing for fine-trimmed lawns, fresh-brick elementary schools or municipal bonds. In here you pay your taxes as you pay your dues and it's all cash money.

It is life in black and white, but the only color that matters is green.

Last weekend, the players came to Son of River City Billiards for the cash, $1,000 for first place, money to eighth. Twenty-eight of Anchorage's best for "The 1987 Alaskan Spring Breakup Straight Pool Championship."

They were pot-bellied men, lanky men, angular types, hard-muscled, clean-shaven, bearded, short-haired and long, chain smokers and teetotalers. They were black, white, Oriental, even female, and they went by names like "Flapper," "Buddha," and "The Rifleman."

They walked through the glass doors into the dimness where fluorescent tubes are the sun, carrying their Canadian maple sticks in small, black cases, or in soft, leather pouches under their arms, cradling them with the gentleness usually reserved for delicate musical instruments.

They came to shoot straight pool, or "14.1 continuous," as it is technically called, because the last ball of the 15 in a rack must be made when a fresh rack is broken. It was play to 100, shoot 'til you miss, or shoot 'til you lose twice. By Sunday night—or early Monday morning if it took that long—there would be one player left, one who outshot, outfinessed, outblinked the others.

"It's like going to war," said Robert Colby, who is called "The Rifleman" because he shoots straight and hard. "The tension is so great between the two people."

Hustlers miss early to win later. They play dumb to play suckers. Tournament pool is the difference between playground basketball and the NCAA playoffs. You lose once here and it costs you.

"A tournament is sort of the ultimate pressure," said John Duclos, winner of six Alaska State Championships between 1968 and 1975 and now making a comeback. "People can go and gamble at pool with a pocket full of money. They lose and they've still got money.

"Tournament pool is a lot of concentration. You get into a state, it gets so deep that somebody could walk up and talk to you and you wouldn't even know it."

★   ★   ★

"How much am I going to win tonite, huh? I'm going to win 10 grand in one night. Who's going to beat me?"—Paul Newman as Fast Eddie Felsen in "The Hustler."

Friday night: The blind draw, done by reaching into a coffee tin for playing cards, produced surprising pairings. Many of the favorites ended up lumped together. That meant that some of the top players would knock each other off and others would get the money.

Some of it depended on who could play straight pool as well as they could play the more often contested 9-ball and 8-ball games. In straight pool, shooting well matters, but strategy, knowing when to play safe and leave the opponent no clean shot, can be as important.

"Straight pool is something a lot of contemporary players sniff at," said Kent Anderson, owner of River City and organizer of the tournament. "But it's the basic game. You call the ball, you call the pocket, you get a point."

The players knew each other and they knew who to watch. They knew that Duclos would be dangerous. They knew that Wayne Boomer could win it all. They knew that Buddha was a threat. And definitely Richard Holmes. And they knew that there were darkhorses lurking in the pack like Al Bryan and Greg "Flapper" Hamilton.

They all knew it would be a long weekend of concentration, pressure, precision and caffeine.

"I'm usually a little uncomfortable in a tournament. Edgy," said Boomer, a favorite. "You're not as relaxed. Your hands sweat."

The smart money—and it was a room loaded with smart money

—was on Duclos, the blond, chunkily-built player with tinted, wire-rim glasses and a past.

Duclos, 40, started in the game in Walnut, Calif., when he was 17. When he was young, the cue stick was an extension of his arm. He was a talent and he attracted money. He once ran 130 straight balls and played in the U.S. Open twice. Much like Tom Cruise in "The Color of Money," Duclos went on the road with a sponsor, playing wherever they'd rack them up.

"I went into different places and just challenged people," said Duclos, who runs The Side Pocket in Eagle River. "I had a stake horse. We split 50-50. I managed to cover expenses."

Then Duclos got married, had three children, and stopped playing. That was 12 years ago. Since 1975 he has only played in three major tournaments. Duclos practiced hard to get ready for this tournament.

"Four or five days a week, five hours a day," he said.

★　　★　　★

"Putting a tuxedo on a hustler is like putting whipped cream on a hot dog."—Minnesota Fats.

Most of the important things in Kent Andersson's life happen on green felt.

He named his pool hall after the town in the hit show "The Music Man," which ridiculed pool playing for youth as the prelude to a wasted life. It's only Son of River City Billiards in the phone book. To everyone else, it's just River City.

River City is a byproduct of Andersson's personality. He's a bulky man who always wears black—black shirts, slacks, shoes. His wife Helen, the only woman in the tournament, said all-black attire means he never has to worry about matching clothes. He's got tinted glasses and greased, black wavy hair. Andersson, 47, is a throwback to the '50s, when he used to play poker with author Nelson Algren, and so's his pool hall.

River City, open 24 hours a day, has large pool balls painted on the outside front wall. The single-room parlor is decorated in Coca-Cola memorabilia motif, its walls and ceiling covered with metal soft drink signs, framed pool tournament and card-playing posters, old sheet music, even the bumper of a 1949 Chevy. The juke box plays exclusively oldies. Except for the Talking Heads. The spectator seats are old barber chairs.

At Andersson's pool hall men are men and children should be in school. He identifies with the Depression-era joke of a newspaper headline, "Pool Hall Burns Down, 3,000 Men Homeless." At River City, direct sunlight is a rumor and the air might fail pollution monitoring tests. Call the atmosphere eau de smoke. There are no hanging plants at River City. You want to go out on a date and eat nachos, you go to The Bank Shot. You want to play serious pool, you go to River City. Action is what it's all about to Andersson.

"I've tried to create an atmosphere," said Andersson, "the kind of place I'd like to be in."

The 4½-foot by 9-foot tables are covered in green felt. The desk in Andersson's backroom office is a green-felt poker table. The dining table in Andersson's apartment is another green-felt poker table.

"My wife kids me that I couldn't eat on a table unless it was green," he said. "When I eat, I always sit in the dealer's chair."

Pool players are supposed to be hard men with no manners or consciences. They've got reputations as shiftless bums who play the felt, but don't play by society's rules.

In "Hustlers, Beats & Others," a sociological study of activities regarded as unsavory, author Ned Polsky writes that President John Quincy Adams installed a billiard table at the White House with his own money, but that others used it as a campaign issue against him.

To Andersson, though, pool players are just folk.

"Pool halls were very important social centers in a bachelor's society," he said. "I feel there's a need for the old kind of pool hall. I think men have the need to socialize with men and compete with men."

★   ★   ★

"Money won is twice as sweet as money earned."—Paul Newman as an older Fast Eddie Felsen in "The Color of Money."

Saturday: The games started at 9 a.m. and ran on all six tables to past 1 a.m. The juke box played constantly—rock and roll, big band tunes, Elvis Presley, the Mills Brothers.

The songs complemented the clicking of the balls and a low hum of chatter. Some players talked between shots. Some stood poker-faced. Some played with cigarettes dangling from their lips and others circled the room while their opponent shot. Duclos withstood a 27-ball run by Mike Thornton to win a first-round match. When he's hot Duclos moves around the table with bounce in his step, yet he can take as long as five minutes to study the lay of the balls, scrutinizing them as if they made up a geometry problem.

Duclos smoked and calmly watched Thornton's run. Once, he said later, he was behind 147-92 in a game to 150 and won it. So he doesn't worry.

"It taught me a lesson," he said.

Buddha, 41, a contract painter who said he uses no other name in pool circles, looks his name. He is from Hawaii, of Japanese extraction, and is short, squat, with little hair on top of his head. He got the nickname, he said, because friends thought he was so good "I shot like God."

Buddha won two difficult games, beating Colby, "The Rifleman," who was recovering from a 104-degree fever, and Bryan. He was down 93-87 to Colby and won 100-93 and was down 54-16 to Bryan and won 100-95.

Like Duclos, Buddha once roamed the road, walking into strange places armed with his cue and his nerve. But he gave up pool for a while in 1974.

"A buddy of mine in Chicago, he won $500 and they shot him in the back as he walked out the door," said Buddha. "I had guns pulled on me. It wasn't worth it."

Boomer, who describes his age as "a Jack Benny 39," is a truck driver with a streak of gentility. He said he dislikes hustling and calls himself a tournament player. He proved it early against Holmes.

Boomer built a lead of 60-37 and then ran the final 40 balls. Boomer stalked the balls, wearing a frown of concentration and chalking automatically after each shot. Stroke. Chalk. Stroke. Chalk. The best can make the white cue ball dance to their song and the blue chalk on the tip of the stick gives the orders.

"What it does is make the leather fluffy," said Boomer. "There are players who can go five or six shots without chalking up, but it's a good idea to chalk every shot so it's got some friction. You can hit it straight with a broomstick, but chalk creates a grip."

★   ★   ★

To play a good game of billiards is the sign of a well-rounded education, but to play too good a game of billiards is the sign of a misspent youth."—Lord Chesterfield, 17th century English Lord.

Pool has had periods of prosperity and periods of decline. Two of the upswings in popularity followed the release of "The Hustler" and "The Color of Money."

They're both about street life, but last year's "Color of Money" was glitzier, culminating at a major tournament in Atlantic City. Andersson hated it.

"There was so much Hollywood hokum," he said. "It created an interest in pool because it put it up on the big screen, but I winced. I cringed."

There is a scene in the movie where Newman tosses young hustler Cruise a Balabushka stick. Balabushkas, named for their deceased maker, cost thousands of dollars. Duclos said they are the Rembrandts of sticks.

"It would be like your wife throwing a Chinese vase from the Ming Dynasty across the living room," said Andersson. "And everybody breaking at one time. That's like those synchronized swimming movies. Yeah, Esther Williams.

"And Tom Cruise twirling sticks. If Tom Cruise walked in and acted like that I would give him one warning and throw him out."

Yet the Billiards Congress of America gave Newman an award for promoting interest in pool. And others, like Bryan, 39, a black man with a cat-that-ate-the-canary grin, who is a salesman by trade, thinks that if pool sells itself by moving from dark halls to resort casinos it can help bring bowling, tennis and golf size purses to pool.

"Pool's got a stigma attached to it," he said. "Pool's been played in the wrong places. Don't get me wrong. I like the green cloth. I grew up in pool halls. But sponsors want to see people in tuxedos."

★   ★   ★

"It's about money; the best is the guy with the most."—Paul Newman in "The Color of Money."

Sunday: By Sunday night, 48 hours after the draw, there were only four survivors: Duclos, Buddha, Bryan, and Flapper.

Flapper once won a pool tournament in his hometown of New Orleans with a first prize of five days in Las Vegas. He stayed there for three years. In his early-round games he wore a red sweater with a gray, wrap-around shark on it. Call him a pool shark: he ran 48 balls to beat Colby.

But Bryan beat Buddha the second time around and knocked Flapper out to set up a final with Duclos.

The championship game was to 150 and the atmosphere in the hall changed. The juke box played on, but idle talk changed to whispers. There were perhaps 20 spectators situated carelessly on stools and chairs.

Bryan was a sartorial delight in red jersey, gray slacks, gray Reeboks and a black beret that kept his long hair to the sides of his face. Duclos sucked on cigarette after cigarette as they picked at the table, playing safe more than playing bold.

Once, Bryan went to the bathroom. When he emerged, Duclos, who had missed, deadpanned, "Forty-four to nothing. Your shot." Bryan looked shaken before he recognized the joke.

Duclos' expression never changed as Bryan began to control the table. "Ten ball," he said. "Six, cross side." "Corner." He called his shots and made them, 35 in a row. It was Bryan 75 balls, Duclos 38.

Duclos was missing, but then his fingers caught fire. Thirty-three straight. Thirty-four. And the chalk slipped out of his hand onto the cue ball. Foul. Bryan took over, ran nine balls that should have been Duclos' and never flinched again. It ended after three hours. 150-113.

And only then, when the final ball dropped, did Bryan smile. And breathe.

"It takes a lot of concentration," he said. "To relax, that's the hardest part. You take deep breaths and try to calm down."

Now he could let loose. And count his money, his $1,000. He was the guy with the most and that made him the guy who's the best.

Harry Caray

BASEBALL

By *BRIAN HEWITT*

From the Chicago Sun-Times
Copyright © 1987, Brian Hewitt

In more than 40 years of broadcasting, Harry Caray had never missed an inning in the booth. For any reason. He had survived scandals, firings, feuds, hangovers, two divorces and a 1968 offseason auto accident that left him with a pair of broken legs, a fractured shoulder and a busted nose. But he had always come back for more. And he had come back more vibrant and more popular than ever with his fans.

People close to him say he is about to do it again.

But just last winter the Mayor of the Street of Dreams woke up in a Palm Springs hospital surrounded by a nightmare. His right arm flopped grotesquely. The right side of his face had been pulled violently to one side. And he was unable to control an annoying drool emanating from the right corner of his mouth. Caray had suffered a stroke.

The cause was a small hemorrhage in the left cerebellar portion of his brain that also slurred his speech and intermittently lapsed his memory. The immediate prognosis was guarded. "We had doubts whether or not he would live," said his son, Skip.

Now his doctor has given him permission to return to work Tuesday when the Reds show up at Wrigley Field. It will have been three months and two days since the stroke interrupted a friendly poker game at a golf course clubhouse near his offseason California home. Jimmy Piersall, one of Caray's many former announcing partners, says it will be years before they get Caray out of the booth again.

Piersall's father was a housepainter who died while painting a house. He suggests it would be fitting if Caray dies broadcasting a baseball game. "That probably would be right," Caray says warily.

"I don't want to try it though." Depending on whom you believe, Caray is anywhere from 67 to 72 years old. "Harry's much younger than I am," is the way Steve Stone, his 39-year-old broadcast partner, puts it.

Meanwhile, Caray's celebrityhood has grown bigger than the national debt of Brazil. And his fame has spread. Not long ago the tiny banana republic of Belize requested that the U.S. State Department deliver Caray to its annual national festival. Scheduling commitments prevented Caray's appearance. During his recent convalescence huge billboards sprung up on the sides of Chicago's expressways like so many Hallmark get-well cards. "Hurry Back, Harry," they said.

Caray was a Bud Man, a Cub fan, and a dancing fool before the stroke. He was a 20-megaton ego with a steel-trap mind patched into a pair of 20-megawatt pipes. He was the guy with the shiny forehead, the oversized pop-bottle eyeglasses and the expressive mouth who brought a butterfly net to games for foul balls. His feel for the pitches and yaws that punctuate the rhythms of baseball was uncanny.

And he wasn't about to let a vascular setback beat all that fun at the old ball park he had been having since beginning his major league play-by-play career with the Cardinals in 1945. "I'm well," he says. "And much quicker than expected. So I think maybe I've done something right."

But initially, Caray admits, the stroke left him "despondent."

"The thing was such a shock to me. I'd never heard of a stroke. If you'd said a heart attack or something like that, I could have understood. But a stroke. . . . I just never knew anything about it."

Yet he never doubted he would return. He was, if you will, wholly uncowed by the strenuous physical therapy that followed. "Expressions of love" in the form of the thousands of letters he received didn't hurt.

His remarkably swift rehabilitation included a strict no-cholesterol diet that forbade fatty foods and limited alcoholic intake to one drink a night. Caray lost 40 pounds. His old voice returned. Then his memory. "You'd never know he had a stroke," says Burton Winston, the California physician who supervised the recovery.

Caray proved it recently from his familiar suite at the Ambassador East hotel. His speech was rich and unhalting. His memory sharp. Names, dates and places were less of a problem than finding a good tailor. The weight loss, he complained, forced him to buy six new pairs of pants and order alterations for his sport coats.

Doctor's orders also include an enforced reduction in nightlife. "Certainly I'm going to cut back," Caray says soberly. "I'm not as well now as I'm gonna be in three months. But there's plenty of time for that other stuff. I can live without drinking and I can live without all the food and all the garbage. What I want to do is just be in good shape."

★   ★   ★

How he sounds and looks on the air will be what counts to his fans. "I'd really be surprised if he's not ready," says former Chicago sports columnist David Israel, Caray's erstwhile biographer. "Whether you think what he does is the right way to announce a game or not, he has a very specific understanding of what he does. My guess is he wouldn't go on what amounts to be national television and do anything that would make a fool of himself."

That same image-consciousness prompted Caray to postpone indefinitely the publication of his book project with Israel. Caray's attorney, Jeffrey Jacobs, insists the book is still on "hold." Says Caray: "David wrote a fine script. But it wasn't me talking."

The suspicion is that Israel, a hard-knocking reporter, didn't want to re-create *Rebecca of Sunnybrook Farm.* Caray probably could have lived with something a little softer.

Caray is more sensitive that way than most of the people who worship his highly stylized delivery realize. He is comfortable with the public part of his life. But in private, he is a private person. He is also shrewder, better read and more astute financially than most people might imagine.

Rarely do the fans who identify with his common touch hear Caray talk about being orphaned at 9. Or about being so poor he was the only boy at his grade school graduation unable to afford white pants. "I think of that often," Caray says. "That might have been the beginning of my drive. I often told myself I was gonna make so much money I could buy all the white pants I wanted." Oddly enough, he is color-blind.

By 16, Caray was living on his own. He left an aunt who had taken him in when his parents died. But he never forgot her. The aunt's children figure prominently in Caray's will even though he barely knows them. After that, he bounced around selling newspapers. Eventually he found work with small radio stations in Joliet and Kalamazoo.

The Cardinals elevated him to the major leagues in 1945. Before settling down with his present wife, a handsome woman named Delores, whom everybody calls "Dutchie," Caray fathered three daughters and two sons during his first two marriages. Skip and Chris Caray, the two boys, call constantly. "The three daughters have gotten away from me," Caray laments.

Few people realize Caray spends hours of research before every game. "What passes off for a non-structured, haphazard, let's-say-whatever-we-feel-like-when-it's-time-to-say-it type broadcast, really is a well-enacted, well-thought-out piece of sports entertainment," Stone says.

★   ★   ★

Even fewer people may remember Harry Caray changed his name from Harry Carabina. "And they don't need to," Jacobs says. "Harry's an entertainer. They trust him and he's honest."

But that doesn't necessarily mean everybody always has been wild about Harry. In 1981, nine months before Caray jumped the Sox to join WGN and the Cubs, he labeled Sox president Eddie Einhorn a "lying bastard."

Two years later Sox chairman Jerry Reinsdorf referred to the broadcast team of Caray and Piersall as "scum." For the record, Jacobs says Caray called Reinsdorf the morning of the announcement of his signing with the Cubs because "he didn't want Jerry to have to hear about it from anybody else."

The Cubs weren't offering Caray substantially more money than the Sox. But the Sox were moving toward pay TV. Caray was convinced it wasn't the airwave of the future. He feared its early limitations would mean professional *hara-kiri,* not professional Harry Caray.

Plus, the national exposure WGN's superstation network provided was too enticing to a broadcaster many of his peers insist should have been inducted to the Hall of Fame years ago. "I don't have any idea why he's not in except he's never been a very political person," Skip Caray says.

"There's no doubt that Harry did not graduate from the Henry Kissinger school of diplomacy," Stone says. "Harry has always said he was the original tell-it-like-it-is guy. And certainly he's paid a price for that."

At the fall news conference called to announce his 1981 signing with the Cubs, Caray spied general manager Dallas Green lurking in the back of the room. "I'll never second-guess you," Caray promised. "You're too big." Green later said he discussed with Caray the harm an announcer can do by "burying a player who's trying."

For his part, Caray insists he hasn't softened his style one whit since leaving the Sox. Meanwhile, he still spells names backwards on the air. And he still has that special hello for Mr. and Mrs. Joe Bagadonuts from Kishwaukee.

Arguably it is Caray, not Green or anyone else, who has emerged as the biggest name in Chicago baseball in the '80s. "I'll buy that," says North Side tavern owner Butch McGuire. If Caray is the Mayor of Rush Street, the gravel-voiced McGuire is its floor leader. He and his fellow 'Street of Dreams' proprietors elected Caray so long ago he can't remember the name of the previous Mayor. "But it was not by accident," McGuire says. "Harry knows as many saloon keepers and restaurateurs as anybody in the country."

Caray literally stops traffic on Rush Street. When bus drivers pause in mid-route to say hello, Caray has been known to oblige by boarding the bus and greeting everybody individually before exiting through the rear door. "Harry's an even better salesman than he is an announcer," McGuire says. "If it weren't for Harry Caray, we wouldn't be selling Budweiser at my place. I'd have a basement full of elephants if he was selling elephants. If he sold big-ticket items, like 747 airplanes, he'd be the top 747 airplane salesman."

Here's Chuck Yeager! . . . If he could ONLY fly one now! . . . It could be! . . . it might be! . . it is! . . . A three-point landing! . . . HO-lee COW!!"

★   ★   ★

Caray and McGuire became fast friends in the early '70s when both regularly roamed from bar to bar bending ears, elbows, and the minds of anybody who tried to keep up with them. "World class," says McGuire when asked to describe Caray's drinking capacity. "And I've never seen the man stiff in my life. Or out of line. I've never seen him offensive."

But the biggest ticket of all for Caray always has been himself. McGuire would have been proud of the way Caray pedaled himself to the Cubs. For starters, all negotiating sessions took place, in secret, at Caray's apartment in the Ambassador East. Top level Tribune Co. executives; power-broking attorneys; the high priests of WGN—they all paid obeisance to Caray on Caray's turf. When things got crowded they moved into the top-floor suite normally reserved for Frank Sinatra.

The late Bill Veeck once described Caray's success as "more than popularity." It was, Veeck said, "a matter of texture." Veeck also claimed Caray was suited uniquely to the Sox team he owned before *Einvision and Reinsdeal.* "Our audience is not at all like the Cubs'," Veeck said. "Theirs is mostly youngsters and people over 50."

But Caray sniffed the possibilities of the switch. "He understood the impact, he analyzed the decision and he asked the right questions," Jones says. "He was very much in touch, very much aware and very much in charge of everything that was going on."

WGN wanted Caray so badly, sources say the station took pains to keep Tribune Co., its parent, in the dark before the final news conference. WGN didn't want Tribune Co. to leak the story to its own newspaper reporters when so many other media outlets also had helped nurture Caray's legend. "WGN didn't want to be accused of favortism," Jacobs confirms. WGN knew Caray wouldn't have approved.

★   ★   ★

Veteran Cub broadcaster Milo Hamilton didn't approve of the Caray hiring from the beginning and he said so publicly. Hamilton eventually left Chicago for broadcasting opportunities in Houston. "I think Caray wanted me out and he got them (WGN) to do it," Hamilton later told Inside Sports magazine. "He wanted me out and someone in who posed no threat to him. . . . His line is how much he loves the game and the fans, but the bottom line is that he's promoting Harry Caray."

Caray's reply at the time: "You have to consider the source."

Reached in Houston last week Hamilton stood by his remarks. "That pretty well said it all," he said.

It wasn't the first time Caray's ego had clashed with another. Stories that Caray had an affair with a member of St. Louis owner

Gussie Busch's family forced his departure there after the 1969 season. So Caray worked for Charlie Finley's Oakland A's in 1970. He and longtime A's announcer Monte Moore crossed swords immediately. "I could feel the knife in my back every time I walked in the booth," Caray told Sports Illustrated in 1978.

Moore, now a salesman in Porterville, Calif., is still bitter the magazine never called for his side of the story. "The first thing Harry told me in spring training that year was, "I'm gonna be No. 1,'" Moore says. "I said, 'Harry, you've got to earn No. 1.' He never did earn it. He did a whole lot of talking. And he couldn't wait to get out of the booth and start drinking."

Yet Moore still says he would choose Caray "if I had to pick one announcer to do the seventh game of the World Series."

More than one White Sox manager avoided Caray like he was jock itch. And there were always wars with players who preferred finger-nails on the clubhouse blackboard to Caray's voice. Earlier this spring former Cub pitcher George Frazier traced his image problems in Chicago to the 1985 season when, he said, Caray started "getting on my case."

"I know you're saying, 'Hey, he's only an announcer.' But Harry Caray pulls a lot of weight," Frazier said. "When he says, 'Frazier is the most inept pitcher ever to pitch in the National League,' people accept it as gospel."

In 1978 Texas pitcher Jon Matlack was enraged when he heard Caray criticizing teammate Richie Zisk on the air. Matlack said he would have "killed" Caray if the remarks had been directed at him. "I've never heard such a vicious attack," Matlack said after the game. "I lost all respect for Caray tonight." Much of Caray's criticism centered around derogatory remarks made by Zisk about Sox fans. Caray's message to Zisk: Attack baseball's fans and you attack me.

Former Sox catcher Brian Downing wasn't the only person who thought Caray was rough on him in his five years with the Sox. "I think the worst thing Harry ever did was when he and Jimmy (Piersall) ran Brian Downing out of town," says Sox announcer Lorn Brown, a former Caray boothmate. Brown thinks so much of Caray that he says it's a "sin" he isn't in the Hall of Fame. "But he and Jimmy were just unmerciful to the kid. Harry started it and Jimmy jumped on the bandwagon. You can quote me on that."

The Sox converted Downing into a catcher at the major league level even though he hadn't played the position in the minors. Caray and Piersall were particularly critical of his defense. By 1977, Downing's last season with the Sox, the fans had turned against him. He wanted out in the worst way. Veeck shipped Downing along with pitchers Chris Knapp and Dave Frost to California for Bobby Bonds, Thad Bosley and Richard Dotson. Dotson made the trade for the Sox. But Downing, now an outfielder, still is producing healthy mid-league numbers for the Angels at age 36.

★   ★   ★

"That's a bunch of crap," says Caray to charges he was unfair to Downing. "Nobody in the world wants his ballplayer to do better than I do." To be sure, Downing didn't fully develop with the Angels until he started a serious weight training program that increased his power and durability.

But he never recovered from his experience in Chicago. Once he had saved everything written about him. But, he said recently, "when all that garbage began, I threw all the stories away. I vowed never again to be drawn by it. And that's the way I've stayed. I don't play both sides of the fence."

Stone led the Sox in victories the year they traded Downing. He says Caray was willing to talk to unhappy players. "The thing I liked about Harry is that he never said anything behind your back," says former Sox first baseman Lamar Johnson. "He'd stand toe-to-toe with you. And if you didn't like something, he'd give you rebuttal on the air."

The people who don't like Caray complain about his ego. They say he is a guy with a gimmick. They say he's a shameless self-promoter—a legend in his own mind. They say he isn't interested in anybody's opinion but his own. But what his critics don't understand is that when Caray deigns to disagree with you, it means he likes you enough to spend the time making his point. He didn't like Milo Hamilton. So he dismissed Hamilton's attacks with a "consider the source."

"A real good night for Harry is if he can get into two or three great arguments and talk for 15 or 20 minutes on each one and just argue vehemently," Stone says. "The next night, if he's sitting at the bar and conversation's lagging, he'll argue the other side. He just loves to bat it around."

During the winter Caray holes up in an airy but unpretentious Palm Springs ranch adjacent to a golf course fairway. Several years ago Kansas City third baseman George Brett repaired to Palm Springs for a week of golf and a visit with his friend Caray. He left after two days. Brett later told Stone the reason he bolted was he couldn't keep up with Caray's nightly peregrinations. "He told me he feared for his life," Stone says.

Caray has suffered fools and Presidents gladly and well. But he says his most memorable encounter occurred years ago in Memphis, Tenn. when the room phone rang and the caller identified himself as "Elvis."

"Elvis who?" Caray demanded.

Turns out Elvis Presley was a big Harry Caray fan. Minutes later a Rolls Royce pulled up in front of Caray's hotel and spirited him off to Graceland. The two talked baseball and music and became pals. "Frank Sinatra's a great guy," Caray says. "But I think that Elvis Presley story will be the one I always remember."

Not even an appearance by the late Presley could upstage what is certain to take place at Wrigley Field Tuesday. "You watch what happens when Harry comes back," Stone says. "I don't know that we will have seen anything like it. The fans that will be there will be just crazed."

★　★　★

And they may have good reason if Caray reverts to form. After being struck by a car on a slippery St. Louis street in November 1968, Caray almost choked on a mixture of blood and rain before help arrived. But he made it back to Busch Stadium for Opening Day '69. After the public address announcer introduced him, Caray hobbled from the Cardinal dugout propped up by two canes. As he crossed the foul line, he threw one aside. The crowd roared. As he neared the mound, he discarded the other cane and raised the hands over his head triumphantly. "Har-ree, Har-ree, Har-ree," the crowd chanted.

Only later did Caray admit the truth. "Well, it's all show business," he said. "I hadn't needed those canes in weeks."

But now he admits he needs the people who listen to him as much as they need him . . . even if he isn't entirely sure why. "I don't understand it, to be honest with you," he says. "Everybody tries to analyze what it is I have. I don't see anything different. I just enjoy my work. I know I don't have as good a voice as some people. I'm not as bright as some people. But I think I enjoy myself at the ballgame as much as the people who pay their way."

Maybe that's it. As Caray steers toward the end of his career, his star is shining brighter than ever. "God willing," he says, "I hope to be broadcasting a long time to come." But maybe there has been a price. Maybe the stroke was a late charge for an overdue billing. Maybe Harry Caray *has* paid his way.

What's in the Future For Women's Sports?

GENERAL

By *CANDACE LYLE HOGAN*

From Women's Sports & Fitness
Copyright © 1987, Women's Sports & Fitness

Nancy Tieman, 22, still calls it Black Friday: that day in April last year when her gymnastics coach at Southwest Texas State University called the team in for an unexpected meeting. Dreading the news they might hear, the women waited in silence until all 14 of them were assembled.

They leaned forward intently as Darlene Schmidt, coach of the team for 17 years, began to speak. That afternoon, just four weeks before summer break, athletic director Bill Miller had called her into his office, Schmidt said, "and dropped a bombshell." Without warning or consulting Schmidt beforehand, Miller had decided to stop offering gymnastics as a varsity sport for women at SWT.

There was no obvious reason for the decision. Coach Schmidt's won-loss record over the past five years was 75-31, one of the best in the athletic department. The gymnastics team had been sending individuals to the nationals since 1980, and the entire team had made it in 1982, 1984, and 1985. SWT would be dropping two All-Americas and two student gymnasts with 4.0 grade-point averages, as well as eliminating a sport that had qualified the school to compete in two NCAA Division II national championships.

Southwest Texas State University, LBJ's alma mater, once seemed more of a haven from bad news than a source of it. Rising like an oasis from the flat Texas plains, SWT's campus of 20,000 students is an expanse of green, flanked by sweet-smelling cedar groves and the sleepy Southwestern town of San Marcos.

An athlete could learn to feel important here, especially if she were a gymnast. SWT's program was nationally recognized, and it was known as the place to go in that state for gymnastics. The school even earmarked one dormitory, San Saba, especially for female athletes.

Gymnastics meant a lot to the women on this team. Nancy Tieman never would have gone to college without the lure of earning a scholarship at SWT. Her teammate, Kristen Melzer, had lost a year of competition because of an injury and was eager for another chance. Gymnastics had given structure and a special purpose to Joan Corder's life since she was 8 years old. Another teammate, Stephanie Dannelley, had doubled up on classes her senior year in high school to graduate early just to compete sooner on the college team of her dreams.

"I can remember that day, when my daughter came home from school," says Cynthia Dannelley, Stephanie's mother. "I thought she was in a wreck or some friend of hers had died—I didn't know. She couldn't talk, she just sat there and cried and nothing would come out of her mouth." Stephanie, now 19, had begun competing in gymnastics at age 10. She'd pushed herself to graduate from high school in December, came to SWT in January; in the spring, the sport was dropped. She would have earned a scholarship by September. Apologizing for having to speak for her daughter, Cynthia Dannelley explains: "She still can't talk about it. Every time she tries, she just breaks out in tears."

Nancy Tieman's story is a little different. Growing up in Austin, Tex., the youngest and least academically inclined of six children, Nancy says she was "a tomboy who wasn't planning to go to college at all." But when it occurred to her that she might be able to make the varsity gymnastics team at SWT, only 30 miles from home, she applied. "Once I got there," Nancy says, "I realized what I could do with college."

Having begun training in high school, relatively late for a gymnast, Nancy was at first unable to perform at the level of her teammates. But she worked out five hours a day, did her homework on airplanes, and took tests in hotel rooms.

In her junior year, Nancy was voted team captain and awarded an athletic scholarship. She had won the Most Improved title twice, and shared Most Valuable Player honors for 1986. "Because of gymnastics, I felt I had a purpose, that I was part of the university and not just another number," she says.

College gymnasts prepare to peak in the senior year. A senior now, Nancy knows "this year would have been my best."

★   ★   ★

How did a school with such a strong sports tradition come to the decision to cut one of its winningest teams? Too suddenly, some say; and certainly unexpectedly. Hays County Clerk Ronnie Dannelly, Stephanie's father, concludes: "It seems obvious to me that they singled out a women's sport and chopped it."

Why? Aren't women's sports programs supposed to be protected by Title IX?

Title IX of the Education Amendments Act, passed in 1972, prohibits sex discrimination in any program provided by educational institutions receiving federal aid. Although Title IX addresses a variety of issues, it is best known for its effect on sports programs. Faced with loss of federal funds if they didn't comply, schools scrambled in the mid-'70s to offer females opportunities in sports where they had none, or few, before.

The gains made by Title IX are evident all around us. Before it was passed, colleges devoted less than 2 percent of their athletic budgets to women. Today, the allocation is estimated at 16 percent by the National Association for Girls and Women in Sport. At the high school level, more than 1.8 million girls participate in interscholastic sports, as opposed to 300,000 before Title IX was passed. Before Title IX, athletic scholarships for women were almost nonexistent; today, more than 10,000 are offered.

But today Title IX is unenforceable. In 1984, the Supreme Court decided in *Grove City College vs. Bell* that only programs—not institutions—directly receiving federal funds would be under the jurisdiction of Title IX. There are very few, if any, athletic programs that directly receive federal funding. As a result, there is virtually no legal recourse under the federal Title IX statute for a woman who feels that athletic opportunities are being denied to her. Indeed, at the time of the Grove City decision, there were over 60 cases of Title IX violations under investigation. All were dropped.

Since the Grove City decision, there has been an erosion in many women's sports. The University of Arizona has cut its women's synchronized swim team. Brunswick Junior College in Georgia has eliminated the women's basketball team. Women's gymnastics has been dropped at the University of Oregon, Southern Illinois University, and Connecticut College. At Northeast Louisiana State University, the number of women's scholarships has been reduced in two sports, tennis and softball.

States and institutions that supported the principles behind Title IX are likely to continue to do so. Even though the federal law has been gutted, 14 states have passed their own versions of Title IX laws to ensure equitable treatment. However, the Civil Rights Restoration Act, a bill that would restore Title IX to its original power, met considerable opposition in Congress last year. It was reintroduced in February.

In some states, the message schools are hearing is that they are safe in dropping or cutting back women's sports. Particularly in school districts and colleges hit by dwindling revenues, women's athletics may be among the first programs to be sliced. "Someone said to me recently that when the economy's bad, we can't afford equality," reports Lee Morrison, who is a former president of the now-defunct Association for Intercollegiate Athletics for Women (AIAW), the organization that created national championships for women in 1971.

"Cutbacks are the name of the game now," says the University of Iowa's Christine Grant, athletic director for one of the few women's programs still growing. "Nationwide, women never did receive equal opportunity, but when it comes to cutting back, suddenly women are more than equal."

The problem is compounded by the fact that female coaches and athletic directors have lost a great deal of clout in college programs. While the average number of women's sports offered by colleges has grown from 5.6 in 1978 to 7.1 in 1986, the number of women coaching them has decreased. Administrators decided that Title IX required the merging of men's and women's athletic departments. Almost always, college presidents put the man at the top with the woman assistant athletic director. An unintended outgrowth of Title IX: the male AD has control of the budget; the woman has a rubber stamp.

Ironically enough, before Title IX, 90 percent of the few women's teams were coached by women. Today only 50 percent are. Five of the 10 most popular NCAA sports for women have more male coaches than female, while only two women are in charge of a Division I men's team. And 38 percent of the intercollegiate programs for women in this country have no female at all involved in athletic administration. R. Vivian Acosta and Linda Jean Carpenter of Brooklyn College, who are researching the decline, note: "These trends encourage the development of a male athletic program for men, and eliminate strong female mentors and role models."

Notably, it is in the nine or so unmerged departments left in the biggest, Division I schools, like the University of Texas in Austin, that women's sports are still growing toward equality, largely because the female AD's control their own budgets.

At Southwest Texas State, athletic director Bill Miller says he cut the popular women's gymnastics team last year because of declines in state funding and "lack of a competitive future." Similar reasoning could apply to the school's football program, the funding of which was not cut: in a deep slump after a recent move to Division I status, the varsity football team had an unenviable won-loss record of 3-8 in 1985. But, as one gymnast's parent put it: "Southwest Texas is football country."

So is much of the United States. "Where schools are cutting sports for 'budgetary reasons'," says Sue Mottinger, executive director of the National Association for Girls and Women in Sport, "so-called minor sports are cut first, and women's sports are considered minor. They would never cut football or boys' basketball."

Indeed, at Southwest Texas State, almost half of the $1.5 million budget is spent on men's football and basketball, with the seven other men's and women's sports sharing the rest. The women's gymnastics team cost SWT only about $47,000 a year.

Unfortunately, Bill Miller has good reason to believe in gymnastics' "lack of a competitive future," given the cutbacks at other schools. Yet, in a recent USA Today poll, women's gymnastics was ranked the most popular amateur sport women watch on television.

★　　★　　★

The demise of gymnastics at Southwest Texas State and elsewhere casts some doubt about whether or not women will have sufficient opportunities in sports they most want to play. "Watching my kids grow up in gymnastics, I think it was the best thing that could happen. They learned leadership, sportsmanship, and courage," says Cynthia Dannelly. "When I think of all the thousands of girls who got a shot in the arm from the Olympics just now reaching high school age . . . they'll look for a college, and there'll be no place to go."

The situation at SWT also raises questions about whether or not women will get to play a role in deciding which sports die and which remain. The year before the gymnastics team was dropped, the governor of Texas warned of shortages in state funding, and college presidents began calling for cutbacks in athletic departments. It occurred to Darlene Schmidt that her upcoming retirement as gymnastics coach might endanger the future of her team. "So I made a special point of asking Mr. Miller to consult me if he ever began thinking of dropping the team," she says. "And he promised me he would."

Bill Miller says he doesn't remember that conversation. He says he had two meetings with the Athletic Advisory Committee, the faculty body typically called upon to approve such major decisions. Schmidt was not included in either one. Associate Athletic Director for Women's Athletics Dana Crafts says four people—Miller, Executive Vice-President Michael Abbott, President Robert Hardesty, and herself—knew of the final decision to cut the team before the gymnastics regionals hosted by SWT on March 22. But Schmidt was not told even then. She was informed on April 11, shortly before the end of the school term.

"That was the worst thing, not having it confirmed in time so we could work it out with the team," says Schmidt. Ronnie Dannelley, Stephanie's father, thinks the school administration timed it that way to diminish opportunity for protest.

Still, the young women mobilized to try to get their sport reinstated. They circulated a petition and got 2,700 signatures, largely from students—whose fees represented three-quarters of the athletics budget. The young women were respected in the community, since many of them taught age-group clinics, open to the public. The administration received scores of letters urging reinstatement of the sport from parents, boosters, alumni, varsity prospects, and even gymnastics clubs across the nation. The gymnasts offered to do anything they could to keep the sport going, with fund-raising aid from parents.

The *University Star*, the student newspaper, pointed out a contradiction: If budget cuts were the excuse, then why had another football coach been added? The paper also pointed out that the big-budget sports, men's football and basketball, had dismal won-loss records that year. Was the jump to Division I big-time in football worth it, if it meant losing one of the school's most successful teams?

The meeting with athletic director Miller did not go well, from Nancy Tieman's point of view. "He reminded me of, say, your father," she remembers. "You know, you're trying to pursue an issue and he won't listen to you, he just turns his head—what he says is right, what he says goes—I don't care what you all say. This is the way it is; this is the way it's going to be."

The team's final appeal to President Hardesty was described as "15 cold minutes in the summer," followed by polite rejection, by letter, of their petition for reinstatement. Although the team members' scholarships remained intact, there was not time to apply to a program elsewhere—and no offer from the school to facilitate such a move.

All but one of the gymnasts are still at Southwest Texas State, with no place to compete. Adjustment has been difficult partly because of the specialized nature of the sport. "I will never be able to do again what I did just eight months ago," says Nancy.

Joan continues her marketing studies; Stephanie has switched to dance; Nancy plans to teach kindergarten. Coach Schmidt remains as instructor, a tenured member of the physical education department.

But they are disillusioned by what happened. "It used to be that you had a purpose," says Joan, who misses the discipline and beauty of a sport that had been the centerpiece of her life since age 8. "You gave something to the school; you didn't only take from it, but you gave something back, a very important part of yourself."

Neither Joan, Nancy, nor the Dannelleys had ever heard of Title IX, and Darlene Schmidt certainly never invoked it. Yet, ever since they dared to disagree, they've been treated strangely, in the athletic department, in the booster club, in the classroom. At last year's awards ceremony, Schmidt was not congratulated on her retirement as a coach. Why? "I can't imagine that we didn't," says Miller. "I don't remember." Today Schmidt feels ostracized. "I walk through the corridors every day," she says, "and colleagues avoid me."

The gymnasts themselves have been called troublemakers since they petitioned for reinstatement. One teacher said in a classroom that they shouldn't have protested an administrative decision. "Now I look back and I can see the good things that we did," says Nancy. "But I also feel crushed. Later on, 10 years from now, when I remember my gymnastics days, this is going to haunt me. It's not that I only had two or three good years, but also that they kicked the program out from under me."

What has she learned? Says Nancy: "The system doesn't work."

Navratilova Still Shows Championship Qualities

TENNIS

By *JOHN FEINSTEIN*

From the Washington Post
Copyright © 1987, Washington Post Co.

When they handed Steffi Graf the silver cup that is named for Suzanne Lenglen Saturday afternoon, the West German teen-ager acted like a teen-ager, if only for a second. She stood there, frozen, not quite sure what to do.

Suddenly, from two steps below her on the victory stand in Roland Garros Stadium, Graf heard a voice softly coaching her. "Come on, hoist it up, you won it, you deserve it. Hoist it up for everyone to see."

The voice belonged to Martina Navratilova.

If there ever was a moment when a loser had the right to be a tad ungracious, this was it. And yet, there was Navratilova, coaching the kid who will undoubtedly succeed her as the best women's tennis player in the world, helping her in a moment when others would only have been bitter. She had lost the French Open final, 6-4, 4-6, 8-6 to Graf, in a match she thought she had won. She had lost two straight matches to the same player for the first time since 1981. She had lost a taut, three-set final here for a third straight year.

And yet, Navratilova made no excuses, didn't cry or whine or try to detract from what Graf had done. But that has never been her style. "I'll be back next year," she told the crowd. "Hang around. Maybe I'll win this thing yet."

People have never really given Navratilova her due. As a tennis player, they have. Now can anyone deny the greatness of someone who has won 15 Grand Slam titles, including seven Wimbledons, and put together the two longest match winning streaks ever?

But as a person, it has been more difficult. Some won't accept her as an American because she is Czechoslovakian by birth. Others won't accept her because she has acknowledged she is bisexual. And then there are those who don't like her because she became a better player than Chris Evert.

Evert has been Navratilova's blessing and her curse. Both have been blessed all these years by the presence of the other. They have pushed each other to better tennis, created some of the most dramatic matches ever played and, together, have been the linchpins of the game for 15 years.

But because Evert is Evert, people have been slow to appreciate Navratilova. Evert has been the world's darling since she was 16, so blond, so cute, so gracious. Navratilova was a fat little kid—"I looked like Porky Pig"—when she first came on the tour as a 16-year-old. She is slender now, blond like Evert, with an easy smile that makes people comfortable.

She understands that people have always compared her to Evert on appearance, on being from Prague instead of Fort Lauderdale and on who they have had relationships with. Long ago, Navratilova made her peace with this. Evert would be the darling. She would be the champion.

But as she has gotten older, Navratilova has, ever so slowly, won people over. They hooted her until she cried during the 1984 U.S. Open final against Evert but pulled madly for her when Graf had her in trouble there in the semifinals last year. Saturday, they cheered her in Roland Garros, a place where she once spoke to the fans in French to win them over.

"I think people have slowly come around to understanding me here," she said Saturday. "I think they appreciate the fact that I never say die, and I like them for that. I like playing here now. I enjoy them, I think they enjoy me."

They enjoyed her Saturday, just as they enjoyed Graf. There is a tendency to root for the youngster, the underdog, the one who never has won. And Graf's tenacity was to be admired. Few people beat the woman who is arguably the best player of all time when they trail, 5-3, in the third set. Graf did that.

Because she did that, and because she has won 39 matches and seven straight tournaments, some are saying Graf is now the best player in the world. Navratilova is not ready to abdicate.

"I'm not ready to step down yet," she said. "Don't dethrone me until I've stepped down." Her eyes narrowed for a minute. "I'm tired of it."

Only then did her frustration show. The same question had been raised in Rome when Gabriela Sabatini, the game's other star teenager, beat her in the semifinals. Navratilova thinks the Grand Slams matter. Saturday certainly mattered. But she lost here last year and ended up putting together a superb year, winning Wimbledon, the U.S. Open and the Virginia Slims Championships.

"I'm disappointed I lost the match, but I'm happy that I played well enough that I could have won on clay," she said. "A month ago, I was playing so bad I thought I might not even win Wimbledon. Now, though, I feel like I'm back. I've got my concentration back, my fight, my spirit. For the rest of the year, I feel good."

She is 30 and she knows that Graf is going to surpass her at some point. But she isn't going to go easily. She held her off at the Open last year, routed her in November—Graf's last loss—and perhaps should have won Saturday.

"I think Steffi felt sorry for me, which I didn't expect," Navratilova said. "She's a good kid. I'm glad she's out here pushing me. I think she's giving women's tennis a shot in the arm. She's good for the game."

And perhaps someday Graf will be a special champion. But not yet. For years now, they have written odes to Evert. They have called her, "Chris America," and, "Amazing Grace," and the most gracious champion in the game's history.

Evert is a marvel. But maybe, just maybe, people will learn to marvel at Navratilova. Saturday evening, she brushed off those who might compliment her for helping Graf on the victory stand. "She'd just never been there before," she said. "I'm sure she'll be up there again. Next time, she'll know what to do. She won't need my advice."

Maybe not on how to hold a trophy. But when it comes to being a champion, a truly special one, Martina Navratilova has been giving people lessons for years.

Safe!

by Dennis (Buzz) Magnuson of the St. Paul Pioneer Press Dispatch. Minnesota's Randy Bush reaches home plate before St. Louis catcher Tony Pena can deliver the tag during the Twins' six-run fourth inning in Game 2 of the 1987 World Series. Copyright © 1987, Buzz Magnuson, St. Paul Pioneer Press Dispatch.

Teamwork

by Larry Alpaugh of the Transcript-Telegram in Holyoke, Mass.
Dick Hoyt of Holland, Mass., strains as he runs the final 100 yards
of the 1987 Holyoke St. Patrick's Day 10K Road Race while pushing his son, Rick, in his wheelchair. Copyright © 1987, Larry
Alpaugh, Transcript-Telegram.

Falling Star

COLLEGE BASKETBALL

By *STEVE FRIEDMAN*

From St. Louis Magazine
Copyright © 1987, St. Louis Magazine

On good days, Marshall Rogers can almost remember what it feels like to be rich and famous. Flipping through the scrapbooks he never allows to leave his room, he is struggling to make this a good day.

"I scored 58 here," he says, and stabs a finger at a yellowed clipping, then at me. "Here," he says, and flips the page, "this is where I scored my 1,000th point. There. That's Lamar. I used them up. I had 18 the first year we played them. The next year I had 44." He flips to another curled piece of paper. "I had 58 points here. This is important. Look at this."

It is late July, the kind of hazy, sweaty day when even little children in this North St. Louis neighborhood stay off the streets and cling to patches of shade on their front porches. We are sitting in Rogers' bedroom, on the top floor of his mother's house. A fan blows hot, stale air around the cramped room, over the chessboard that sits on a footlocker between two beds, ruffling the pictures of naked women that plaster the walls. In a corner, nearly hidden, is a shiny, bronzed basketball engraved on its base. It says, "Marshal (sic) Rogers, The National Scoring Champ, NCAA Division I 36.8." Rogers received it in 1976, the year he scored more points than anyone else in major college basketball. He picks it up, rubs the top of it, mutters something to someone who is not there.

Then he shouts. "Hey, you've heard of Willie Smith (former basketball player at Mizzou)? They retired his number, right? Willie Smith never scored 58 points. They're crazy. Don't you think so? See what I'm saying?"

★　　★　　★

People remember Marshall Rogers. He was one of the inner city's success stories. A role model. By the time he graduated from Sumner High School in 1971, he wasn't just a high school All-America basketball player. He was also the school's Scholar-Athlete. And when he left Pan American University on a spring day in 1976, he held, as well as a slew of scoring records, a bachelor's degree in history.

Did mothers tell their little boys about Marshall? Did they say it was OK to run outside and play, as long as they remembered to study—like Marshall? The children surely paid attention, because Marshall was living their dream. People paid him to play basketball. He was on television. For a few glorious months in the winter of 1977, he worked for the Golden State Warriors, and on days he wanted to tool around the San Francisco Bay area, he hopped into a green Cordoba, or a lavender Mark V. Sometimes he tooled around in a yellow van with "Warriors" emblazoned on the side. He made $45,000 a year. That was a long time ago.

This past June, a downtown drugstore manager spotted Rogers stuffing something into his gym bag. When the manager searched it, he found a bottle of Mennen Skin Bracer, a stick of Adidas deodorant, a pair of white sunglasses and three Baby Ruth candy bars. Total value: $13.

Rogers has lived with his mother for at least three years. He hasn't worked steadily this decade.

Hometown heroes often fall, but rarely from such dizzying heights, and seldom to such public lows ("Ex-Sumner, Pro Player Held in Melee," said the headline in the *St. Louis Post-Dispatch*). Marshall Rogers seemed to have it all, and when he lost it, those who knew him groped for explanations.

"Living in the past," said a man who played against Rogers in high school. "Like a lot of inner-city kids," said one of his college coaches, "who can never give up that dream of playing big-time basketball."

Impatience, said his mother. "He always wanted to jump fast. You can't jump fast if you're new."

Pride, said one of his two ex-wives. "He probably feels that things should be better because they were better. . . . He will have to go back down, in a sense, to get back up."

Rogers is proud, of course, and impatient. Those qualities, as much as his enormous physical gifts, helped him claw his way to success. And yes, he clings to the past, and to the dream he should have long ago abandoned. But those are small problems. What's wrong with Marshall Rogers is more serious. And more frightening.

★　　★　　★

"I was drafted number 34 in the second round, but I would have been in the first round, playing with the New York Knicks. But some important people didn't want me in New York."

We are sitting in Pope's Cafeteria in Central City Shopping Center. Rogers is halfway through his lunch—a pork steak, a plate of roast beef, a large salad soaked in Thousand Island and Italian dressing, a roll with six pats of butter, green beans, a large pickle, two cartons of milk, a piece of apple pie and a bottle of Budweiser. Before he digs in, he shakes salt over everything but the drinks and pie for five seconds, then pepper for three seconds, until there is a gritty layer of black and white covering his food. "Hey," he yells when a waitress walks by, "where's the ketchup?" She promises to bring some. "And bring some Tabasco and A-1 sauce, too."

Between huge bites, Rogers talks about basketball, and college, and women.

After he left the pros and before he returned, for good, to St. Louis, Rogers went back to Pan American University in Texas to take some graduate-level courses. He dropped out because "every time I went to take a test, they were using a machine to clear my mind."

"A machine?"

"Yeah."

"Who?"

"I can't tell you. You know what this place is called?"

"Pope's?"

"Yeah, exactly."

He attacks his pork steak, and we eat in silence. Then he tells me how he and his team almost defeated the University of Nevada-Las Vegas basketball team 12 years ago. "We were hooping 'em to death," he says, until "they were using some kind of animation machine to help them score in the second half."

"An animation machine?"

"They have these rays that grab the ball in midair."

"Who does?"

"I can't tell you."

Roast beef and green beans then, and more silence.

I ask how many children he has.

"I don't really know."

"Five?"

"No, about 12. I have some white ones, too. When I was at Kansas, I had some white girlfriends, and they had my kids. They wanted some money for the kids, and cars, and stuff, and they asked the regime, and they got the cars and money and places to live."

"You mean the athletic department got that stuff for them? Coaches? Alumni?"

"No, the regime. Pope John Paul, Queen Elizabeth, King Arthur and Hercules."

★   ★   ★

Marshall Rogers was the sixth of seven children. A bright little boy, he paid attention and worked hard. Before long, he was riding the bus to Sportsmen's Park with all the other straight-A students to watch the baseball Cardinals. He decided he wanted to be a teacher when he grew up. That, or a professional baseball player. His heroes were Ken Boyer, Mike Shannon and Bob Gibson.

In third grade he discovered basketball. He was the best player in his class, "but the big dudes used to beat on us." For a while, anyway, Marshall stuck with marbles and hopscotch. But his mother bought him a shiny new basketball that year, and when he wore it out, she bought him another. By the time he graduated from Sumner in 1971, Marshall's mother had bought her baby boy 10 new basketballs. Every year, a new ball.

In the summer, he went to the baseball games with the other straight-A students. In the spring, he set sprint and long jump records for the Sumner track team. And always, there was basketball.

He played for the state championship team when he was a sophomore; when he was a senior, he averaged 26.7 points per game and led his team to a 22-4-1 record (a near riot forced the tie with Vashon). When practice was over and the rest of the team had showered and gone home, Rogers stayed in the gym. Coach John Algee stayed, too, and when Rogers dribbled and shot, Algee slapped his star's wrist. Or he smacked his star's elbow.

"I wanted to make him get his rhythm down," Algee says, "to help him learn to shoot with people hitting him."

He learned—on the court and in class.

"My favorite course was probably history," Rogers says. "Math was good, too. Cutting class was the best, though. Just to talk about what happened yesterday, or last night."

John Algee: "I can't say enough about him as a high school athlete. He was one of the greatest basketball players that ever played for me. . . . He was a very good student, carried himself well.

"But he more or less was a loner—stayed by himself. I don't think he had any best friends."

★   ★   ★

"My mother stole one of my tank tops." He has finished everything but the pie. He will take that home. He is sipping his beer and smoking a cigarette. "Someone probably called her—the Pope or the Queen, and told her, "Steal Marshall's tank top, so he won't look so good.' "

★   ★   ★

Rogers left St. Louis and moved to Lawrence, Kan., where he had accepted an athletic scholarship at the University of Kansas. He led his undefeated freshmen team in scoring and assists and enjoyed the social opportunities available to a healthy young athlete in a college town. He averaged 24.3 points that year. His freshmen coach, Bob Frederick (now athletic director at KU), says he "really enjoyed" Marshall, but remembers that "he did have a little bit of a temper. He'd flare up pretty quickly."

He had plenty of chances to flare up the next year. The Jayhawks employed a slow-down offense which could not have been less suited to the insect-quick Rogers. His scoring average fell to 7.6. The team went 8-18. "I was unhappy," Rogers remembers. "We were winning quite a few games in the first half, then losing. There were some inner-squad squabbles. The teammates got upset."

During his sophomore winter of discontent, Rogers happened to pick up a magazine on one of the Jayhawks road trips. He spotted a story about a coach named Abe Lemons, legendary in basketball circles for his explosive offenses.

"Dear Coach Lemons," Rogers wrote, "My name is Marshall Rogers. I'm 6-foot-2-inches and 180 pounds. I averaged 24.3 points and 6.0 assists respectively for the Kansas freshmen team last year. My main strengths are speed and quickness. . ."

Fourteen years later, Lemons still has the letter.

"I just thought he was the nicest kid," the coach says. Lemons was especially impressed that Rogers didn't badmouth his Kansas coach. "And he wrote a real nice letter."

After his sophomore season, Rogers left KU and transferred to Pan American University, where Lemons was coaching. When he showed up at the campus in Edinburg, Tex., and laid eyes on his new coach, the "nice kid" demanded money. "He asked if I was going to give him plane fare for his trips back to St. Louis," Lemons remembers. "I said no. He asked if that was the way it was for everybody on the team. I said yes. He said, 'Well, I can live with that.' "

While Rogers was waiting to become eligible to play for Lemons, he joined a city league in Edinburg. "They kicked him off," Lemons says, "and they told me he would never be able to play for me, because he shot too much."

They didn't know Lemons. Famous for his cowboy boots and his drawling one-liners, the coach never met a jumpshot he didn't like. And if some of Marshall's shots were—shall we say, inventive?—well, Lemons took to splash and dazzle the way other coaches take to crew cuts and blazers.

For two years, the city kid and the country coach created a defensive specialist's worst nightmare. Their supporting cast could have been dreamed up by Ring Lardner. At one guard was Jesus Guerra, a short (5-feet-10-inches), skinny kid who grew up on the Mexican border. He penetrated and passed. Teammates called him "Chewey." Fans called him "Little Jesus." In the pivot was Pete "Pizza" Severa, a 6-foot-5-inch, 250-pound manchild who worked during the day at—where else?—Pizza Hut, then threw opponents around at night. "He was what we jokingly called our center," says Lemons, who now coaches at Oklahoma City University.

The Pan American Broncs often scored more than 100 points in a single game. And the biggest scorer and main attraction of the hardwood circus was Rogers.

"He was the best pure shooter I've ever seen," says Jim McKone, Pan American's sports information director for the past 18 years. Likeable? Rogers is one of two Bronc athletes McKone ever had to his house for dinner. Tough? McKone remembers a game—it was January 29, 1976—against Houston Baptist University. Rogers drove the lane in the opening minutes, and when he stretched toward the basket, Houston Baptist's 7-foot center caught the nation's leading scorer in the jaw with an elbow. "He was out on the floor," McKone remembers, "absolutely cold." A minute passed. Rogers didn't move. Two minutes. Nothing. Three minutes. Rogers got up, walked to the free-throw line and sank two shots. He ended up with 45 points. Final score: Pan American, 81, Houston Baptist, 79.

Rogers averaged 26.7 points per game his junior year. The team went 22-2. In his record-setting senior season, he hit 36.8 per game. The team was 20-5.

"He was amazing," says Guerra, now head basketball coach at Roma (Tex.) High School, in the border town where he grew up. "Coach Lemons kept stats every day, and Marshall would shoot 40 out of 50, 25 out of 30. He was the most dedicated player I've ever been associated with."

"He was one of the best," Lemons says. "He had the size, the ability. There wasn't anything he couldn't do in the game. . . . He was what you'd call an All-American boy. He made his grades, worked hard, got along with everybody. He was a coach's dream."

★   ★   ★

Rogers: "We were playing the University of Hawaii. The Queen called me on the phone and said we had to beat them by 15 points. I scored 47 points, but we had to play them the next night again, and I was too tired. So one of my brothers, who looks just like me, from Africa, he played."

★   ★   ★

Rogers was selected in the second round of the National Basketball Association's annual draft, and in the fall of 1976, he signed a $45,000 contract with the Golden State Warriors. He played in 26 games that year and averaged 3.8 points. "I was hooping 'em to death," Rogers says. "I should have been" playing more.

The next fall, he attended veteran's camp, where he continued to ride the bench. In October 1977, the Warriors played the Los Angeles Lakers in an exhibition game in Reno, Nev.

"I should have been starting," Rogers says. "I got kind of upset. . . . You get real upset and feel like hurting somebody. It's best just to get away so you don't get into trouble."

He left the team.

★   ★   ★

We are driving to Shoney's, in North County. Rogers is in the passenger's seat, stroking an invisible baby he holds in front of him. He is talking out of the right side of his mouth, addressing something outside the car.

When we sit down, he calls to a waitress. "I'll have an apple pie a la mode while I order," he says. She brings it, and he asks for spaghetti with extra meat, and a turkey club sandwich, and the salad bar. He gives it all the salt and pepper treatment and asks for ket-

chup and A-1.

"On May 30, 1976," he says, "I went to the Olympic camp in Raleigh, N.C. There were two practices a day for three hours each time. It was grueling. It made you tired. And mean and mad. I did real well before the animation machine got in my way.

"Wait," he says, after we finish and I start to stand. "I have to do something." He stands in the aisle, turns and crosses his arms under his chin, elbows outstretched. He stands that way, rigid, for almost five minutes. "That was the Pope," he tells me later, "telling me to do that."

★　　★　　★

After leaving the Warriors, Rogers stayed in the Bay area. He played in pickup games, in tournaments. He was a substitute teacher in Hayward, Calif. And he was unhappy.

In September 1978, he tried out with the San Antonio Spurs. "I was doing good enough to be in the top seven. I didn't see anyone else hitting as many jumpshots as me. (But) people in the underground were saying, 'Marshall likes himself too much 'cause he scores too much.' That's why I didn't play. But I'm thinking about trying out again."

"The last I heard from him," says Coach Lemons, "seems like he was down in San Antone. He called and said he needed $100, so I telegrammed it to him."

★　　★　　★

Rogers is standing at the free-throw line in the gym at Vic Tanny on Dorsett and I-270. His right arm is cocked in a U, and a scowl splits his face. He hits 34 free throws without missing, and without smiling. Then he hits 31 without missing, then 17. The only sounds are the clanking of the weight machines nearby and the rock music being piped over the fitness center's sound system. That and the occasional bounce of the basketball on the floor, and the swish of the net. And Marshall's muttering. He is talking to the voices.

★　　★　　★

KU's Bob Frederick heard from Rogers last winter. "He wanted to know if I could put in a word for him with" Topeka's semi-pro basketball team. "He told me how he and his friend were hooping everybody at Forest Park Community College."

Frederick clears his throat. It pained him to hear from Rogers. It pains him to talk about him.

"I don't want this to sound wrong," Frederick says, and clears his throat again. "It was like he was just a year out of college, instead of 11 years."

Roma's favorite son, Guerra, doesn't know what to say when he learns of his old teammate's troubles. First come the adjectives: "hardworking," "gifted," "dedicated." Then memories of specific games, particular feats of athletic heroism. There is a realization that "it was very rare when we got together" socially, and a few half-hearted attempts to understand why some people succeed and others fail. Finally, there is simply a request.

"Do you have Marshall's phone number?" Little Jesus asks. "I need to call him."

       ★   ★   ★

We are driving to O'Fallon Park with a photographer to shoot some baskets and some pictures. Rogers is expansive—laughing, smoking, jiving. He is telling us how he played one-on-one with a local teenager a few days earlier. "He was woofing on me. I smoked him. I'm gonna steal his mother from him now. She knows me from high school. She knows me from when I was a superstar."

It is Thursday afternoon, August 27. Today, Rogers turns 34 years old.

       ★   ★   ★

Narrating his own life story, Rogers will gladly rattle off dates and statistics. December 2, 1974: The Broncs steal the ball three times in the final 30 seconds to erase a 5-point deficit and beat Arkansas State in Jonesboro. January 3, 1976: The Broncs lose to the University of Nevada-Las Vegas, and Rogers feels the "animation machine." May 16, 1976: Rogers graduates from Pan American University. September 1978: He tries out with the Spurs, but is cut.

And "that's it," Rogers says. "Right there. You don't need to write about any of that other stuff."

       ★   ★   ★

Kurt Gull used to work as a security guard for St. Louis Centre. He was on duty Wednesday, June 24.

"We got a call from Walgreens. They said they had a shoplifter in custody. I was the first person on the scene. When I got there, Marshall and the manager were arguing and pushing and shoving. . . . (The manager) explained that he had seen him take some items, and that he and the assistant manager had talked Marshall into going into the backroom, and they checked the gym bag and found the items. What they were pushing and shoving over was that (Rogers) didn't like the idea of them getting into his gym bag.

"I said, 'OK, I'm placing you under arrest.'

"He said, 'OK, what's going to happen now?'

"I said, 'I'll have to handcuff you until the police arrive, and you'll probably get a summons, and you probably won't have to go anywhere.'

"He said, 'OK,' and I put one handcuff on his left hand and he went crazy. He jumped back, slammed me against the wall. He swung, he pushed, he shoved."

By then, two more security guards and a police officer had arrived.

"I'm 5-foot-9, 225 pounds, 50 inches across the chest, and he was tossing us around like we were rag dolls."

In September, Rogers was convicted of assault. He was placed on probation.

       ★   ★   ★

After the Spurs cut him, Rogers returned to St. Louis. Except for a brief attempt to take graduate courses at Pan American in the fall of 1979 (where the machine "cleared his mind"), Rogers has never ventured out again. One of college basketball's greatest scorers hasn't done much the past 10 years.

He taught at McKinley High School and O'Fallon Technical Center in 1978-1979. He left McKinley because "the principal was upset ... because the students were acting crazy, and one girl especially, and I started to curse her out." He has been married twice and has at least two children. His second wife, who asked that her name not be used, says "he probably feels that things should be better because they were better." His mother says he "does funny things with his hands." She wishes he would see a doctor.

Rogers spends much of his time sleeping and eating. He wakes up early every day—sometimes 5:30 or 6 a.m.—and makes breakfast. A typical meal is two eggs, two hot dogs, two pancakes, milk and Kool-Aid. After that, "sometimes I go back to sleep. Sometimes I cut the grass. Sometimes I just sit on the porch. Sometimes, but not all the time. Sometimes it's fun. Sometimes it's boring."

He usually skips lunch, and after a typical afternoon of "just relaxing," his mother cooks dinner. After that, he usually hangs around the house until he decides to go up to his room and go to sleep, which could be any time between 7 p.m. and 2 a.m.

"Sometimes I get mad at the voices," he says, "and I can't go to sleep. And I say, 'Leave me alone.'"

★   ★   ★

We are sitting in a courtyard on Laclede's Landing. Rogers is here with mixed feelings. He doesn't want anything written about his recent troubles with the law, and he would rather talk about how many points he scored against Lamar than his difficulties finding a job. On the other hand, without a car, he doesn't get a chance to leave the house much. And I'm buying lunch.

I ask who his friends are.

"No one."

"No one?"

"Sometimes, I'll be with friends, but not very often. Nowadays, I'll be by myself at home."

"You ever get lonely?"

"Sometimes. Sometimes. But not all the time."

"What do you see yourself doing in five or 10 years?"

"Some type of work. . . . With a job, I could get around and do more things I want. I could go to a discotheque and buy some drinks that I like—that's why I need to get some work. You know, I haven't been having a real good time lately."

"What plans do you have for looking for work?"

"I don't know. I haven't thought about it."

"You have any regrets about what happened at Walgreens?"

"It's over with."

"Do the voices bother you?"

"I'll be trying to lay down, and it really upsets me when I'm

trying to lay down and go to sleep and I don't feel like standing up and they tell me to stand up."

"You told me you talked to a doctor about this once."

"That was someone else. That really wasn't me.

"Sometimes they say things to me that don't pertain to what I want to do. They tell me to do something while I'm playing and I don't feel like doing it, and I just say, 'Shut the fuck up.' Sometimes it gives me a headache."

"Do you ever think now about seeing a doctor?"

"I don't need a doctor. I just need to go to sleep and not talk to them anymore."

Playing at Home Can't Help the Bears

HUNTING

By *GENE COLLIER*

From the Pittsburgh Press
Copyright © 1987, the Pittsburgh Press

Today marks the halfway point of bear season, or at least it is officially recognized as such by hunters and bears alike, in part because the season started yesterday and ends tomorrow, and I just thought it would be a good time to take a look at how things are going.

Maybe it's not, but I'm doing it anyway.

My sources in the woods tell me that, as you might expect, the bears are losing big-time.

Again.

They are definitely not going to make the playoffs.

Unless they come up with a startling second half tonight and tomorrow, the bears are looking at their landmark 200 millionth consecutive losing season.

The bears have not had a winning autumn since the invention of the hand-held club.

The post-club era (sometimes called the dead-bear era but never to be confused with the live ball or big-band eras) actually began not with the club itself but with the dispute over the inclusion of the club amidst the hunter's legitimate equipment.

To this day, what we have in bear season is not merely a battle of nerves between man and beast. What we have here is another in a series of annual disputes about the rules of the game.

The rules for bear season, published in this newspaper Sunday and which, I thought, looked suspiciously like those used in Australian Rules Football, might have something to do with the bears' skid in this long series.

One of the things that is just killing the bears is that the hunters insist on a liberal interpretation of the rule on clothing.

In Pennsylvania, and I'm quoting from the published rules here, "hunters are required to wear a minimum of 250 square inches of fluorescent orange on head and chest areas."

The bears, understandably, prefer strict adherence to this rule because it helps them see the hunters advancing toward them with firearms.

Hunters, however, are virtually ignoring this rule.

Already a report has reached me that a bear was dragged to one regional check station by a man wearing only a fluorescent orange cumberbund, a woods-brown wet suit, and a fez.

Well that's just great.

And then people call the talk shows and say, "What's wrong with the bears?"

To think that the 250-square-inch minimum was erected as a result of good faith collective bargaining makes the hunters' ignorance all the more distasteful.

At one point, hunters were allowed into the woods wearing anything at all. A hunter could hunt bear dressed as a bear if he liked.

The bears—and this is regarded as one of the all-time blunders in the history of the sport—actually dropped their demand for bulletproof vests just to get them to agree to the 250-square-inch minimum.

Another rule the hunters have found their way around is the roster limit.

In Pennsylvania—and I'm quoting directly again—"parties of five or more persons hunting together must maintain a roster that includes the name and address of each hunter. A copy of the roster must be carried by the captain of the hunting party."

Hunting parties routinely expand, however, by taking hunters off the injured-reserve list.

Since parties cannot replace him in that list with an uninjured hunter, they must move a hunter onto the physically disinclined to go near a bear list, for which a 48-hour cooling off period is required.

As a result, parties often get into the woods numbering nine, 10, 11, 30 hunters.

Given this climate of distrust, it is amazing that any agreement on even the most insignificant of rules ever has been reached.

So the pregnant bear/hunter rule is certainly a landmark.

It arose over a dispute on the number of bears that could be "taken" or in the colloquial, "blown away."

In Pennsylvania, to quote again the published rules, "a hunter may take only one bear and a party of three or more may take no more than three bears."

The bears insisted that the "taking" of a pregnant bear constituted two bears.

They did this after discovering that lone hunters were arming their pregnant wives for bear season to qualify for the three-hunters, three-bears clause. Starting this season, either violation costs the hunters a draft choice.

But the primary remaining rule that prevents the bears from achieving parity is the rule that covers the tagging of the bear.

In Pennsylvania—and again, I'm not making this up, not this part anyway—"successful hunters must fill out the tag attached to the hunting license and attach it to an ear (the bear's ear) before moving the bear."

Toward a more equitable competition, then, I propose that the final phrase of this rule be amended to read "before shooting the bear."

The bears have argued this point since the advent of tagging, saying, quite rightly, that a hunter required to tag a bear's ear before discharging his weapon has a much higher risk of being "taken."

I could support such a rule, but only on the promise that if it did result in a winning season for the bears, they would not write any books.

He Fought His Way Up

BOXING

By *RON BORGES*

From the Boston Globe
Copyright © 1987, the Boston Globe

Marlon Starling's story is about America the way we used to be before condo conversions and insider trading and wars we didn't want and wars we couldn't win and deficit spending and drugs that make kids crack in the night.

It's a simple story about a guy who went to work every day for 20 years, punching people instead of a time clock, paying his dues but never paying a price so high it killed his dream.

It's just a simple little story you don't see enough of anymore in boxing . . . or anywhere else . . . about a guy who finally got what he deserved and earned everything he got.

Every single thing, including the welterweight championship of the world . . . and a whole lot of pain.

       ★   ★   ★

ROUND 1

There are a lot of things that make people fight for a living but poverty is the most common. You need something special happening in your life to decide that a punch in the nose is the best way to make a living. The thing you need is desperation.

There is plenty of that in the north end of Hartford, enough to fill a half-dozen housing projects and a lot of gyms. But other things can drive you into fighting, too, although they're usually all part of that same desperation.

"Jealousy," Starling recalled while standing in the shadow of a crowded, noisy and dangerous piece of not-so-real estate in north Hartford called Stowe Village.

It is a multi-building housing project identical to the one two miles away where Starling lived 29 years ago. It is not a place where hope springs eternal because at best hope comes around like city services—sporadically.

"That's why I started boxing," Starling continued while an outside light flickered undecidedly between on and off, although settling on off for longer and longer periods as he talked.

"Jealousy. I was looking out a window just like that one up there with no curtains. I was looking across the projects and I saw into another kid's apartment and he had a boxing trophy.

"I decided I was gonna get me one of those. I didn't think it'd be that hard to come by."

★   ★   ★

ROUND 2

From the start, Starling was no fan of fists to the face. At 9, he first walked into Johnny (Duke) Galuchi's gym in the Bellevue Square projects and didn't like what he saw.

"I said, 'I'm not going in there,' " Starling said. "Man, they was punching. It's not something you would like."

Assuredly not, but from the beginning, the ring was one place where the West Hartford kids with blond hair and straight teeth didn't have the built-in advantage over him. Money didn't count in the gym, and neither did the clothes or the books, because everyone was in his underwear in the ring and there wasn't much to read at the end of a boxing glove.

"You see any champions coming out of Weston?" Starling asked. "Nah. No champions in Weston. I don't know of a champion come from the rich, do you? Champions come out of the inner city because what else they got?"

They come from the places where Starling was spawned, tough and dangerous places where what counts are the things he had in abundance—speed, aggressiveness and heart. And what counts the most down there is heart.

But heart is not the same as confidence. Heart keeps you going through the doubts and lets confidence grow, but when you start at the bottom, you had better have a lot of heart because there will be a lot of doubt.

"I remember getting a call," Duke said. "They needed a 147-pounder for the (Junior Olympic) Nationals. Marlon was 15 and about 140, but I believed in him. I told him he could do it.

"Three weeks later, we're flying out. It's his first flight, and he says, 'Mr. Duke, tell me what you said in the gym.' I didn't remember what I said, but he says, 'You can do . . .'

"I can still remember that. I told him, 'You can do it, Moochie.' I told him that every day. When the fights started, we were back in the 10th row, and each time you win, you move up a row. Every time he moved up, I said, 'You can do it, Moochie.'

"In the championship fight, I told him that going up the stairs to the ring. I told him that after the first round and after the second. He came back after the last round and I didn't say it again. I just looked at him and said, 'Hello, champ.' You should have seen him smile."

★   ★   ★

ROUND 3

Marlon Starling had been a professional boxer for a year when his world fell apart.

He'd fought 110 times as an amateur and was 5-0 as a pro and the hottest thing in Hartford since humidity. *Snap,* just like that, he was a guy with a future, which is not something that comes easy in the north end.

Everything was going right until they put him in the Civic Center Exhibition Hall on January 9, 1980, against a kid he grew up with named Charlie Newell.

Newell was a prison inmate by trade, a guy serving 6 to 12 for armed robbery up at Enfield, the state's minimum-security facility. Like a lot of prisoners, he boxed on the side, and everyone agreed they'd put him in with the skinny kid and let 'em mix it up for a few bucks.

Starling dominated the bout, knocking Newell out in the seventh round. Newell's head hit the canvas twice. He did not get up.

For nine days, Newell lay unconscious before he died of a blood clot on the brain without ever coming out of his coma. Charlie Newell had been scheduled to be released in April.

No one really blamed Starling. It was part of *the game.* It *happens.* Just *forget it.*

But it wasn't easy to forget when people he didn't know drove up to the gas station where he worked late at night and called him a murderer. That wasn't a part of *the game* they tell you about when you get in it. They didn't tell you people died.

So Marlon Starling went off by himself, walking the fields of a farm owned by his manager then, Hartford attorney F. Mac Buckley. He walked alone. Moochie and the cows. The cows and Moochie.

"He called me in Vegas the day the guy died," Buckley recalled. "He was hysterical. I flew right home and made him go to the funeral. He wanted to stick his head in the ground, but he had to face it."

"He doesn't talk about it, but I know it was a tough time in his life," added Donald Bowers, Starling's recently deposed manager. "The best thing that happened was that Mac made him go to the funeral. Charlie's mother told Moochie to keep fighting. She said it wasn't his fault. She told him he could do it."

"Tell me, Mr. Duke . . . Tell me, 'You can do . . .'"

★   ★   ★

ROUND 4

Less than two months after the Newell fight, Starling was back in the ring and he quickly ran his record to 19-0 before getting his first real break. He would go to Las Vegas to spar with Thomas Hearns, who was preparing for his fight with Ray Leonard.

It was a way to get noticed and a way to see if Johnny Duke was right about him.

"I was ranked seventh or eighth but I wanted to see how I could do with the champions," Starling recalled. "I was too wise for Tommy. I could see that early.

"But one day he caught me with a shot. If we'd been in a regular gym I'd have said, 'Hold up.' But no way I'm going to let him beat the crap out of me. I got some pride. I kept fighting. If you watch the film, you can't tell when he broke my jaw."

Marlon Starling had learned that Tommy Hearns could punch . . . and that Marlon Starling could take it.

★ ★ ★

ROUND 5

By the end of 1982, Starling was 24-0 and owner of the U.S. Boxing Association welterweight title. It wasn't much, but you had to start somewhere, which is something no one had to tell him.

He had produced a spectacular first-round knockout of Kevin Morgan the first time he fought on national television, and the lights were on again October 3, 1982, when he went in with Donald Curry in an elimination bout. The winner earned a chance to fight for the vacant World Boxing Association welterweight championship.

The fight was in Atlantic City, where Curry, a Texan, was considered the hometown favorite. He was the Lone Star Cobra, a name given him by the national media. Starling, meanwhile, was The Magic Man, a name he'd given himself.

This was Starling's chance, and he had some magic that night, but he also played the fool, winking at his supporters, waving at Leonard at ringside, clowning in the ring like a street kid ill at ease at being invited to boxing's country club.

Apparently, he irritated the judges enough to make Curry a winner by a split decision, which in boxing often means the other guy won but *psst,* don't tell anybody.

Buckley was furious. Later they went up to their hotel room, where Sam Kane, one of the 30 original investors who put up $2,000 to start Starling's career, was waiting. Kane was suffering from Lou Gehrig's disease.

"If I could open this window, I'd throw you out," Buckley shouted.

"I was having fun," Starling answered.

"Tell the guy in the wheelchair who's dying you had fun," Buckley snorted with disgust.

★ ★ ★

ROUND 6

Donald Curry had been champion for just under a year when he called Starling again, and this time the outcome was beyond dispute.

The determination was there that night, but so was the doubt, and on this night doubt ruled Marlon Starling. He went the distance but he didn't spend much time fighting.

"I lost," he said. "It was close, but Curry won it. He was the better fighter. My corner kept saying, 'Back him up. Back him up.' Why do you think I didn't? It was because I couldn't. Not that night."

"Tell me, Mr. Duke ... Tell me, 'You can do ...' "

★   ★   ★

ROUND 7

They were beginning to write the obits for Starling the minute the referee raised Curry's hand a second time, but it was nothing like what they said after Starling put Pedro Vilella in the hospital and still came out on the short end of a Brinks job at Madison Square Garden four months later.

He punched Vilella around for 12 rounds, but on his record they said it was a loss, and when it was over, Buckley exploded.

"They got close to the top, but they fell off," Bowers explained. "After Vilella, there was a tremendously heated exchange. There was a lot of sailor talk and name calling. Anyone who witnessed it knew that was the end.

"It was like a marriage gone bad. It couldn't be reconciled, and the end was almost a relief. But there had been stability there, and I think Marlon was scared at the loss of security."

"Tell me, Mr. Duke ... Tell me, 'You can do ...' "

★   ★   ★

ROUND 8

Marlon Starling did not fight again for 10 months.

But the real point is that eventually he did fight again, as he always would, and he won five straight, setting up a USBA title match with Johnny Bumphus, another fighter who had been hovering on the welterweight periphery too long for his own good.

After five rounds, Bumphus had a big lead, but Starling had begun to wear him out. Bumphus' hands were dropping, his legs were gone and Starling was waiting to unleash a left hook that would more than even the score.

But their heads came together first, and the other side of boxing came out. Bumphus' manager, Lou Duva, was screaming, hands were waving and doctors were shaking their heads even though the blood had stopped running into Bumphus' eye. Marlon Starling was quickly declared a "technical" loser.

"They screwed me bad," Starling said. "I didn't have a chance. I should have seen what was coming. They stole it."

Stolen or not, they were writing goodbye to him after that.

"They'd been doing it for three years," Starling said. "But every time there was room for doubt, victory came my way."

★   ★   ★

ROUND 9

Five fights, five wins, five guys you never heard of, but so what? In the interim, while everyone was saying Marlon Starling's day was gone, Tommy Ayers was losing a tuneup fight that cost him a shot at WBA welterweight champion Mark Breland.

Ayers was out, but Breland had to fight somebody. Hey, Duva thought, how about Starling? He's all done. He lost to Bumphus, didn't he? Let's give him the shot.

Quietly this time, Marlon Starling agreed.

"Tell me, Mr. Duke... Tell me, 'You can do...' "

★　　★　　★

ROUND 10

For most of the first 10 rounds they fought at the Township Auditorium in Columbia, S.C., on August 22, Breland popped Starling in the face with two- and three-punch combinations. He scored and scored and scored again, and the punches that landed were the kind that hurt and kept on hurting.

But as each round passed, Breland grew wearier, eventually falling down of his own accord a ridiculous eight times until Round 9, when he landed what should have been his best punch of the night.

Breland had set himself as Starling moved in and exploded a massive right hand directly on the chin of the challenger. It was a knockout punch, but nothing happened.

"He hit me with his best shot, and nothing," Starling said. "That can discourage a fighter."

Or it can convince one that Johnny Duke was right again.

★　　★　　★

ROUND 11

Three solid shots—bang, Bang, BANG—and Mark Breland's legs were spaghetti.

One more left hook as crisp as burned toast to the chin and Marlon Starling's 20-year search was over at 1:38 of Round 11. Breland was down and would not know when he was standing again for quite some time.

"After 20 years in this cruel sport, I now can say I'm the champion of the world," Starling said. "I beat the system. I had to beat him. I got hit more tonight than I ever have because I fought with my heart and not my head. I just plowed in. That's not me, but I had to gamble. What did I have to lose?"

"You can do it, Moochie. You can do it."

★　　★　　★

REALITY, ROUND 12

It is two months since the Breland fight, and Marlon Starling is back in Stowe Village. Back at work. He is the champion of the world, but not much else around him has changed.

"Bring my belt down here?" he says. "Into this neighborhood? You crazy?

"Now I can always say I was the champion of the world, but I don't kid myself. That ain't gonna pay the mortgage. I been fighting 20 years. I broke my jaw, cut my eyes, broke my hand, neglected my son. I want to get some back pay for that. My son's 10. He asked me this week, 'When you gonna hurry up and retire?'

"I told him, 'This is why you wear Nikes when your friends wear

$4 sneakers. This is why you have this and that and go on vacations. I didn't take any vacations when I was your age.'

"But he doesn't want to listen to that. He's a kid from the suburbs (South Windsor). He doesn't want to hear about boxing."

Marlon Starling Jr., age 10, is the son of the champion of the world, a kid with advantages growing up in a place where they don't make champions.

"If my parents had money, I'd have gone to college," Starling said wistfully. "I wanted to get something they couldn't take back from you, but I got into this working world and the money became more important than the education. If I could have done it any other way, I would have. But I couldn't."

"Tell me again, Mr. Duke . . . Tell me, 'You can do . . .'"

Gansz: A Closer Examination

PRO FOOTBALL

By *MIKE FISH*

From the Kansas City Star
Copyright © 1987, the Kansas City Star Co.

Military records do not substantiate the public image of Chiefs Coach Frank Gansz, who has allowed himself to be represented in reference guides for the media, newspaper stories and job resumes over the last 15 years as a jet fighter pilot with experience flying dangerous combat missions.

Gansz is on record as saying his squadron was "shot at practically every place we flew." His military personnel records show he flew jet trainers and propeller-driven military transports. It also shows that he never was stationed as a jet fighter pilot nor was he involved in any combat missions while a member of the U.S. Air Force.

Records and interviews with military officials and former associates also do not substantiate assertions Gansz has made regarding other aspects of his experiences as an aviator, coach and athlete.

Among other things, the records do not support assertions that Gansz lettered in football at Navy, that he was special assistant to the athletic director there and his version of a military flying experience that earned him the nickname "Crash."

"When I first got hired here in '81 and '82 and again last year, the only thing I can remember saying was the fact that I was an Air Force jet pilot. I don't write this stuff," Gansz said Saturday when he was asked about these discrepancies. "I was a qualified jet pilot from '61 to '66, so I don't know what else you would say.

"I was qualified as a single-engine jet pilot. That's what I was. I got my commerical rating as a single-engine jet pilot."

In a review of more than 25 stories published nationwide, there are no quotes from Gansz saying specifically that he was a jet fighter pilot. However, he has been described in many publications, including guides prepared as reference material for media representatives as a jet fighter pilot, and he has been quoted extensively about his flying exploits. He often draws comparisons between his military background and his current occupation.

"If I were a fighter pilot, would I be preparing to come close and make the playoffs?" Gansz was quoted September 12, 1987 in the *Kansas City Times*. "You only get one loss as a fighter pilot. I'd want to win every time I got into the cockpit against everybody."

In a question-and-answer interview September 13 in the *Kansas City Star,* Gansz responded to a question about burnout: "If you think this is pressure you ought to strap on an F-14 (fighter plane) sometime. Everything is fine here. No matter how bad it gets, I'll walk away. It's not true in that business."

Over time, a persona of Gansz as a daring aviator has developed. The opening of a 14-page brochure mailed by the Chiefs to season-ticket holders after the hiring of Gansz as head coach last January begins with the words: "Whether it's flying jet aircraft through danger zones or coaching a football team towards end zones . . ."

The news release put out by the Chiefs when Gansz was hired described him as a former jet fighter pilot. The Chiefs' 1987 media guide says he was a jet fighter pilot for six years. When Gansz was an assistant coach at Philadelphia, the Eagles' guide said he was "a military jet pilot."

Air Force officials, backed up by Gansz's Air Force Form 11, a military personnel record, said Francis VanRensselaer Gansz received his primary and basic training in a T-37, a twin-engine subsonic jet, and a T-33, a single-engine jet. The records show that Gansz flew those aircraft, designated as trainers by the T before the number, as a student pilot and the T-33 while he was on the coaching staff at the Air Force Academy. His only other technical flight training was a 12-week program with the MATS Transportation Training Unit at Tinker Air Force Base in Oklahoma City.

According to those same records Gansz never served in a command that had aircraft designated as jet fighters, and he flew a C-124—a large propeller-driven troop and cargo carrier nicknamed "The Aluminum Overcast" because of its size and relatively low normal cruising speed of 272 mph.

Mike Fixman, lead archives technician for Air Force correspondence at the National Personnel Records Center in St. Louis, said Gansz had the aeronautical rating of: "pilot at the squadron level for C-124-type aircraft . . . and he assisted the aircraft commander."

Gansz's final three years of active duty were served as an assistant football coach at the Air Force Academy. Former Air Force football coach Ben Martin said Gansz and other officer-coaches often got their flight time by piloting the T-33 on recruiting trips.

Air Force records do not show any combat service for Gansz. Records show the only individual awards bestowed on him were for small-arms marksmanship and the National Defense Service Medal, given to anyone on active duty during the Vietnam conflict.

There are other assertions made about Gansz's background that are not substantiated by records.

• The Chiefs' 1987 media guide lists Gansz as head freshman coach at the Naval Academy (1969-72). Dick Duden, a former All-America end at Navy, was head coach of the plebes at that time. The Navy media guide of 1972 describes Gansz as a plebe assistant coach and football recruiting coordinator, which Navy officials say was primarily an administrative duty that included escorting high school prospects during their on-campus visits.

• The Chiefs, in their 1987 media guide and in information given out when he was hired as head coach, said Gansz served as a pilot flying commercial airliners for Continental Airlines in 1967 and '68. Gansz reiterated that in an interview Saturday morning.

A resume Gansz submitted to another NFL team lists his time with Continental only as "1967." Airline records show he was employed for seven months—April 3, 1967 to October 31, 1967—and nearly half of this time was spent in flight training. Because of Gansz's brief stay with the airline, Continental public-relations director Rick Scott, based in Houston, said Gansz likely was a flight engineer, occupying the third seat in the cockpit.

• Army and UCLA media guides in Gansz's employment at those schools stated Gansz lettered in football at the Naval Academy. Navy records show Gansz never lettered in a varsity sport at Annapolis. He played 14 minutes of football as a sophomore in 1957, 11 minutes as a junior and 48 minutes as a senior. While on the coaching staffs at Oklahoma State, Army and UCLA, the media guides stated Gansz lettered in baseball and lacrosse at Navy. Not true, Navy officials say.

• And, there is the incident for which Gansz earned the nickname "Crash."

Gansz's account of piloting an aircraft on a low-level training mission when it struck 12 power lines has been reported in publications across the nation. According to Gansz, he then "was able to bring the plane down safely."

Air Force records show the incident occurred July 13, 1961, about 12 miles southwest of Tulia, Texas, but that an instructor, William J. Groves, "took the aircraft, climbed it back up and returned to Reese" Air Force Base.

Military records state the T-33 jet trainer incurred damage to its left tip-tank and slight skin abrasions on the nose section, an estimated repair cost of $404.50.

★   ★   ★

Frank Gansz was commissioned in the U.S. Air Force after graduating 694th in a class of 797 from the Naval Academy in 1960 and, according to military records, compiled a military career that does not square with the legend that Gansz has promoted, or has allowed to be manufactured.

In the November 4, 1976, edition of the *UCLA Daily Bruin,* Gansz indicated he risked his life on many occasions while serving in the Air Force and is quoted as saying: "Any crisis mission my squadron would be assigned. Whether it would be the Congo, the Red Chinese, India or Vietnam, our squadron would fly the mission and we were shot at practically every place we flew."

That article was included by Gansz in a resume he submitted to an NFL team.

Capt. Thomas Johnston, chief of the media support branch at MAC headquarters in Belleville, Ill., said a Military Air Transport Service squadron to which Gansz was assigned at the time took part in an airlift in the Congo. Roger M. Vaunius, command historian for MAC—MATS took on that name in 1966—reported he had no way of knowing whether Gansz was involved in that operation.

Rear Admiral Donald Boecker, a former Navy test pilot, said MATS' primary mission was assisting the other branches of service in the transportation of troops and cargo. Boecker, who roomed with Gansz during football road trips at the Naval Academy, said the C-124, an aircraft widely used by MATS, would not ordinarily have been assigned to combat areas.

"They flew them into relatively safe air fields or they wouldn't be going in there with cargo planes," he said. "They can't evade or maneuver as well as fighters or attack airplanes."

According to Air Force officials, MATS had no jet fighter aircraft.

"MATS or MAC always have been in the transport business," Capt. Johnston said. "We have had no fighters in our history."

As an athlete at Navy, Gansz is remembered by teammates and coaches for his hustle and enthusiasm. He was undersized for an offensive center, then carrying 180 pounds on his 5-foot-10 frame.

"He wasn't an all-star player, but he volunteered to do anything to be one of the guys," said Martin, an assistant coach at Navy when Gansz played there. "He was a gregarious guy. He'd play any position in practice to prepare the team."

Navy teammate Jim Maxfield, a retired Air Force colonel, said: "Frank was the most tenacious person I ever met. He was a heck of a ballplayer for his size."

Gansz served his final three years at the Air Force Academy in Colorado Springs, Colo., and worked almost seven months for Continental. He was the head freshman football coach at Colgate in 1968.

According to school records, Gansz returned to the Naval Academy, beginning in 1969. The 1972 Navy media guide said he was plebe assistant coach and football recruiting coordinator.

In an article in the *UCLA Daily Bruin* that Gansz includes with his resume, Gansz is quoted: "Once I got the job at Navy I thought I would never leave. I was a special assistant to the athletic director and in charge of the recruiting for the 23 sports."

By the time the Chiefs chose Gansz as their head coach, the biographical information the team released described Gansz's duties at Navy as special assistant to athletic director, assistant football coach, head freshman coach and recruiting coordinator.

"I hired Frank," said Rick Forzano, then head coach at Navy. "He was an assistant with the freshman team and he did some recruiting for us."

Capt. J.O. (Bo) Coppedge, the athletic director at Navy then and now, was asked whether Gansz was his assistant. Coppedge said, "No."

As for Gansz's duties as football recruiting coordinator, Coppedge said: "He was off and on the phone. It was mostly giving tours (to recruits) and that stuff."

Coppedge said he can't remember Gansz being involved in any non-football recruiting, although Gansz for a time helped process applications for athletes in other sports because recruiting for football and the other sports were in the same office.

"I don't remember any instance where Frank had any involvement in recruiting other than football," said Steve Belichick, administrative assistant on the Navy football staff. "I don't see how he could have been other than the fact that the office itself is involved in it. A broad interpretation being that these secretaries in this office handled the correspondence for athletes in all these sports. Maybe you could say that, but it would be stretching it."

'Doc': An Aviator For the Ages

PRO BASKETBALL

By *TONY KORNHEISER*

From the Washington Post
Copyright © 1987, Washington Post Co.

Julius Erving has not quite reached the end of the road, but he can see it from here. Today, at Capital Centre against the Washington Bullets, he'll play his final regular season game. From now on, it's just a matter of time until he is gone, *vaya con dios,* taking along the gifts, the portraits, the golf clubs, the tennis rackets, the trips, the proclamations, the patch of wood from Boston Garden's parquet floor, and taking irreversibly with him a piece of the game, as well.

Watching him, I often thought he didn't pattern himself after other players as much as after distant eagles. To see him glide and soar and swoop was to appreciate the awesome possibilities of flight. The excitement began as soon as he got his huge hands on the ball, building in a crescendo as he raced toward the basket. From midcourt, it took him only three dribbles to reach the foul line and rise into the air, hang and hang and hang there, mysterious and sinewy like a python, finally jamming the ball down through the hoop with a contemptuous fury. I always hoped that just once he would lift off and go over the glass, out of the arena and disappear into space.

Although it's almost incomprehensible now to think of him as anything other than a supernova, in Erving's first few years in professional basketball he was little more than a rumor. The ABA wasn't on national television. Beyond New York, it had no presence in vital basketball cities such as Los Angeles, Chicago, Philadelphia and Detroit. Indeed, ABA strategy disdained direct competition with the NBA, settling in smaller markets and attempting to appeal to regional interests in states with little or no NBA history: Virginia, North Carolina, Kentucky, Indiana and Utah. Consequently, as great a player as Erving was, the basketball establishment hadn't seen him. And since the NBA regarded the ABA as an outlaw league, stocked with young, undisciplined players and pensioners looking for a last payday, quite a few skeptics wondered if this "Dr. J" was the genuine article.

As an example, one night in 1974, good friends and basketball cronies Kevin Loughery, Bob Ferry, Slick Leonard and Jack McMahon were seated around a bar in New Orleans arguing over Doc. Loughery was Doc's coach in New York, and Leonard was coaching against him in Indiana. They knew what he could do. But Ferry, who was the Bullets' GM, and McMahon, who was an assistant with the 76ers, were part of the skeptical contingent. Finally, Loughery got tired of listening and stood up, faced the others, all middle-aged and packing some serious bellies, and said, "The four of us could take Doc and right now go out and play .500 in the NBA."

Apparently enough people believed as Loughery did, because within two years the ABA-NBA merger was effected primarily because of Erving. We can imagine the negotiations that took place between the commissioners, Larry O'Brien and Dave DeBusschere.

O'Brien: Your league has no credibility. Your franchises are folding every 15 minutes. Your players leave a forwarding address at the laundry. We've got TV. We've got the best cities, the best players and the best arenas. What have you got that we need?

DeBusschere: Heh-heh, we've got the Doc.

O'Brien: Okay. I know when I'm beat.

People who couldn't see him truly wanted to see him. On the day the merger was announced, one J. Smiley took his $200 paycheck to Detroit's Cobo Hall and said, "Gimme all the tickets this'll buy for The Doctah!"

There have been arguably better forwards: Rick Barry and Larry Bird, the preeminent forwards on either end of Erving's career, were more accomplished shooters and passers and slightly more productive scorers. But neither understood or expressed the rhythm of the game as spectacularly as Doc. More than anyone before him, including the saintly Elgin Baylor, Doc took the game off the ground and into the air—reinventing it with each flight—playing a kind of jazz that was as accessible as it was futuristic. No single reel in sports ever was as heart-poundingly thrilling as seeing Dr. J with the ball in the open court, the promise of something theatrical and improvisational hanging fragrantly in the air.

He came along when pro basketball needed him most—in the white flight days of the 1970s—when the game was suffering at the gate and in the ratings because its racial composition had changed from mostly white to mostly black. Dr. J became the rarest of pro athletes, the black superstar beloved by white America, rightly perceived as an open, honest, gifted worker who cared for his family and never got the swelled head. His crossover appeal was so great that in recent years white America has paid him the highest compliment: Approving of his style and his substance, his classically understated wardrobe, his sensible haircut, his central politics, his character, his integrity—the whole conservative, responsible package—white fathers select him as a role model for their sons. And ultimately, race has become a nonfactor. As Bill Cosby is now everybody's father, so Julius Erving, the articulate, pensive, gregarious suburban son of the American dream, is everybody's athlete.

Time and age have extracted their fee. The days of condor dunks and Houdini levitations are behind him and despite a glimmering brilliance, in truth, he hasn't been a consistently great player for three seasons. But the crowds attending his triumphant victory tour indicate there are still legions willing to put their money down to see The Doctah, if for no other motive than respect, if for no other reward than the sweet, intoxicating whiff of memory. In his aristocratic grayness, the Doc is the NBA's legend emeritus, its ambassador at large. The NBA has made him a rich man, and he has given the NBA a richer, fuller imprimatur, a good deal all the way around. There are billboards in Philadelphia that say everything necessary, and say it in nine words. The artwork is two colossal sneakers, and the words are: We'll Never Fill Your Shoes. Thanks for Everything, Doc.

The Anatomy Of an At-Bat

BASEBALL

By *DAVID GRANGER*

From Sport Magazine
Copyright © 1987, Sport Magazine

Mike Scott has given the question some thought. Asked yesterday to think back over the history of his encounters with Dave Parker, he is ready with an anecdote.

"The only one I remember, I remember because I outsmarted myself," he begins, sitting in the visitors' clubhouse at Riverfront Stadium in Cincinnati. "It was two years ago here and it was his first time up. I threw him a changeup and he hit the ball about 500 feet foul. After the at-bat I came into the dugout and said to our pitching coach, 'I'm not throwing that guy another changeup as long as I'm in this league.'

"So the next time he comes up, before the first pitch I'm thinking, 'There's no way he's thinking changeup here after he hit that ball, so I'm gonna throw him one.' I threw him one and he hit it 500 feet fair. And I'm standing there watching him run around the bases thinking, 'What a stupid son of a bitch I am.' That's what I remember about facing Dave Parker."

Sitting in the clubhouse with Scott, it's easy to wonder why Parker wouldn't hit one out every time. Mike Scott, unlike most athletes, seems smaller than he is. The Astros say he's 6-3, 215, and once you scutinize him you see that it's probably true. But the way he walks (and even sits), kind of slumped forward, the way his uniform bags around the shoulders, midsection and knees, the glasses he wears off the mound and his soft voice with its gentle lisp—these things conspire to make the premier starting pitcher in the National League look very much like the average American male.

Parker, on the other hand, is a specimen. He's sitting on a stool in his cubicle, dressing the lower half of his body. Over his shorts and jock, he dons leotardlike black pants; over those he adds sanitary hose, tapes them near the tops of his calves and rolls the top of the socks down over the tape; he pulls up the stirrups, puts on his uni-form pants and finally laces up his shoes. The long muscles in his arms jump, and his immense chest flexes with each motion. When he stands, the Reds' slugger is suddenly 6-5 and you trail after him, looking up to listen, talking up in the hope that words travel that high.

A few minutes later you believe the 230-pound Parker when he tells you, "My whole concept of hitting has a lot of intimidation in it. If a pitcher comes inside I don't give him a chance to think about how he brushed me back. I jump out, then I'm right back in the box. I take a cut or take a pitch, then I look the ball all the way back to the pitcher. It's a natural reaction, but I'm letting him know, hey, I'm here to hit. I'm in the box to hit. I'm ready to hit *at all times.* So there's no need to brush me back, because you're not gonna intimi-date the kid."

Three times today, Mike Scott and Dave Parker will go one-on-one. It's the most basic struggle in sports—as simple as three rounds in a ring. For even though the dimensions of the field of play shift with each sideways step a fielder takes, though the particular goals of pitcher and batter—getting a ground-out, moving the runner over—change as the score or the number of baserunners change, the fun-damental confrontation is unaltered: *I will hit you.* I will get you out.

They have faced each other 39 times in their careers prior to today's game. Parker has 13 hits. Much of his success, though, came against the pre-splitfinger Mike Scott. Last year in 13 at-bats against Scott, he managed but one single.

By the time they confront each other for the third time in this game they have established a new, smaller history. Parker has dou-bled off Scott in the first inning, and Scott has struck Parker out looking in the fourth. "Every at bat against Scott," Parker promised before the game, "is going to be a major challenge for him and for myself."

In the sixth inning, Parker steps up to the plate, carefully keep-ing his right (front) foot outside the batter's box until his left foot is precisely where it belongs. There are two outs, nobody on. Houston leads, 6-1. Scott looks in for the sign from catcher Alan Ashby.

★   ★   ★

COUNT: 0-0. PITCH: SPLITFINGERED FASTBALL.

For the third time today, Parker is up with the bases empty. Advantage Scott. "Not having men on base gives him more options," Parker offered earlier. "He can mess with the splitfinger away. He can mess with that fastball up and away or up and in, until he gets in a situation where he's behind. With men on base I think he's gotta be a little more deliberate with me. With men on base he wants to bust me inside, but he also wants to throw strikes because he doesn't want to put another man on base with Eric Davis coming up behind me.

Having no runners on base definitely opens up his whole repertoire of pitches."

Scott calls himself "basically a two-pitch pitcher." His main pitch is a fastball over 90 miles an hour. The "other" pitch is the splitfinger fastball. But it's deceiving to refer to the splitfinger as a single pitch because both the speed and movement of the ball vary widely with the way in which he grips it.

"I never know exactly how I'm gonna throw it," Scott has explained earlier, "but I adjust its speed by how I split my fingers. The wider I split them, the pitch will break more, it'll be a slower, more erratic pitch. The closer I put them together, it'll be harder, it won't move as much and I have a little better command of it."

These pitches are particularly effective, because Scott's various splitters are delivered with the same motion and the same armspeed as his fastball. And because Scott is not sure of what the pitch is going to do, a hitter, even if he is expecting the splitter, can't really anticipate.

So far, Parker has seen just one splitfinger all day. It was the previous pitch Scott threw him, the 0-2 pitch that got Parker looking in the fourth. "I *hate* taking the third strike."

Yesterday, Parker talked about what he would be looking for if he got behind in the count. "He gets two strikes on you, he's gonna waste a pitch. He'll throw that fastball up and away from the plate or he'll throw that splitfinger in the dirt."

Indeed, ahead of Parker 0-2 in their second confrontation back in the fourth inning, Scott tried to throw one out of the strike zone. "I got ahead," Scott will recall after the game, "and I thought, 'I'll throw the harder forkball and if I bounce it, fine.' The ball tailed. It went down and away. I don't know where it started out, but I wanted to either throw a ball and miss down and away or throw a perfect pitch."

That pitch *was* perfect. It started out numbers-high on the inside of the plate and ended up on the outside corner at the knees. Parker took his short stride into the pitch, but, expecting it to be out of the zone, never got the bat off his shoulder. As the ball came across the plate, Parker looked it into the catcher's glove. When he saw it was a strike he straightened up, then hung his head before walking back to the dugout.

Scott starts Parker off in the sixth with the same pitch. Parker leans into it, wanting to swing, but somehow has the discipline to again watch it into the catcher's mitt. It's away.

Parker remains in the batter's box between pitches. First, he resets his left foot and steps out with the right. He blows a bubble, brings his right foot back in and, holding the bat with just his right hand, taps the far side of the plate. He straightens, takes a single leisurely practice swing, twirls the bat in windmill fashion and is again ready to hit.

★   ★   ★

COUNT: 1-0. PITCH: FASTBALL.

Of the nine pitches Parker has seen today seven have been fast-balls, all but one up and in. The 1-0 pitch is also high and tight.

"Parker is one guy you simply don't let hurt you if you've got an open base," Scott will say later, explaining his pitch selection. "You don't intentionally walk him every time, but if you throw him three pitches up and in you make sure they're up and in. You don't want to hit him, but if you do, that's part of the game. You just don't want to miss on the other side where he'll knock the crap out of the ball."

Parker had in fact anticipated that Scott would be coming at him high and inside. "Before the game I went through my bats and got the two with the best grain," he will point out. "I also was using a lighter bat than what I normally use because of his good velocity."

Before Parker's first at-bat, the double, he was kneeling in the on-deck circle, thinking about what Scott would throw him. "I try to swing at only pitches below my hands. I hold my hands at the top of the strike zone. I definitely did not want to chase that high heat."

On the 3-1 pitch then, Scott came with a fastball just below the 39 on Parker's chest. "It wasn't a real good pitch to hit," Scott will remember. "I got it right where I wanted to—right where I wanted to."

As Parker strode into the pitch, the right side of his body opened up fast, but his hands stayed back, close to the left side of his chest, patient even as he was trying to hit a 90-mile-an-hour fastball. He then whipped his hands, rolling them through the ball, hitting over it while keeping the knob of the bat handle right up against his chest so that the fat part of the bat could meet the ball.

"It was a fastball," Parker will explain, "but I think he cut it a little because it ran in on my hands. I just got the bat head out in front. My thing was to make sure to be quick on a pitch like that, because with my long arms I couldn't extend. When I made my approach on the ball it had a fastball rotation, but it started running in, so I just opened up a little bit and threw the bat head and hit a double down the right-field corner. I think he had it right where he wanted it, but I was fortunate enough to get the bat head out."

Parker normally places his left foot along, or even on, the back line of the batter's box. For his at-bat in the sixth, though, he has moved up about six inches, hoping to hit the splitfinger before it sinks. Having doubled off that high inside fastball back in the first, he is looking for the splitter.

As a result, Parker is startled when Scott comes with the heat. "I was still trying to catch the forkball he had dazzled me with in the last at-bat. I think Ashby had a lot to do with it because he watched my feet. Some of the good catchers in the league will call the pitches according to your feet. When he saw me closer to the plate and bent over a little more, I guess he said this is the time to bust him in. But I still got the bat head out." And, body opening up again, hands hanging back and then whipping through, he rips the ball foul just beyond the Reds' dugout.

Scott waits restlessly on the rubber for a new ball from home plate umpire John McSherry. As usual, he is ready to go. He removes his mitt, rubs up the ball, slides his left hand back into the glove, brings it with the ball in it to his chest, keeps both hands together, adjusts his grip on the ball and starts his windup.

$\star$ $\star$ $\star$

COUNT: 1-1. PITCH: SPLITFINGER.

There are pitchers who are tacticians on the mound. Thinking three pitches ahead, they use the first pitch to set up two more, plotting to get an out later in the count rather than with a single pitch.

Looking at his pitch sequences—throwing the splitfinger at the start of this at-bat after he had made Parker look bad on the same pitch in the fourth, figuring there would be no way for Parker to keep from chasing the pitch—it is tempting to see Scott as a tactician. Didn't he bust Parker in with the next pitch to set him up for a splitfinger down and away? No, Mike Scott does not plan. He reacts. "I basically throw my pitch. If I keep throwing a guy up and in and he keeps getting hits, it'll eventually sink in that this guy's been ripping that pitch, so I don't throw it. Other than that I just throw my game, mix up my pitches and hopefully get 'em out.

"I think of situations rather than pitches. 'I want a ground ball here' or 'I need a strikeout here' or 'We can't afford to let this guy even make contact.' But I don't over-think. Like I said, when I pitched to Parker two years ago I thought too much and he hit the ball 500 feet."

No, Scott doesn't throw this splitfinger with some scheme in mind. It bares no relation to any of the other pitches he has thrown Parker. Actually, he throws this one and the pitch that follows, in part, to get a little practice in. "We had a pretty big lead and I'd thrown two or three during the game that had stayed way up in the strike zone (including a Kal Daniels home run on Scott's second pitch of the game). I just wanted to get a better feel for the pitch. I didn't want it to hang, but if it did, and he hit it out, it wouldn't affect the game that much. I wanted to show it to him and work on it a bit."

The pitch starts about knee-high and breaks down. Parker golfs at it and still misses it over the top. Ashby catches it in the dirt.

"It was on the outer half of the plate," Parker will recall. "It broke down real quick. Excellent pitch."

For the first time in the game, Parker shows some emotion at the plate. He's always animated, but rarely emotional. He steps all the way out of the box and turns his back on it. He slides his left hand up the barrel of the bat, lifts it to eye level, stares at the label for a moment and shakes his head. He blows a bubble before stepping back in. Parker takes two forceful practice cuts and one deep breath. He's set and ready.

$\star$ $\star$ $\star$

COUNT: 1-2. PITCH: SPLITFINGER.

The ball is out over the plate, moving slightly away from Parker, who strides into it. The front leg stiffens. He bends from the waist, reaches out and down with the bat and flicks at the ball with those massive wrists and forearms.

"It was the same pitch as the second at-bat," Parker will say later, "the one he punched me out on. And when you get in that situation you can't gamble and take a pitch. See, as you make your initial approach to a splitfinger it looks like the ball is still gonna be at the same level. But it drops. That was one of those pitches where I was kind of fooled but I still got the bat on it."

The fact is, this isn't the same pitch Parker struck out on. It's the slower, more erratic variety. It may be that one reason batters find Scott so difficult to hit is that they treat all his splitfinger pitches as if they were the same.

"The last two I threw to Parker in the sixth I split my fingers farther apart and just aimed at the plate. The first inning, when Daniels hit the home run, I had 'em split pretty far apart. That makes it move a little bit more, but can also make it flutter and hang. That one hung. On these two I lowered my sights and they turned out to be good pitches. I just tried to hit the plate. If I was gonna miss I didn't care if it bounced three feet in front of the plate.

"Those are the pitches you hope they chase and hope they're pretty good pitches. I was gonna keep throwing those and see if I could get him to chase one."

Parker does get the bat on the ball, but you can see him realize he's been fooled. His strength does him no good here. He manages only a weak pop-up beyond third in foul territory. Phil Garner gloves it and Parker's turn is over.

The at-bat has taken 55 seconds.

James Lofton's Trying Times

PRO FOOTBALL

By *MARK HEISLER*

From the Los Angeles Times
Copyright © 1987, the Los Angeles Times

Time hangs ominously in an upstairs room of the Brown County Courthouse, where the next word spoken can mean 10 years. Minicams are trained on the accused. Visitors squirm on hardwood benches.

James Lofton sits erect and waits.

This is a rape case. He's the defendant.

Oh no, this just can't be happening.

Maybe to some hard-shelled mercenary who's been bribed, flattered, recruited, fought over, pandered to, paid off under the table and passed along in class until he can't tell the Ten Commandments from a laundry list, but not to James Lofton.

This is the best and the brighest: B+ student in engineering at Stanford; Wisconsin chairman of the Mental Health Association; Packer United Way spokesman; volunteer worker for Special Olympics, the March of Dimes, the Boys Club of Milwaukee, the Urban League; member of the board of directors of the National Football League Players Association, the Milwaukee Ballet.

This is also the second such accusation made against him in 27 months.

Behind him sit relatives, former Packer teammates and the little group from Iron Mountain, Mich., the family of the woman Lofton is accused of assaulting.

During recesses, the Packers walk 20 feet across the hall for the rape trial of another teammate, Mossy Cade. It is a singular week in the history of Green Bay, and if there is never another like it, no one will complain.

The verdict is handed to Judge Alexander Grant, a homey-looking man with a round face and a forelock that falls over his forehead the way a kid's does. The mini-cams zoom in on Lofton. Whatever he's feeling, it's betrayed only by a single lick of his lips.

Behind him, his wife, Beverly, "is just about to lose it.

"I knew in my heart what the verdict should have been, but when you're relying on 12 people you don't know . . ." she says later.

"He could have been convicted and taken away from me right at that minute. All I kept thinking was, 'Gosh, I didn't let him say good-bye to our son, like a real goodbye, this morning.'

"And, 'If he's convicted and they don't let him out on bond, would I just be standing here in my shoes, wondering where to go?' "

Grant says he'll announce the verdict and then ask the jury a question. Lofton's lawyer, Stephen Glynn, confident until that moment, says his heart feels as if it has fallen into his stomach.

James Lofton sits erect, unflinching, waiting to hear how the rest of his life will come out.

★   ★   ★

THE RIDDLE

James had a beautiful personality. Let me put it this way, of all the young men I coached, if there's anyone I would want my sons to pattern themselves after in terms of their attitude towards people, towards athletics, toward academics, toward life in general, it would be James Lofton.

     —RON FOWLKES, Lofton's football
      coach at L.A. Washington High

Me. Gary Hart. Jim Bakker. Richard Nixon. Ronald Reagan. Hey, I'm in there with some good guys.

     —JAMES LOFTON

Lofton was acquitted.

And in the previous case, resulting from an accusation by an exotic dancer in a Milwaukee bar that Lofton and teammate Eddie Lee Ivery had sexually assaulted her in her dressing room, the Milwaukee district attorney's office refused to file sex-related charges.

Before the law, Lofton is clear.

He is now a Raider, having been traded to the Los Angeles team a month before the trial, and the world is spread before him anew.

But still, how could it have happened?

Putting the best face on it, why would this man—gifted, generous, admired, married, humiliated by a prior accusation—meet a woman in Green Bay's busiest downtown night spot, engage in a public flirtation and wind up with her performing oral sex on him in a stairwell?

Lofton concedes all this. The only issue was whether the woman was forced, as she claimed, or consented, as he claimed.

Whether he was having a problem at being in Green Bay; or of having to grow up and settle down; or of realizing, where previously there was a sense of invincibility, that there are limits to the athlete, there does seem to have been some kind of rebellion going on in his life.

That's the short answer. What follows is the long answer.

★   ★   ★

YOUNG JAMES

This is the bittersweet saga of the family of Emmanuel Michael Lofton Sr., a career Army man turned bank operations manager, industrious and personable, blessed and burdened.

Violet, Emmanuel's wife and James' mother, left the family when James was 8 and he didn't see her again until he was 19.

James' big brother, Michael, drifted through life and last year, at 38, was bludgeoned to death while sleeping overnight in a park in southwest Los Angeles. James says the reason that Michael drifted was "probably drugs."

Emmanuel was born in Texas and attended Prairie View State College where he played football, basketball and track. Like James, he was a long jumper. Emmanuel fought in World War II, stayed in the Army until 1964, then retired from the service and moved his four children to Los Angeles. Violet didn't accompany them. Emmanuel doesn't like talking about it.

He borrowed enough for a down payment on a pleasant house in a middle-class neighborhood a few minutes east of the Forum and still lives there. Now retired, he does volunteer work for the active blind, the Urban League and the NAACP.

One of James' sisters is at San Francisco State, doing graduate work in sociology. The other is a writer living in New York. He isn't in close touch with either.

"I think it was a relatively close family," James says. "I don't think it was as close as 'Father Knows Best,' or 'Family Ties' or 'The Cosby Show.' I think we were probably the average American family, where some of the kids talk to the other kids more than some others, and things that you had in common brought you closer together.

"Me and my brother had sports in common and probably our sisters rebelled. If you're in a house and they're watching sports all weekend long, I think you might get tired of that.

"Being the youngest, I was catered to by my brother and sisters. They probably fought over me like a toy. So when we moved to California, I really didn't miss my mother. I remember realizing a few months later, when my brother and sisters were talking to her on the phone, that she wasn't going to come. And I didn't understand that. I didn't understand the concept of divorce."

Was it hard on his father?

"For some reason, I really don't think so. The older kids were at the age when they're pretty self-sufficient."

James loved Los Angeles. At Washington High, he wasn't so much admired as revered. His coaches loved his intelligence, his industry, his easy sense of humor, his independence, his leadership. They marveled at his overwhelming self-confidence.

It wasn't because James was a superstar, either. Anyone who has seen him bounding past NFL defenders like an elk among tree stumps, or remembers his days as a one-man track team at Stanford, would be surprised to learn that he made himself into an athlete.

As a high school sophomore, he played B-team football. Ken Stumpf, his track coach and a football assistant who is now at Banning High, said that at a big program—say, Banning's—James might have had trouble getting a uniform. He was state long jump champion as a senior, but only a pretty good quarterback. Not good enough to interest USC or UCLA.

"He had no real tools going for him but he had a goal down the line," Stumpf said. "He lifted weights on his own. At that time, lifting at the high school level wasn't a real big thing."

Lofton today has a huge upper body. Asked by Sport magazine why he still lifts so much, he said, laughing, "Because it makes me look good."

You might also think that being one of four kids raised by a single parent, James would have been out there alone. You'd be wrong.

"I have four sons and I just don't know how the father could be so dedicated," Fowlkes said. "He was at every football game, every track meet, I don't care where it was. Anything James was involved in, the father was there, always in a suit and tie, smiling, a very personable man. There was a unique closeness between father and son."

It was late in his college career that James really happened. He didn't start in football until his senior year, when he exploded under new Coach Bill Walsh. He long-jumped 27-0 that spring, best in the world in 1978.

He was the sixth player chosen in the National Football League draft. A fraternity brother of Lofton at Theta Delta Chi said that when they heard where he was going—Green Bay—the whole house let out a collective groan.

★   ★   ★

THE BEST OF TIMES, THE WORST OF TIMES

It may have been a small fiefdom but it was his.

Lofton was the most outrageous talent the franchise had seen in the post-Vince Lombardi era. He made the Pro Bowl as a rookie, ruled the locker room almost from the day he walked in and dazzled the fans. The press thought him cocky—this is the first stage in his life where you begin to hear this characterization—but usually charming.

The Packers went 8-7-1 in 1978, their first winning season in six years. There was fun, fun and more fun.

A year later, they went 5-11. Lofton hurled his pads into his locker during the postgame prayer and had words with Coach Bart Starr after one loss.

During another, he was booed and made an obscene gesture to the crowd. Packer publicist Chuck Lane subsequently called him "a prima donna" during a speech to a group of fans.

Lofton would often marvel that he had only gestured for an instant and that the photographers happened to catch it, suggesting he'd been victimized by some fast-draw photog. Then, as later, he had trouble accepting consequences.

At a New Year's Eve party in Los Angeles on the last day of 1979, he met Beverly. She was a singer, a born-again Christian who had been second runner-up in the Miss Arkansas contest. They married a year later. James became a born-again Christian.

Beverly once told Sports Illustrated: "(He) had a real desire to change. He was unhappy and he knew he had to get down off his high horse and stop thinking he was better than everybody else."

Says Beverly now: "He's had a lot of girlfriends. There were a lot of women up here who wanted him. He was the big do in Green Bay. He had a lot of women in California. He knew beautiful women, but he just didn't seem like he was at a pleasant place in his life."

Overnight, it seemed, James was happy again. He laughed once more. He joined community organizations throughout Wisconsin. He went back to the Pro Bowl. Beverly was said to have "matured" James, as if maturity was something one person could hand another.

But they were as engaging as a couple could be. Before the '81 season, newly married and living near the Stanford campus, they were interviewed by Mike Littwin, then a *Times* writer, who found them a delight.

"He picked me up at the airport," said Littwin, now a columnist with the *Baltimore Sun.* "He had a Porsche. We kidded about it.

"We went back to his condo, where I met Beverly. She was just a knockout. She's so smart. I really enjoyed the day and you know me, there aren't that many of these guys I want to talk to.

"His whole thing, he didn't want to play in Green Bay. The quote I used, I asked him how long he stayed after the season. He said, 'Only as long as the first flight out.'

"He said once he had stayed overnight because there wasn't a flight till the next morning. Green Bay was too white, not hip enough. He was hip. He was handsome, well dressed. He was a Yuppie before they had the word."

Lofton says now he didn't really want out of Green Bay. He was renegotiating his contract and his agent told him to say that.

It's a point on which there has been some confusion, aggravated in no small part by Lofton's favorite practical joke, telling one writer, "Yeah, I can't stand it here," then five minutes later telling another writer, "Oh, no, I'm perfectly happy."

Maybe he wasn't sure, himself.

In fact, he never asked to be traded, or refused to report. He signed a long-term contract worth $935,000 a year. In 1983, he was one of five finalists for NFL Man of the Year, an award for players with exemplary off-field lives. He and Beverly had their own weekly TV show. They had a beautiful house set in the woods of the Green Bay suburb of Ashwaubenon and another in Milwaukee, where they spent the off-season.

Then came the incident in the Milwaukee bar in October, 1984. The D.A.'s office brought no sex-related charges but stated, 'We believe the conduct of the two men to be reprehensible, shameful and depraved.' "

Lofton and Ivery were found guilty of trespassing in the dancer's dressing room and ordered to pay $500 each to the owner of the nightclub. Lofton's image had been tarnished. The TV show was not renewed. His demeanor changed again.

"As dramatic a change in a good way as there was after he married Beverly, there was a change for the bad after Milwaukee," says Rob Schultz of the *Madison* (Wis.) *Capital Times,* who was close to Lofton. "As accessible as he'd been up to that point, suddenly he was that inaccessible."

Even at that, the situation stabilized. There were several other court challenges relating to the Milwaukee case, and Lofton won them all. He made the Pro Bowl in '84 and '85. His picture was on milk cartons throughout Wisconsin. The Loftons enlarged the Ashwaubenon house, figuring they were there for the duration.

But there was one more disaster left on the horizon.

★   ★   ★

THE TRIAL

Last December 17, three days before the end of the season, the Packer receivers had a dinner. Afterward, Lofton and teammates Mike Moffitt and Walter Stanley went to the Top Shelf Lounge where they got acquainted with three women who were down from Michigan's Upper Peninsula for two days of Christmas shopping.

The six spent some time together in the bar, although who was with whom and for how long was disputed.

Defense witnesses said they saw the complainant, a 30-year-old housewife, standing between Lofton's legs as he straddled a bar stool. One of her companions, 26-year-old Paris Stanchina, said it was she who had stood between Lofton's legs.

A waitress, testifying for the defense, said that Lofton had asked her what she was doing when she finished work.

Lofton and the complainant later took an elevator downstairs and entered the stairwell, where the woman performed oral sex on him. The woman said that Lofton forced her to do it, holding her by her hair.

She didn't report it, however, for several hours, after telling one of her friends back at their hotel. The friend mentioned it, in passing, to a hotel security man who called the police. No physical evidence— e.g. bruises, torn out hair—was found.

The jury, chosen in Janesville, about 170 miles south of here near the Illinois border, deliberated for less than two hours. A few days later, several of the jurors talked to a reporter from the *Beloit Daily News.*

Edith Fiebig, one of two women on the jury, said: "It was an easy decision."

John Denninger said: "We agreed right from the beginning he wasn't guilty."

Robert Glenn said: "I don't think it's a case that should have been brought to court because they didn't have enough evidence to convict the guy."

★　　★　　★

JAMES

Just for starters, what was he doing there in the first place?

"Oh, c'mon," Lofton says, reclining on a sofa in the Ashwaubenon house. "Anybody could be in that bar. And anybody could sit around and let women flirt with them.

"And how many men turn down sex? I think that really is the question."

How many are married public figures who have been accused of sexual assault?

"At some point, you think to yourself, 'Now c'mon, relax, be at least a normal football player,' " Lofton says. " 'Be like everybody else. Don't be so guarded.' "

But a public flirtation in Green Bay's hottest night spot?

"OK, you look at that and you say, 'Well . . .'

"At some point the brain just cuts off and he said, 'Well, I'm having a good time, what the heck.'

"Think if you were sitting here with Gary Hart. Here's a man who probably would have been the next President. Look at what he was risking and look at what I was risking. That somebody would tell my wife? And the next day, I'd say, 'No, I wasn't.' Really, that's all I was risking in my mind.

"That is the answer. The question is: 'Weren't you aware that there might be evil forces out there, that people are after you?' At some point, you don't *want* people to be after you. You want to relax. You want to let your guard down. . . . It's just a denial that something bad is going to happen to you. And that's all I did.

"People say, 'Didn't you think?' No, you don't think. Do you think when you're changing lanes and you forget to use your turn signal?"

Put another way, if you've had it both ways long enough, you begin to think that having it both ways is an inalienable right. Chalk up another one to experience: It isn't.

Lofton is wearing shorts, a T-shirt from his "Superstars" competition days and a Rolex. He's friendly, soft-spoken, shows a good sense of humor and entertains all questions.

He's also hard to read. He talks about what you'd imagine to be painful memories—the death of his brother, the absence of his mother—matter of factly, briefly, and without changing the tone of his voice.

He argues with most characterizations made of him. Do his high school coaches say he always had a plan? He says he was just a kid who loved sports. Does the press think he was dying to get out of Green Bay? Not r-e-a-l-l-y.

Do they say he's aloof and arrogant? No, it's just there are so many times he has nothing to say.

Beverly says: "There were times when we were first together when that's what I noticed most. You could just tell, the tenderness— James had to fend for himself a lot. James spent a great deal of time alone.

"Usually it's your mom who calls you after something like that (the obscene gesture to the crowd) and says (sweetly), 'Now James, what are you doing?'

"James grew up with his father and men are tougher in that way. James' father is the type who would tell him but he'd tell him quickly and then he's done. His father was a military man so he dealt with things in a military style: 'You're a man and this is what you're supposed to do.'

"A lot of people have criticized James the past few months when they've been doing all these psychoanalytic things. But when you have a wife like Chatty Cathy and you've spent your life being silent, there really is no reason for him to open up.

"For the people close to him, he's open enough. There are people who are close friends who will still say, 'Gosh, I don't know when he's kidding or when he's teasing, or angry.' That's a part of his nature.

"At the same time, he's very, very sensitive to other people's feelings. And very non-judgmental. That's one of the things I liked most about him. He doesn't have great expectations of people. Except athletes. He doesn't like it when players don't have discipline, when players don't have heart.

"He doesn't drag his problems home. When the Packers were having problems last year—they changed the system on him—he struggled but I could barely see it. (The Packers went to a short-pass game, Lofton's per-catch average dropped and he missed the Pro Bowl for the second time). I knew by my seeing it a little, he was struggling a lot.

"His quarterback of eight years (Lynn Dickey) was gone. His roommate of eight years (Mike Douglass) was gone. His receivers coach of eight years (Lew Carpenter) was gone. Greg Koch from the offense line, Paul Coffman.

"The day Lynn Dickey was waived, he said, 'I still had to go out to the second practice and I practiced all out. I couldn't go, "Oh gosh, I'm so depressed, my best friends are gone." ' I know how he dealt with that. He just totally avoided it. He thought the only way he could survive was to continue to go on as if it hadn't happened."

Similarly, after the '84 incident in the Milwaukee bar, Lofton turned to the game.

"Maybe I felt I had something to prove and that was the only way I could prove it," he says.

"If that changed me, maybe this incident and being vindicated has taken me back to before that all happened. Maybe I have more knowledge.

"I've gotten a chance to look at myself and look at possibly what God is doing to me. And perhaps He just wanted to say, 'James, I want you to be a little more compassionate.'

"Maybe, being an athlete who does nothing but train as hard as you do, who thinks it should hurt when things don't go right on the field, that other players should be able to disregard their problems and get out there and do what they have to do, that could have caused my attitude.

"And God might have just said, 'Unh-uh. Because I've given you so much that you're unable to see other peoples' hurt, I'm going to let you experience a little hurt. So that maybe you can help somebody else down the road.'

"I think Jesus hit it on the head—'Let he who is without sin cast the first stone.' And that's not to make me sound self-righteous. I made mistakes. I've asked for forgiveness. And I've just got to go on.

"Most people live in fear that somebody will find out something horrible about them. People know more than the worst about me. It's better this way. Now, if people like me, it's because they like me. I don't have to think, 'I hope Mark doesn't turn this up when he goes back to the hotel.' I mean, what more can you write?

"This is the first time in a couple of years that I've felt good. The cases are over. For a while it was like the worst soap opera ever written: 'What's going to happen to me now? Woe is me.'

"Now it's been taken care of. All I have to worry about now is getting in the starting lineup."

★   ★   ★

BEVERLY

Does Beverly Lofton remember the night of December 17?

Try minute by minute.

"It was a weird thing," she says. "That night I kept feeling strange. I just didn't feel right. I almost got in the car and went down there.

"What would have happened if I'd gone down there? We wouldn't have been in all this mess, but hindsight is 20-20. But I had this gut feeling that was what I wanted to do. The only reason I didn't, I was making an angel costume for our child's Christmas program the next day and I had to finish it.

"I had a sense there was some hanky-panky going on. When he got home, there was a guilty look on his face. I was still up, pretending I was cleaning. It was 2 in the morning.

"Once he had disclosed everything (the next day, after being arrested), I asked him, 'Is there any way, that by any little inkling you could be considered to have forced anything to happen?' And he said absolutely not.

"It wasn't like he was saying this because this is what the wife wanted to hear. When you've gone through as much as we've gone through, there are no more secrets, there are no more games.

"So I was convinced he was innocent. We knew what he had done wrong but it had nothing to do with the criminal system. It had to do with us.

"Honestly, I think he knows my feelings. If he'd assaulted someone, I'd have wanted him to be prosecuted.

"It's ironic. I used to work with female victims here in Green Bay. I was on the board of directors of the Family Abuse Center. When I first came up here, it was one of the first organizations I became involved with. My sister was a victim of domestic abuse. She was murdered by her estranged husband.

"What I think could have happened—James had his pick of women here. I mean, I've had women come up to me and ask me what it's like to wake up next to this man, with this body. Women would come up to him and want to kiss him—young and old. Women will say the darndest things to me. I can't imagine—I *can* imagine— what it's like when he's not with me.

"Of course, he knew he was being watched, but he hates that kind of scrutiny. He hated not having anonymity. It's not like it's a death wish but it's the same sort of thing as Gary Hart. James knew he was being accused of having an extra life. But what is it in a person that says, 'I'm going to do this. I'm just going to do this because it feels good right now.'

"There are some things I feel bad for him. I don't want him to get a reputation as a womanizer. I've heard stuff like that: 'Oh gosh, she's known he was like that for years.' No, I have not known he was like that. If so, that's going to be a great surprise for me. I didn't marry somebody to put up with that kind of stuff.

"People have said things about my own sexuality: 'Is she frigid? Doesn't she like oral sex?'

"People asked me all sorts of things: 'Did you spend too much time with your child? Was James jealous?' I said to James, 'People don't look at it like there was a flaw in you but that there's a flaw in me.'

"I think he's OK about knowing his life will change. He's had incredibly bad fortune. But for us, there are blessings in everything. Either this man is going to be totally committed and . . . faithful and committed to this marriage. Or he's going to blow the whole thing apart.

"A lot of people don't get to test their commitment. Mine has definitely been tested. I've never questioned that James loved me— no, I shouldn't say that. Let's just say I've always known he loved me and I've never thought he was unhappy in marriage.

"He bottomed. Don't let James fool you. We bottomed in hurt and everything else. It just turned us over and allowed us to look at everything in our lives, football, our friends.

"I've heard people say, 'Oh, their marriage won't come out of this.' (Laughing) If you'd asked me ahead of time if I could have withstood something like this, I'd have probably said, 'No. I'll feed him poison, make him impotent and *then* I'll leave him.' "

She tries to think if there's anything she's left unsaid.

"Just don't forget," she says, "to say that I love the man."

★   ★   ★

EPILOGUE: FAME IN A SMALL CITY

It seems there are some people in this world who want to take from others, who are never satisfied with what they have accomplished and therefore feel a need to take what someone else has gotten through hard work and perseverance.

I'm sick and tired of people not knowing and understanding what it takes to become a successful athlete. If professional athletes get some sort of special treatment, it is because they have earned it.

No one knows what a person has to give up to be a professional. It takes more than ability. He has to have a certain drive that will place him above others.

—FORREST GREGG, Packer coach

Two days after Lofton was found innocent, one day after Mossy Cade was found guilty, Gregg really said that to a *Milwaukee Sentinel* reporter, referring to the Cade jury that had prayed for five minutes before beginning deliberations.

Does it have to be said? Many other people work hard and make sacrifices for less glory and profit, while providing more enduring contributions to society. Gregg, who administers what amounts to a state religion, must have forgotten for the moment.

Celebrity tends to warp perspective on the part of the celebrated and the celebrant, alike. And it isn't just a problem in Green Bay.

Workin' On
The Chaney Gang

COLLEGE BASKETBALL

By *JOAN MELLEN*

From Philadelphia Magazine
Copyright © 1987, Philadelphia Magazine

"Sit facing me," Coach John Chaney instructs the Temple University basketball team, "so I can look in your faces." Stranded by snow last January at the Hershey Hotel in Philadelphia, their game against Alabama-Birmingham just 24 hours away, he talks to his chosen 10. The team lost two members to Proposition 48, the NCAA rule prohibiting freshmen with College Board scores under 700 to play basketball, and one to illness (prized recruit Robert Liburd would die of Marfan's Syndrome in May).

If the players, dressed for travel in shirts, ties and sweaters, are anxious about missing the game, their first to be broadcast on network television, they don't show it.

"Some things that happen are out of our control," Chaney tells them. "Big things there is no point to worrying about. The little things, we can." The little things include basketball games. As Temple coach since 1982, Chaney has won nearly 80 percent of the time and would finish the 1986-87 season at 32-4.

Before the boys are off to rest in hotel rooms while waiting for the skies to clear, Chaney issues a warning.

You are not talented players, he tells them, and it is true. John Chaney has suffered in the recruiting wars because he won't cheat, and highly talented players who were likely Temple prospects have mysteriously ended up elsewhere. "You must compensate for weakness with intelligence. What happened to the great fighters who approached their sport with sheer muscle when a new era came in and you had to use your head? Take David and Goliath!"

It's a lesson John Chaney had to teach himself, growing up poor in a kerosene-lit house in Florida. He never knew his real father, and he was whipped by his stepfather for playing basketball. Chaney went to college, at a time when black athletes were not showered with scholarships, only because his coach at Benjamin Franklin High School, Sam Browne, saw to it that he did. Then it was on to Bethune-Cookman College down South, where John Chaney arrived with all his belongings in a small cardboard box tucked under his arm. For John Chaney, who began his coaching career at Sayre Junior High and was 50 before he became a Division I coach at Temple, winning meant much more than victory or defeat in a game. Winning meant leaving behind not just poverty, but the impoverished life.

Now on this long journey to Alabama, out of this moment of adversity caused by the weather, John Chaney offers his team a lesson. It is about despair and survival: "Some people think when the river bends, it's all over. But the river only made a little turn! It's still on course! No situation you're in is life-threatening! Every situation you're in requires you to think! 'I would that I would,' " he will quote Mary McLeod Bethune as the day stretches into night and still they remain stuck in Philadelphia.

"You look outside," Chaney tells them. "You see snow. You see rain. Let the sunshine be in you!"

The sermon over, the players can finally complain of more earthbound concerns—like hunger. They never challenge their coaches, but manager John DiSangro receives no small amount of abuse for his meal choices.

"Didn't you eat *yesterday?*" Chaney jokes. Skinny Derrick Brantley, with his flat-top haircut, pleads for room service. They argue. They win a half-hour's liberty, deadline 12:30 and then to bed. "I'll call your room and if you're not back, it's punishment," Chaney threatens.

The rules had been set back in October in Chaney's annual opening lecture, when he offers the ideal of the balanced man, the scholar-athlete. On October 15th each player is told his role. They are a family now, no longer mere individuals, and how they build the foundation of their house this first day of practice predicts how they will finish.

Squealing on your teammates is expected; a paddle sits concealed in the closet of John Chaney's office, and once the entire Cheyney State team John Chaney coached to a 1978 NCAA Division II championship was whacked because they failed to report on two players Coach himself caught in a bar.

If they fail to attend class, they won't play. John Chaney's predecessor, Don Casey, had a less than 33 percent graduation rate of his own recruits. One of these, Terence Stansbury, who plays in the NBA with Seattle, was surprised one day when Chaney noticed that he had dropped his summer classes.

"What did Coach Casey say?" Chaney asked Terence.

"He didn't get involved with things like this."

"Well, this coach gets involved. I'm going to know two weeks before you even think about doing anything."

Drugs are inconceivable. There are no Len Bias-style late-night dorm scenes here. "Alcohol is for celebrating and we have nothing to celebrate right now," Chaney tells them. If he had his way there would be no sex either during basketball season. "Girls like basketball players," he tells them, "and there aren't enough of you to go around!"

Be unassuming, he tells them. "Don't announce that you're on the basketball team. Don't brag. Always give the other team credit." It was watching a tape of one of these October lectures that led Mark Macon, Michigan's 1986 "Mr. Basketball" and most valuable player in last spring's McDonald's All-American high school game, to sign this year with Temple. "I love the coach," he said. "They take you in like family."

"They didn't recruit me," said Shoun Randolph, his teammate, who will also play for Temple this year, "I recruited *them.*"

Two seasons ago, 6-foot, 10-inch, ordinarily mild-mannered Ramon Rivas threw a punch during a game. Last season, attacked by Bonzie Colson of Rhode Island, Ramon kept his hands at his sides and did not retaliate. How did Coach help Ramon? Ramon's large dark eyes widen. Ramon considers and arrives at this answer: "He looks at us."

"He looks mean," teammate Howard Evans explains, "but inside he's a little teddy bear."

Mike Vreeswyk, a 6-foot-7 junior, a pure shooter with a stern game face that resembles Larry Bird's, is the least sentimental of Chaney's players. One cannot imagine him speaking Howie's line.

"He's not sentimental because he has a father who thinks he's wonderful," Chaney says of Vreeswyk, suggesting that for some of the others, *he* must be that father.

Practice is invariably scheduled for 5:30 a.m. And as in the ancient Greek model of the balanced psyche, manliness does not exclude emotion. In basketball emotion is what liberates you to look ahead to the next encounter, as soon as the final horn of a game sounds.

"Some games where we'll lose, he breaks down and cries," Timmy Perry says. "And some games where we'll win he'll cry because he's so happy. In the locker room he embraces and hugs you. He starts crying and he says he can't help it. Everyone in the locker room sits and cries and the whole team are like big babies." At Kansas, Chaney cried during the halftime intermission.

After that Kansas loss, having missed two chances at the three-point shot that would have tied the game, Nate Blackwell also sat down and cried bitter tears. Chaney walked over and hugged him. "I didn't want him to walk away thinking he had let us down for one minute," Chaney says. "Life didn't end."

At 4 p.m., cabs take the team from the Hershey Hotel back to

McGonigle Hall, on the Temple campus, the storm having put off the flight indefinitely. When they arrive, there is no vacant gym. The women's team is occupying one, the wheelchair players the other. Despite Temple's consistent ranking in the top 10 almost all last season, this is not big-time college basketball, where university-owned airplanes transport the team to games. McGonigle Hall seats a scant 4,500, compared to Indiana's 17,000-plus. Spectators perch on benches rather than seats. Assistant coach Dean Demopoulos knows better than even to ask the wheelchair players to move. Chaney wouldn't like it. "This wouldn't happen to Bobby Knight," assistant coach Jim Maloney says.

Chaney's target at practice today, it turns out, is the unflappable, impossibly slender (despite assistant coach Jay Norman's weight-training efforts), Nate Blackwell, the 6-foot, 4-inch guard and the team's only senior. Now being scouted by the NBA, he is the soul of this team, its coach on the floor. And he is the one young man here who has crossed that threshold into adulthood, although at times he tries not to show it. John Chaney hears the clock of Nate's final year ticking. He wants him to have his chance.

Opposing players will be rushing out of the locker room obsessed with the idea of stopping Nate Blackwell, Chaney says. And what is Nate Blackwell to do? Chaney becomes inspired in his search for the appropriate analogy.

Let Nate become Cyrano, Cyrano de Bergerac who came into town with a knife. He chopped off one head. All he had to do the next time was simply walk into town. "You can be Cyrano de Blackwell! You can do it on national television! Once you come into town, everyone else will get you. You won't even have to pull your knife again!" Nate has been newly baptized—Cyrano de Blackwell. ("You shouldn't have said that, Coach," Derrick whispers a few minutes later, "Nate has a big nose.") In June, Nate Blackwell would be recruited 27th in the country, high in the second round, by the San Antonio Spurs, with whom he would sign the first week of October.

There's good news on the weather front, so it's back to the airport, a trip that includes a visit to the North Philadelphia Burger King. Grown-ups on the court, the team reverts to childhood at mealtime. But not entirely. Quietly, Timmy has given his hamburger to a street person.

Howie takes a ribbing for leaving his shoes at the hotel. Mike, hounded for his defense, begins a story about a coach who appreciated offense.

The airport seems normal. The flight to Birmingham has been delayed for another hour, but that's to be expected. Chaney and Demopoulos repair to the Half-Shell Tavern for clams doused in horseradish and hot sauce. Assistant coach Maloney prefers an ice cream cone. Timmy, Ramon and Howie play cards. When Chaney passes, Timmy palms the deck.

But now hour after hour is passing. The players are weary. Eastern Airlines provides a room where they can rest, and seven pizzas are produced from somewhere in South Philadelphia. "It's good, but it's not enough, " says Ramon, Temple's big man.

"Who discovered America?" someone wants to know.

"Americus Vespucius," Chaney says.

"You can't pronounce it!" sassy freshman Tom Katsikis challenges.

"This from a Greek!" Chaney laughs.

"Ponce de Leon," offers Ramon, a native of Puerto Rico. "He discovered the Fountain of Youth."

"A trickle!" Chaney says.

The Eastern agent is a defensive, tiny man with a flowing brown mustache and a chip on his shoulder. Suddenly he announces that the Birmingham leg of the flight has been cancelled. The plane will go to Atlanta as scheduled, but then to Pensacola, Fla. There will be no connection to Birmingham until 6:57 on the morning of game day.

Chaney is beside himself. "Let me talk," he commands, towering over the little man. "We should have been told!" Here is the angry John Chaney that fans and television audiences see. The little man remains supercilious, further inciting Chaney's fury. A major incident seems about to erupt.

Suddenly, out of nowhere, Blackwell comes over and slips an arm around John Chaney's shoulders. "Take it easy, Coach," Nate says softly. "It's all right. We'll take a bus. As long as we get there by 11, we can play."

"Shut up," Chaney snaps, filled with pride at the player he calls his "firstborn son" because he was his first recruit.

"He is like a daddy," Nate says. Nate's real father, who attends every home game, has been known to refer to John Chaney and Nate as "him and his son." So seamless is John Chaney's conversion from discipline to affection that one minute at practice he'll yell at Nate— "You *used to be* the smartest player on this team"—and the next Nate will call him "Coachie Woachie."

"Coachie Woachie, let's eatie weatie," Granger Hall, a former Temple player would say, putting his arm and big hand around John Chaney. "Get your big feet off me," Chaney would growl.

Midnight has come and gone. It's past 1 a.m. as the team piles into a moving luggage wagon where they sit smiling, two by two. "As long as we get there by 11:59, we can play," Howie says. Chaney decides to discuss the semester's grades. The team boasts a respectable 2.7 average with three on the dean's list. Two have not done so well. Whistles identify the guilty.

At 2 a.m., the plane races its engines and the players try to snuggle down for the two-hour flight to Atlanta. "Who scheduled this game?" Chaney demands. "National television, you said national television," he ribs Jim Maloney.

In Atlanta he will *not* rent buses for a drive to Birmingham. "Take the known and leave the unknown alone," he says. Trudging from terminal to terminal in the cavernous, silent Atlanta airport at 4 a.m., he offers spicy salami to Tommy. Deadpan, Katsikis backs away. But Ramon, whom Chaney is constantly urging to lose weight, accepts a piece.

The players search for dark corners, to rest. They lie on the floors and cover themselves with their jackets.

At 6:30 a.m. the team boards a Delta flight to Birmingham. Only Ramon has not stretched out; he hates the noise. "How do you manage in the dorms?" Dean asks. "I *make* them be quiet," says Ramon. Chaney, of course, has not stretched out either.

Curled up, three seats each not nearly enough, they are oblivious to the pilot's wishes of good luck to the Temple team. Outside, a ribbon of scarlet lines the horizon, the sun about to rise. A sliver of moon hovers. Snow covers the Alabama rooftops and gardens, where the temperature is a bitter 34 degrees. "The sunshine inside you," Coach repeats on his way off the plane.

Without waiting for their bags, the players are hustled to the Hyatt, where Chaney instructs them to take warm showers: "Not one of those steamy showers that sap your energy." They will be taped and dress in the hotel, then ride over to the arena, just across the street. It is 7 a.m. in Birmingham, 8 a.m. in Philadelphia.

At 11 they board the team bus. Always, on the ride to the game there is absolute silence. The players do not sit together, nor do they look at each other.

The game begins and at once it's clear that their shooting is way off. Worse, in violation of their credo, they commit the unpardonable sin: turnovers. The offensive rebounds are all going the other way. Basketball requires precision, the unlikely tool of people, however young, who have not slept.

As ordered, Cyrano takes more shots, but they don't fall in. Vreeswyk loses his man; a three-pointer is scored against him. Chaney screams. Vreeswyk comes out of the game. With two minutes and 34 seconds remaining in the first half, Temple is down by 10. At the end of the half, they're down 33-26.

In the locker room at halftime Chaney yells at them for their errors. No excuses are made. But when the second half begins, Temple has changed its defenses. They call on both the box and one and the triangle and two. At once they shut down the UAB guards.

Meanwhile, Vreeswyk starts hitting; he will finish with 26 points, his career high. Eleven for 32 attempts in the first half, Temple will go 14 for 29 in the second. Jumping high in the air to protest a traveling call on Howie, Chaney is doing business as usual.

With 28 seconds left, Coach orders Nate, "Stagger around as if you're drunk," to run down the clock. The end is a bit messy, but then it's over. Temple is victorious, 67-60. The players leave the court quitely, not a fist raised, not a hand slapped.

It's a typical Chaney team effort. Exhausted, off-balance when they began, by the end they have surpassed themselves. And in the middle of the second period, when it all became clear, there was Chaney breaking down in tears. As they depart the Birmingham-Jefferson Civic Center, Maloney takes tissue and rubs out his diagrams from the locker room blackboard. "We aren't giving them *anything*," he says in his fiercely mild manner.

Among them, there is no glee, no euphoria, for Chaney has taught his team to treat victory and defeat identically. They head for McDonald's. Nate does the best imitation of Chaney so far. "Stagger around as if you're *drunk*," he mimics. He jokes about a teammate's defense: "What he ain't done for 20 years, you can't put into him now."

Then a few decide to try "Miss Winner's" chicken dinners. Darren Pearsall has bought one, got one free.

The coaches relax together. John Chaney remembers the words of Sam Browne: Put more where there are few and few where there are more, the secret of basketball offense. The talk is of the many NCAA violations of which they are aware and of the myriad problems of recruiting. Chaney praises the UAB coach, Gene Bartow, because when the game clock was not properly reset near the end, Bartow had said, "John, take four, five seconds, whatever you think is fair." Such courtesy, it appears, is rare in the world of college basketball.

The team comes dressed for dinner, always taking the same seats for each meal on a trip. First comes the blessing. All stand, heads lowered, as tonight Vreeswyk offers thanks for their having come through this ordeal.

Chaney has come not to eat but to talk, to encourage them to grasp the moment. Something important has happened that must not pass without notice, he says. "The sound of a tree bursting through the earth." This is what he heard today. If he had a painting of such a tree, it would bear the inscription, "No one was heard clapping." Now he is clapping for them in their triumph. He tells them they have earned "self-esteem."

The waitress delivers all the courses at once: fruit cup and vegetable soup, salad and fried chicken, potatoes and broccoli, milk and carrot cake. All is quickly consumed, and then the boys are gone. "We're not much for dinner," Mike explains. "They have places to go and people to see," trainer Vic LeMaster explains, no matter that they're not permitted to go far from the hotel. He knows they might all too easily melt into the Birmingham night. (In 1982, when Temple played Rollins in Orlando during Christmas week and the team was offered a trip to Disney World, Chaney did not let them go.)

The bus trip to the airport the next morning occasions old and new nicknames. There are always Huckleberry Hound and Buster Crabbe. Howard is "the usher," because, despite his iron confidence as a ball-handler, someone got by him and he "ushered" the opponent to the basket. Nate remains Cyrano de Blackwell.

"What name should I give you?" Coach asks Mike Vreeswyk.

"Mike Threeswyk," quips a player for whom the present three-point range is easy.

But this is not to be. "Never let a kid off the hook," is John Chaney's motto. On his desk sits a pad with the phrase "Because I Say So."

Undaunted, a week later "Threeswyk" will stage-whisper in Chaney's ear, "Atlantic 10 Player of the Week, two weeks in a row."

"I don't want to hear about last week," Chaney retorts.

At the airport Chaney learns coffee costs 95 cents. Once he went to a farmers market with his grandmother. Grandma looks at a peach pie. It costs $12. Grandma takes another look, a good look. "What you done to it?" she wants to know. How could a peach pie cost $12?

Before heading home Chaney will visit his mother, who had called him at 4:30 a.m. on Friday worried about whether they could fly. "Your mother," he says, "You'll be going up the river for a thousand years and she'll be screaming, 'He's innocent.' " Dean Demopoulos, who lost his own father at age 6 and for whom John Chaney has filled that role, concurs.

A final question goes to Timmy. "Will you be in the library this afternoon writing that paper, getting rid of that incomplete?"

"How did you remember that?" Timmy wants to know.

These innocents, Chaney wonders. Will they ever know such fellowship again?

Blacks in Sports

GENERAL

By *EDWIN POPE*

From the Miami Herald
Copyright © 1987, Miami Herald Publishing Co.

My first reaction to the Rev. Jesse Jackson's ultimatum to baseball was vague annoyance, as it is to most ultimatums. Jackson asked black former big-leaguers to picket ballparks July 4 if baseball did not come up with a "coherent" plan for hiring blacks in administrative jobs by then.

My second reaction was to remember that about the only way blacks have ever gotten anything in this country has been through ultimatums.

My third reaction and final reaction was that black former pro football players should do the same thing Jackson asks in baseball.

The subjugation of blacks in positions of authority represents an outrageous blight on these two sports.

Pro baseball has had three black managers—Larry Doby, Frank Robinson and Maury Wills—in more than a century. Pro football has had no black head coaches in more than six decades.

It has been that way for precisely the reason my first feeling was annoyance: It is easier to go with the flow, no matter how stupid or cruel that flow is, than to help do anything to change it.

Decades were required merely for blacks' playing skills to overcome managements' antediluvian attitude toward blacks as performers. Their eventual ascendancy as athletes gave rise to a national myth that sports are essentially democratic—that you can make it if you are good enough.

You can't, if you're black.

At least you haven't been able to, yet, because the white power structure has been either too prejudiced or too thoughtless to bother to implement the simple justice of racial equality.

In 1977, after *Roots* shocked and shamed me, I wrote that the TV series "brought to sharpest focus yet the innermost and largely unspoken feeling of many blacks that coaches and managers, stunningly white in terms of numbers, are merely extensions of overseers and/or slavemasters of ages past."

One general manager in the NFL has called me "Roots" ever since. And I have not said one word about it since.

Thus, I and others like me share the blame for the travesty spotlighted by Dodger Vice President Al Campanis' televised remarks that blacks are essentially unqualified for leadership.

Like most of the sports hierarchy, Campanis emerges more as insensitive than malevolent. That means we are far more guilty of laziness than the stereotype with which the black has been criminally stigmatized for centuries.

Unqualified to manage or general-manage in baseball because they are black? Reggie Jackson? Bill White? Don Baylor? Dave Winfield? Willie Stargell? Frank Robinson? Hal McRae? Joe Morgan? Henry Aaron? Elrod Hendricks? Lou Brock? And hundreds more?

That is as absurd as it would be to blame the championship shortcomings and subsequent recyclements of Gene Mauch and Billy Martin on their sheer whiteness.

Unqualified to coach or general-manage in the NFL? Nat Moore? Tony Dungy? Jimmy Raye? Marvin Powell? Brian Holloway? Mel Blount? Larry Little? Mean Joe Greene? Roy Foster? Gene Upshaw? Johnny Roland? And hundreds more?

That is as ludicrous as it would be to blame the abject failure of John McKay in the NFL on his whiteness alone.

In his 1966 book "Everything but Money," Sam Levenson wrote, "What a horror it must be for a child to discover that his skin is the wrong color."

Sports was supposed to be an escape tunnel from this horror. It has been, for some multimillionaire black athletes. But the tunnel ends where management begins.

My most poignant conversation involving sports racism took place in the late 1960s with a splendid columnist, Milton Gross of the *New York Post.* As we shared a cab to a World Series game, Gross said with some resentment, "I was the first white sports columnist to stand up for equality for black athletes. Even so, when I try to talk with them, I can get just so far. It bothers me that black athletes don't appreciate what I tried to do for them."

Gross added instantly, "But after everything else that's happened to blacks for so long, why should they?"

Gross was one of the few who cared enough to try in the first place. Most of the rest of us have done nothing. Now is the time to mend the terrible wound our indifference has created. Ours, and all sports'.

If sports has a conscience at all, let it step forward right now and at least start to assign blacks their earned place in sports management.

Even right now is disgracefully late.

Double Trouble

COLLEGE FOOTBALL

By *RICHARD HOFFER*

From the Los Angeles Times
Copyright © 1987, the Los Angeles Times

Here's a sociological snapshot: A year ago, the most visible college football player in the land was Oklahoma's Brian Bosworth, a kind of Mad Max with an attitude.

He wore an earring, went out in the noon sun, and promised, by word and deed, to subvert everything you believed in. His Doberman pinscher ran to a far corner when he stooped to pet him. His hair was purple.

Today? Everybody's darling is Gordie Lockbaum, of the Holy Cross powerhouse.

Lockbaum's stolid mug might well have been lifted from a Norman Rockwell print, his story from a John R. Tunis book. He is the guy you'd vote least likely to wear jewelry about his head or otherwise tamper with a crew cut. His school puts his academic transcript —GPA 3.167—in the football guide. Favorite food? Book says mom's meat loaf.

Perhaps, we stretch a point. But how else to acknowledge the overwhelming popularity of a Division I-AA player, somebody who may or may not have the gifts to even make an Oklahoma football team?

Here come ABC and "Good Morning America," People magazine, altogether 36 interviews in his first 10 days back on campus. These are different times. We need another hero, evidently. Another kind of game, certainly. Maybe the one Lockbaum plays.

Look at it this way. In the year since we first celebrated Brian Bosworth and all that was outrageous and, we thought, fun about football, the game has been characterized by cheating at SMU, greed in the premature signing with agents, drugs—steroids at the very least—astonishing arrogance as characterized by any Miami-related police action, and academic inadequacies just about everywhere.

Perhaps the backlash was being signaled on January 2 when gloriously old-fashioned Penn State, a team whose players do not even wear names on their jerseys, overcame the bigger, better, brasher Miami Sound Machine for the national championship, in a game that took on all the important aspects of a morality play.

In that time even the Tide has turned (see: Bill Curry, Alabama).

And now comes Gordie Lockbaum, two-way throwback, from the Department of Too Good to be True. So good even his publicist blushes.

"Now, Gordie's kind of a straight arrow," he warns, just as Lockbaum is loping into view, stepping out of 1956, apparently. Licking an ice cream cone. Vanilla.

"Aw, geez," the publicist sighs, stopped in his own tracks. It is a daunting thing for publicists when they cannot anticipate the pleasing innocence of even their own candidates.

Lockbaum, besides being a swell guy, of course had a hook going into all of this, in its way no less outrageous than Bosworth's haircut. The team's best defensive player his first two seasons, Lockbaum was pressed into emergency duty as a tailback his junior year. Of course, he didn't give up defense; he simply played both ways.

The result was not simply effective from a football point of view, but from a publicity angle. When this was being done, Holy Cross was still thought of, when thought of at all, as the school whose football coach had hanged himself. Yet, from under his shadow emerged one of the season's brightest stars.

What Lockbaum was doing was challenging everything about the game as played. The game had become complicated, too demanding. It was an age of specialization, players hand-tooled for specific roles.

And here was Lockbaum, in his team's upset of Army, rushing 11 times for 40 yards, catching four passes for 73 yards, making 19 unassisted tackles. Of Holy Cross's 1,599 plays last season Lockbaum was on the field for 1,005.

Mighty good hook. Reporters came to town to eyeball this little novelty—he's 5 feet 11 inches and 195 pounds—and then craft their own gags. Should get two scholarships. Probably a double major. He was posed in 1930s togs, even holding a leather helmet.

But in eyeballing Lockbaum, they discovered that the metaphor was not just skin deep. He really was a throwback.

Here's a guy talking about his off-season conditioning program: "Well, my girlfriend lives two miles away and I don't have a car, so I run back and forth to her house."

Reporters have heard a lot of things. They heard this and slapped their pencils down and just looked at each other. It's the dawning of an old age.

"The timing is right," said Holy Cross Coach Mark Duffner, explaining Lockbaum's appeal. "The atmosphere is right for a guy like Gordie, who attends class, will graduate on time and in addition is a very efficient football player. With all the problems in athletics, here comes Gordie representing the traditional things, even things that go as far back as two-way football."

★   ★   ★

Holy Cross never set out to break ground. Nobody said, hey, it's been 20 years since Leroy Keyes played both ways at Purdue, we could get some attention here. Duffner didn't want a two-way player any more than any coach does. It's just that the Crusaders were a little thin at tailback going into spring practice before last season.

"I talked to him about learning a few running plays, just as a buffer for us," Duffner said. "He was all for it, but we had no real intention of giving him up on defense."

The defensive coaches didn't think that much of the little experiment, one way or another. Except, said defensive coordinator Kevin Coyle, "the first day he goes over there, he's the best on the field."

The offensive coordinator, Tom Rossley, got this glint in his eye. More like a laser beam. "We had to have him," he said. "No two ways about it. You could say, that's when the fight began."

The idea of there being two ways about it, figuratively or literally, didn't occur at first. At first it was simply an un-civil war between offense and defense.

"It got ugly," Rossley admitted. But he had to have Lockbaum, the way he could move the ball.

Yet there was no way Coyle, whose own backfield was young and inexperienced, was going to surrender his top player.

"He's a natural to run," whined Rossley to his boss. "I don't even know why he fools around with defense."

Rossley began making bold statements, that he'd fix it so Lockbaum wouldn't be missed on defense. "If we have Gordie, he'll give us 28 points a game. You won't *need* anybody on defense."

Coyle, meanwhile, was becoming anxious about the way Lockbaum was being flipped from unit to unit. He was worried that the player's abilities on defense would become diluted.

"It got to the point where he was doing more than buffing, seemed to me," Coyle said.

The coaches' meetings were stormy. Rossley recalled that the defense stooped to a certain pettiness. "We'd be driving the ball downfield in scrimmage and then the defense would take him back," he said, the hurt still in his voice. "We'd never score. We didn't know if it was because we had Gordie stopping us, or because he wasn't carrying the ball."

Duffner remembered "the offense ripping his jersey toward offense, the defense tugging their way. Finally I said, 'Enough. We need him both places.'"

The coaches campaigned vigorously as to why this was impossible.

"Quit telling me what we can't do," Duffner told them. "Let's try it."

Just 10 days before the opener, the staff reluctantly concluded that Lockbaum would play both ways.

"We felt it was a gamble," admits Duffner. "But it was a necessity. It came down to us having to do it. 'Let's put Lockbaum on offense, ease the freshman in, take it from there.' So first game, he's in 90 plays."

Lockbaum was in for 97 plays, actually, making five tackles, recovering a couple of fumbles—one for a touchdown—returning an interception 34 yards, rushing six times for 29 yards and catching a 20-yard pass.

"By God, we won," Duffner said. "So we thought, if it's not broken, don't fix it."

Here's how the gamble worked out: Lockbaum made 46 tackles, caused two fumbles, recovered two and intercepted a pass; returned 21 kickoffs for 452 yards; caught 57 passes for 860 yards and eight touchdowns; gained 827 yards and scored 14 touchdowns rushing. He was voted Division I-AA All-America on both offense and defense. He was fifth in the Heisman Trophy balloting.

And so history, if not made, was revisited. The position coaches haven't stopped grumbling ever since.

"I think we were more receptive than the offense," said Coyle, self-approvingly.

Not so Rossley. "I hated it, I hated it, I hated it," he said, and he still hates it.

Rossley got a look at Duffner's practice schedule and cracked anew when the coach entered the room the other day. "Coach," he moaned, "you've got him on defense for the heart of our practice, the very *heart.*"

Duffner smiled lamely and got out of the room fast.

The struggle is natural, given the evolution of football. It hasn't been a simple game for a long time. Practices are specialized. The competition is at such a level that no coach can afford to lose the edge of intensive practice, where a player does "reps," repeating skill or plays until they are robotic in their efficiency. Then there are meetings, of course. Films for offense and defense.

"It's become such a technical game," Rossley said. "So much technique to teach. You just can't get enough (teaching) time. Individual time, group time, team time—and if he misses any part of it, he just can't get it done."

Rossley, like most of today's coaches, is too young to remember that all-around Lockbaum would have been commonplace in the 1950s, when unlimited substitution was outlawed. In those days, it could get done. Had to be done.

It might shock him to know that Johnny Unitas also played defensive back, that Frank Ryan played linebacker, that Howard (Hopalong) Cassady, who won the Heisman Trophy in 1955, played both ways.

But that was a simpler time. It has been a long time since Lockbaum could have been classified as commonplace.

★   ★   ★

In the nurturing of any legend, it is important to go back as far as possible to the source material. When William (The Refrigerator) Perry was becoming a folk hero, reporters interviewed all the fast-food franchisers in his hometown. Lockbaum's parents do the job here.

So far, the anecdotes look like this:

—During church communion, young Gordie would run past people in line so he could be first up, first back in the pew.

—He came home from first grade and announced to his mom that he'd be going to summer school because there was a girl in his class further along in reading skills than he.

Kind of a driven kid, seems to be the point. Three-sport star—wrestling, football, baseball—at Glassboro High in New Jersey. National Honor Society. Ranked second in a class of 147. Getting the picture? Narrowed colleges down to those in a six-hour driving radius so he could get home to family easily.

He was recruited as a free safety by Syracuse and a running back by Navy, and heard from Rutgers and West Point, among other Division I schools. But being a student at Holy Cross, a small Jesuit school which has turned out the likes of Bob Cousy and Joseph Califano, held an appeal for him. He wasn't thinking Heisman Trophy at the time.

Now that everybody else is, well, Lockbaum is still not swept off his feet. He's been playing along and he obviously enjoys the attention. But he hasn't lost perspective or that annoying team-oriented humility that coaches foster among their players.

"We laugh about it," said Lockbaum of the attention he's been getting. "I mean, when I came here, I expected to play good ball but I never expected I'd go to a newsstand and see my face on a cover. Seems silly the way it's happened. If we'd had a good tailback, I'd have been on defense last year."

That is as outrageous as he gets. Although he admits to being goal-oriented, he couches all talk of his personal achievement in the inevitable team talk. "If I do well, the team does well," he typically says, noting semi-correctly that his team's 10-1 record has helped his stature as much as his own statistics.

For all the attention, though, he understands the fragility of his fame, how lucky he's been. Not to be good, but to get the opportunity he has had.

"It's been a combination of things, another of which is I've never really been injured," he said, ticking off another circumstance leading to celebrity. He shrugged.

His modesty is appropriate in at least one respect. IIe'd be having as much fun doing this even if nobody noticed. Individual stars do well to remember how much fun being part of a bunch is. In fact, Lockbaum is smart enough to regret anything that takes him from the team.

"That's the one part I miss, since I began playing tailback, when I don't feel part of the defensive back group," he said. "You know, when you have your little friendships, your own jokes, your own busts on people. Sometimes, I feel a little left out."

If he no longer belongs to one group, he still belongs to the team, and the others good-naturedly tolerate his national profile. They kid him openly when he rushes onto the field with a towel for a muddied teammate, as he did in one game last season.

When a reporter entered the locker room last year, inquiring after Lockbaum, the players explained that he was unavailable as he was lunching with the Reagans at the White House. And so on. Before the spring game, the alumni team chained Lockbaum to the fence to keep him out.

But all these are side dishes to Lockbaum's entree, playing football. He understands he's doing "something uncommon and that I had a chance to make a name for myself." But he understands, too, that he's getting to play twice the amount of football he expected.

"It's a lot more fun than I imagined," he said. "It's great to be on the field, to have an effect on the outcome of the game, not just standing on the sideline hoping the defense will hold them off. Isn't that where a football player would want to be, on the field?"

The amount of time Lockbaum wants, and now expects, to be on the field is almost irritating.

"I've created a monster," said Duffner, who in the past thought he was doing the responsible thing by resting Lockbaum on defense. "I'd be watching the play and I'd feel this tap-tapping on my shoulder."

Argues Lockbaum: "I have to keep reminding them I want to play defense."

The demands off the field are sometimes extreme, with both the defensive and offensive coaches offering special tutoring to make up missed meeting time. And they do not forget at Holy Cross that Lockbaum, besides carrying two playbooks, may well be carrying 19th-Century Russian Plays (Up the middle, through Poland, on One!).

But Lockbaum is obviously up to it. He makes few-to-no on-field mistakes and his grades actually improved when he became a two-way player.

"I'm just one of a bunch here," he explained. "Everybody studies at night. It's just what you do."

These demands are clearly worth it, as well. He enjoys the hustle and bustle of the practice field, no standing around for a two-way player.

"I just switch jerseys and go to the other end of the field when they start giving the second team their reps," he said.

What player doesn't want to be in on every play? Maybe that's what's so old-fashioned about him.

Rossley was musing about his little throwback. "He was probably one of the great all-time backyard players," he said of the irrepressible Lockbaum.

Backyard player? What kind is that?

The kind that plays for the fun of it, he explained.

See what we mean by throwback?

Follow Through

by Wayne Roper of the Brantford (Ontario) Expositor. Gary Schaff, a paraplegic from Calmer, Alberta, follows through on the discus throw that shattered the Canadian record and narrowly missed a world mark at the Canadian Foresters Games for the disabled in Brantford. Schaff, who had trained two years for the competition, beat the Canadian record by nearly eight meters. Copyright © 1987, Wayne Roper, Brantford Expositor.

Helping Hands

by Robert Bunch, a free-lancer for United Press International. Dallas soccer star Tatu, shirtless and ecstatic, high fives eager fans after the Sidekicks had defeated Tacoma in Game 6 of the 1987 MISL championship series. Copyright © 1987, Robert Bunch.

Bad Boxers

BOXING

By *MARK KRAM*

From the Philadelphia Daily News
Copyright © 1987, the Philadelphia Daily News

A van is parked at the door of the Uncle Sam Boxing Club in Troy, N.Y., and in steps Sam Lee Youngs, dressed in sweat clothes and sporting a new haircut. That evening, some four hours away in Massachusetts, he would be headlining a boxing show at a high school in Attleboro, and he had stopped at the Sanitary Barber Shop to have the sides of his head decorated with "lightning bolts." While the other boxers in the van erupt in the side-splitting laughter—and agree he looks like "some kind of fairy"—"Lightning" Sam announces: "I am a soldier at war."

Sam Youngs is 26 years old. He is a junior welterweight. He is single, has a 2-year-old son, and works in a packing plant that processes 750,000 pounds of hamburger a week. The area of the plant in which Youngs works is kept at 50 degrees or below, and while Sam is careful to dress warmly—wearing a helmet, gloves and coat—his trainer, Carlo (Pops) Litz, is of the considered opinion that this continued exposure to the cold has held Youngs back as a boxer.

"That could be the answer, Sam," says Litz, 67, and equipped with two hearing aids. "Working in the cold air throws off your whole system."

"Could be, Pops," Youngs says. "Could be."

While Pops pursues this theory in elaborate detail with one of the other passengers—and dissolves into a discourse on the dietetic evils of ice cream—Youngs chuckles to himself and peers at the passing landscape, the colors of which on this October Saturday are deep and vivid. Since 1980, the year he started boxing professionally, his career has been anchored in both obscurity and in the perpetual belief that he still can escape his circumstances. While he has won less than half of his bouts—and has won only four of 23 bouts since January 1984—Youngs says this: "I never win away from home. I have to knock the other guy out to get the decision (sic)."

That would be the scenario awaiting Youngs in Attleboro. His opponent, David Rivello, would seem to have some incredible advantages: not only does he hail from Attleboro and have a big following there, he attended the school where the bout is to be held and even starred in football there. Home again from Miami, where he had been under contract to Angelo Dundee, Rivello now has Goody and Pat Petronelli in his corner, while Sam has the obscure tandem of manager Bob Miller and Pops. The Petronellis guided Marvin Hagler to the middleweight championship and plan to have Rivello pursue the New England lightweight crown.

Youngs intends to upset those plans.

"I am an animal today," Youngs begins as others on the van continue laughing. "I plan to crush this boy like a jellybean."

The van continues toward the Massachusetts Turnpike; Attleboro is still 180 miles away.

★   ★   ★

The New Jersey State Athletic Commission banned Sam Lee Youngs and 34 others in June from ever again boxing in that state. Commissioner Larry Hazzard explained his actions as an effort to cleanse the sport of the "sophisticated fix." Unlike the old Hollywood B-films, in which the "fix" is orchestrated with bribes and threats, the "sophisticated fix" is the practice of building the career of one boxer at the expense of an "opponent" who has little or no chance of winning. The Sam Lee Youngs-David Rivello bout qualified as a "sophisticated fix."

That Hazzard acted and banned 35 boxers is commendable. However, it also is inadequate. A six-week investigation by the *Daily News* disclosed hundreds of other boxers who have shown little or no skill, but continue to obtain licenses and are in high demand. Using records supplied by Ralph Citro, a consultant to the Association of Boxing Commissions, the *Daily News* identified 772 boxers who are both dangers to themselves and discredits to a sport brimming with abuses.

The *Daily News* interviewed dozens of state commissioners, promoters, trainers and boxers in its investigation, and found:

• Boxers who never win—301 of the 772 boxers identified never have won a bout, and 60 never have won in eight or more bouts. One of those boxers is Michael Grant, a Philadelphia middleweight, who had 20 losses between February 1982 and February 1984.

• Knockout victims—67 of the boxers were knocked out in each of their bouts, and 365 were knocked out in one-half of their bouts. Moreover, 192 were knocked out six or more times, 75 were knocked out eight or more times, and 32 were knocked out 10 or more times. Carl Oville, a junior middleweight from Texas, has been knocked out in each of his 13 bouts.

• Losing streaks—386 boxers have had six or more consecutive losses at some point in their careers, 101 have had nine or more, and 35 have had 12 or more. Jimmy Mitchell, a junior welterweight from Mississippi, had 30 consecutive losses from 1982 to 1986.

• Violations of suspensions—184 have boxed while on suspension, or within 30 days of being knocked out (the Association of Boxing Commissions recommends a 30-day suspension after a knockout). Moreover, 48 boxers appeared within 10 days of being suspended or knocked out.

• Boxers who use aliases—dozens were found to have competed under assumed names in an effort to camouflage woeful records. For example, Stanley Johnson is a heavyweight from Milwaukee and has been knocked out in 15 of his 19 bouts. Johnson boxed Tex Cobb in Arkansas in March, but was promoted as Stan White, of Billings, Mont. Johnson/White never had been to Montana. He was knocked out in the first round.

One state athletic commissioner declared: "Boxers have more different names than a bag of popcorn has kernels."

• Falsification of records—this is the charge that led New Jersey to suspend Sam Lee Youngs in 1985. Citro lists Youngs at 11-26-1. Youngs said he is "25-15, or something like that." The promoter for the bout in Attleboro, Paul Morrisette, advertised Youngs as "25-10." Dr. Stuart Kirschenbaum, the Michigan state boxing commissioner, called such altering of records "a total deception intended to defraud the public." He added: "When I hear a boxer is 28-8 I automatically assume he is 8-28."

• Failure on the part of some state athletic commissions to govern the sport—J.W. Steinsiek, the secretary for the Arkansas State Athletic Commission, said it is "standard procedure" for promoters to operate without licenses in Arkansas, and added that he had "no idea" that the Cobb-White bout even had taken place. Nor had the Massachusetts commission been "aware" that the promoter Morrisette had advertised Youngs to be "25-10-0." Said commission aide Frank Lehan: "We will look into this."

That boxing is in such a state of utter chaos is not surprising. Unlike other professional sports that are subject to the dictates of a single commissioner, boxing is an organizational catastrophe. As evidence, consider welterweight Eddie Flannings, of Georgia (4-24-4, 17 losses by KO), who was knocked out on March 17, 1985, in Florida. Flannings went on to be knocked out on March 20 in Louisiana, on March 23 in Tennessee, on March 25 in Maryland, and on March 30 in West Virginia. A Midwest-based commissioner referred to Flannings as "the Greg Louganis of boxing." Louganis is the Olympic *diving* champion.

Commissions in New Jersey, Michigan and elsewhere have adopted a strong stance toward boxers such as Flannings. However, while strides seemingly are being made in some states, others such as Arkansas and South Carolina continue to be havens for abusers.

Kirschenbaum said there are "some boxers I will not allow to cross the state line," but added he has no power to prevent them from boxing in an adjacent state. "Opponents are like moles," Kirschenbaum said. "I can set a trap for them here, but there is no stopping them from tunneling into another state."

Unlike Kirschenbaum, who objects to the use of boxers as "cannon foder," others contend that "opponents" fill a need. The traditional (and, indeed, prevailing) belief is that club shows such as the one in Attleboro will perish and that potential "contenders" such as Rivello will have no place to develop. While Rivello is 11-0—and has appeared with what Citro terms "some decent opponents"—Goody Petronelli observed:

"(Rivello) still has to develop. There is no way I would take him down and feed him to the animals in Philadelphia or Atlantic City. Youngs is the perfect opponent for him at this point in his career."

★   ★   ★

The van from New York arrives at Attleboro High School less than an hour before the official weigh-in. Scheduled for 5 p.m., less than three hours before the bouts would begin, the weigh-in had precluded Youngs from eating much more than a poached egg and a piece of bread this day. When the van stops at a fast-food restaurant on the Massachusetts Turnpike and the others eat burgers and fries, Sam pokes at part of a salad and speaks effusively of his plans to order "a big plate of spaghetti" that evening for dinner.

"Protein, Sammy," Pops tells him as the two stand in the parking lot. "Order a piece of beef tonight, and have a baked potato and a roll with it."

"I always eat spaghetti," Youngs says. "Carbohydrates, Pops."

Weighing himself the evening before on a scale at the Uncle Sam Boxing Club, Youngs had been ecstatic to discover he weighed 136 pounds. Weighing himself again before the official weigh-in at Attleboro High School, he discovers that he has somehow added three pounds and weighs two pounds over his contractual limit. While it seems highly unlikely that the Petronellis will withdraw Rivello from the bout—an option—the possibility exists that Youngs will have to forfeit a portion of his purse.

"I have to get this weight off, Pops," Youngs says.

"Take a (bleep), Sam," Pops advises. "See if that helps."

When Youngs emerges from the lavatory and discovers he still weighs 139 pounds, he dresses and starts out the door for the school athletic field. Wearing two layers of clothing and a jacket with a towel protruding from his collar, he steps onto the asphalt track and begins running laps. While Pops stands to the side, his hands in the pockets of his wind-blown trousers, Sam runs up, down and across the bottom row of some bleachers, does eight trips around the track, and finishes by sprinting the length of the school football field. Breathing hard, his forehead soaked with perspiration, he wipes his face with a towel and says, "I got it off, Pops, I know I did."

"Cool off inside, Sammy," Pops says. "The air out here is cold."

The New York boxers and the Petronelli stable are assigned to opposite ends of the school locker room. Amid the crowd that has formed there—including a wizened doctor who examines the boxers with a stethoscope—commissioner Jimmy McCarron spots Youngs and tells him to weigh in. "Hop on there, Sammy," McCarron says. Youngs strips down to his briefs and steps on the scale.

McCarron adjusts the weight at 136. He peers down over the top of his glasses and adjusts it again at 137. Slowly, ever so slowly, he slides the weight to 137½, 137¾ . . . 138. When he adjusts the weight to 138½—and the bar still does not budge—McCarron hurriedly slides the weight back to zero, tells Youngs to step off the scale and writes on his commission sheet: 137 pounds.

Sam dresses into his street clothes and heads for that plate of spaghetti.

★   ★   ★

Sam Youngs was crushed when he learned he had been suspended by New Jersey for "poor performances." Later, during his shift changes or breaks at work, friends would tease him and say, "Sammy, we thought you were better than that." The co-workers would laugh and Youngs would shake his head and laugh with them. They never would know how deeply it hurt him.

The morning of the day before the trip to Attleboro, Youngs sat at the counter of a coffee shop in Troy. While Pops sat on a corner stool and stirred his coffee—and remembered warmly the days he and his cohorts shot dice behind City Hall—Youngs poured four bags of sugar into his coffee and began to speak of how wronged he had been by New Jersey.

"How can they say I gave a 'poor performance?' " he asked. "I have never given a 'poor performance.' "

Promoters and others who have seen Youngs agree. Philadelphia promoter J Russell Peltz, who stages boxing events at the Blue Horizon, had Sam on a show in June 1985 and remembered him dropping a close decision to Philadelphian Andre "Sharp" Robinson. Michigan matchmaker Lindy Lindell had Youngs come in as an "opponent" for Hilmer Kenty in March 1984, and while Lindell said he was "somewhat disappointed" (Kenny won on a third-round knockout), he added: "I remember him as a 'quality opponent.' "

Both Peltz and Lindell can point to others of decidedly lesser caliber. Philadelphians Michael Grant (0-20-0) and James Lyons (0-15-0) both have been cited by Citro and have dropped out of circulation. So have Ron Washington (2-10-0) and Maurice Young (0-7-0), both of whom had been attached to trainer Johnny Barr. Barr had been a principal supplier of "opponents" before the commission started adopting stricter standards. (Barr claimed, "I am retired from boxing," and answered an interview request by saying, "Go (bleep) yourself.")

Of the 37 Philadelphians cited by Citro—28 of whom have appeared on shows promoted by Peltz—only nine have had bouts in 1987. Mike Brown, a junior lightweight who is currently 5-14-1, has two victories this year and has dropped two split-decisions to Frankie Mitchell and one to Ali Muhammad. Peltz promoted those bouts and said that Brown "easily" could have won two of three decisions. Brown agreed. "I should have won," he said, "but I always seem to be in there with someone the promoter is trying to build." Mitchell is 18-0; Muhammad is 7-2-3.

Brown has boxed professionally for four years. He is 23. Abandoned at age 15 when his parents divorced in 1979—his father, the boxer said, had been an alcoholic—Brown dropped out of school in the 12th grade and started living off the streets. He carried scissors and cut hair for $2 a head. He helped people carry bags home from the grocery store. He fished for eels in the Schuylkill River and sold them, and he foraged abandoned houses in North Philadelphia for copper and sold that. He started boxing at age 17.

Brown appeared one evening not long ago to spar at a North Philadelphia gym with Ron Woodley, an amateur junior middleweight. Standing off to the side, his eyes hidden behind a pair of dark sunglasses, trainer Leonard Pate ordered Brown to "throw the jab, throw the jab." Pate has trained Brown for six years, both as an amateur and a pro, and said that Brown has the "potential" to be one of the top junior lightweights in the world. How Pate is able to discern that is curious indeed—he has been legally blind since the Korean War.

"I know," Pate said. "I can hear his punches. When he comes back to the corner, he describes the action and I tell him what to do. Mike has talent and he could have been even better if he had had better training habits. I would get him a contract (for a bout) and he would only train two days for it."

"Those days are over," Brown claimed. Inactive since July, when he grew frustrated with the course his career was taking and dropped out of training, Brown said he has a job with Acme Manufacturing in Philadelphia. He spoke of the day he will open his own mail-order business. He said he no longer views boxing as "a way to make money."

"I look at boxing now as a sport," Brown said. "I will never make any money at it."

Brown has earned between $150 and $750 for an appearance. Others, such as Bill Hollis, of Pontiac, Mich., have done as well as $1,000 or more. Hollis, a light heavyweight who is 1-14-0, has a wife, six children and 14 consecutive losses dating back to September 1982. Without a manager or a trainer—a typical state of affairs for "opponents" of his caliber—it has not been uncommon for Hollis to prepare himself for a bout by performing conditioning drills in his dining room. "I say to myself," Hollis said, "this is it—no more boxing. But then I think, well, it's one more dollar."

Michigan has banned Hollis from ever boxing again in the state.

He is 38 and his wife, Pam, had been starting to worry. "He could come home a vegetable," she said. She also observed some subtle changes in Bill: where once he had been a person with hope and desire, he evolved into a person with neither. He has been an auto worker, a security guard and a cook. He was fired from his job as a cook for allegedly stealing and eating a piece of cake.

"I never stole that cake," Hollis claimed.

Pam shook her head. "I worry for him," she said. "Poor Bill is a defeated man."

Hollis never seemed to care who his opponent was; nor, would it appear, does Youngs. Still seated with Pops at the Troy coffee shop, the windows clouded with steam, Youngs referred to his opponent in Attleboro as "Luis Rivero." When a friend stopped to say hello, and the discussion turned toward the bout, the friend said, "Rivero, huh? Never heard of him."

"Neither have I," Youngs said.

*   *   *

The Attleboro High School gym darkens and suddenly a beacon sweeps the crowd. Then, beginning slowly but building to a crescendo, the audience hears the theme from "2001: A Space Odyssey," and the hometown hero appears and the red, white and blue sequins on his robe sparkle in the spotlight. Flanked by the Petronellis, and followed by a long line of handlers, David Rivello walks down the aisle from his dressing room and steps into the ring.

"Lightning" Sam Youngs is already there. Standing in his corner with Miller and Pops, both of whom are dressed in the traditional attire of their profession, Youngs waves to the crowd as his name is announced and proceeds to the center of the ring. While the referee dispenses his instructions—and Sam and Rivello exchange glares—a spectator at ringside declares, "Youngs looks tough. Rivello could go all the way if he wins this one."

A crowd of close to 600 is seated on the wooden chairs and bleachers surrounding the ring. Youngs had planned to pressure Rivello, and at the sound of the opening bell Sam does exactly that. He pursues Rivello to a corner and begins throwing punches to the head and ribs. The crowd roars as Rivello spins from the ropes, and they are delighted as he appears to win both rounds 1 and 2. Youngs is unable to generate an effective attack.

While his adoring fans begin to chant "Rocky, Rocky, Rocky," Rivello sits in his corner between the second and third rounds and asks to see the ring doctor. Rivello apparently injured his left hand in the second round. Concern begins to circulate through the crowd as the doctor steps through the ropes and asks Rivello some questions. When the doctor leaves, and Rivello stands in his corner for the third round, someone in the bleachers shouts, "Come on, Dave, give him a one-way ticket on the 'Rivello Express.' "

Rivello remains poised. Although he is unable to use his left hand —which later would prove to be sprained—Rivello begins adding to his lead with long right hands and controls the tempo between rounds 3 and 8. Pops shouts from the corner for Youngs to "get a hold of that arm," but Rivello continues throwing long right hands and does not allow himself to be trapped either on the ropes or in the corner. Youngs has no punching power.

The crowd renews its chant of "Rocky, Rocky, Rocky" as the 10th round draws to a close, and when it does, Youngs hugs Rivello and Rivello hugs Youngs. Goody Petronelli and Miller step into the ring and shake hands. Pops offers Sam a drink from the water bottle and begins to cut off the gloves. As Pops strips off a piece of tape—and assures Sam he has a "big shot at (the decision)"—the ring announcer begins:

"Ladies and gentlemen . . . in the main event of the evening . . . we have a decision . . ."

★   ★   ★

Promoter J Russell Peltz sat in his Fairmount office and discussed the difference between a "stiff" and a "bum."

"A 'stiff,' " Peltz contended, "is someone who rarely ever goes the distance. He always gets knocked out.

"A 'bum,' on the other hand, is someone who will come in and lose a decision. Somehow, they always seem to find a way to lose."

Peltz has no doubt that New Jersey acted properly in banning Eddie Flannings and others like him, but he is not so certain of some others. As he scanned a copy of the New Jersey 35—10 of whom have appeared for Peltz—the Philadelphia promoter shook his head.

"Here," he said, "Thomas Baker, for instance. I have had Baker here before and I would have him here again."

Peltz continued, "Or here—Joey Soler. Joey Soler has some talent. No way would I include him here."

Nor would Peltz include Sam Youngs. "Youngs is definitely of a higher caliber than Flannings or some of the others," Peltz said. "Flannings is . . . like delivering a corpse."

That Peltz would assess Youngs and others somewhat more liberally than Hazzard would is understandable. Whereas a promoter is in the business of "making" bouts, a boxing commissioner is in the business of "breaking" them. Hazzard, a former boxing referee who began as the New Jersey boxing commissioner in 1985, said he expected some "disagreements" to evolve from his action. But he is comfortable with his decision.

"A person who obtains a license to box is obtaining a privilege—just like a person who obtains a license to drive is obtaining a privilege," Hazzard said. "A privilege can be taken away.

"Boxing is not a sport to be taken lightly. We have to protect the boxers—from themselves. And secondly, we have to protect the public from bouts that I call the 'sophisticated fix.' "

Some have been critical of New Jersey's decision. Miller is one; he has written Hazzard a letter protesting the suspension of Youngs and has asked Hazzard to reconsider. Others, such as Peltz and

Goody Petronelli, question the wisdom of basing a suspension strictly on wins and losses.

"Records have their place in the evaluation process," Peltz said, "but relying on them too heavily can produce a distorted picture." Peltz said he does not allow his ring announcer at the Blue Horizon to give records.

"Americans are obsessed with statistics," Peltz said. "For instance, if a person hears that the boxer in one corner is 20-10 and the one in the other corner is 8-16, he will have a preconceived opinion of the two that could be unfair. The one who is 8-16 could be superior."

That opinion is shared by Goody Petronelli. "I wish I had a dime," he said, "for each boxer with a winning record who was beaten by someone with a losing record. Some of those '10-20 opponents' are tougher than some of those '20-10 contenders.' Boxing needs people like Youngs."

Carlo "Pops" Litz would not disagree. "Sam is a real crowd-pleaser," Pops declared. A former bar owner—"I had a straight place and a gay place," he said—Pops began working with Youngs in 1980 and said, "Sure, Sam could have been better."

Youngs agreed. A member of a street gang as a teenager who in an altercation once stabbed someone—but not fatally—the story he tells of himself is a familiar one. "I wanted to become someone," Youngs said. So, he began training at the Uncle Sam Boxing Club, won his pro debut, and at some point came to realize that in the dispassionate world of pro boxing there are "opponents," and that "opponents" never become champions.

         ★   ★   ★

"*. . . The winner, from Attleboro, Massachusetts . . . the future New England lightweight champion . . . Daaavid Rivelllllllo.*"

The crowd erupts in cheers when the decision is announced, and while the ring announcer adds that there will be a celebration in honor of Rivello at an Attleboro bar, Youngs crosses the ring, shakes hands with the winner and is cornered for an interview by a cable TV commentator dressed in a tuxedo. Youngs says the "decision was fair" and "Rivello is a tough kid." The tuxedo says Youngs has "nothing to be ashamed of" and Youngs is escorted by Miller and Pops to his dressing room.

Neither Youngs nor Miller are especially distraught by the decision. "We had to knock (Rivello) out," Miller says. "We knew that."

Standing off to the side, his voice angry and hoarse from shouting, Pops says, "The kid (Rivello) is a hometown hero. He had been a big football star here." Pops begins to pack some belongings in a small carrying case and looks over at Youngs.

"I told him to get a hold of that arm," Pops says. "I would have taken that (injured left) hand and torn it out of its socket."

Pops shakes his head sullenly and mutters a curse at Sam.

Young glances at Pops and says, "Watch that heart of yours, old man. Be cool."

Pops continues packing as Miller delivers the purse to Youngs. Sam counts it—$750—and then strips out of his boxing trunks. He showers, dresses in his sweat clothes, and heads for the door. Two of his cousins had attended the bout and Youngs decides to ride home with them. He curls into the back seat, and falls asleep. Home is hours away.

Why is Baseball So Much Better Than Football?

GENERAL

By *THOMAS BOSWELL*

From Washington Post Magazine
Copyright © 1987, Washington Post Co.

Some people say football's the best game in America. Others say baseball.

Some people are really dumb.

Some people say all this is just a matter of taste. Others know better.

Some people can't wait for next Sunday's Super Bowl. Others wonder why.

Pro football is a great game. Compared with hockey. After all, you've gotta do something when the wind chill is zero and your curveball won't break. But let's not be silly. Compare the games? It's a one-sided laugher. Here are the first 99 reasons why baseball is better than football. (More after lunch.)

1. Bands.

2. Halftime with bands.

3. Cheerleaders at halftime with bands.

4. Up With People singing "The Impossible Dream" during a Blue Angels flyover at halftime with bands.

5. Baseball has fans in Wrigley Field singing "Take Me Out to the Ball Game" at the seventh-inning stretch.

6. Baseball has Blue Moon, Catfish, Spaceman and The Sugar Bear. Football has Lester the Molester, Too Mean and The Assassin.

7. All XX Super Bowls haven't produced as much drama as the last World Series.

8. All XX Super Bowls haven't produced as many classic games as either pennant playoff did this year.

9. Baseball has a bullpen coach blowing bubble gum with his cap turned around backward while leaning on a fungo bat; football has a

defensive coordinator in a satin jacket with a headset and a clip-board.

10. The Redskins have 13 assistant coaches, five equipment man-agers, three trainers, two assistant GMs but, for 14 games, nobody who could kick an extra point.

11. Football players and coaches don't know how to bait a ref, much less jump up and down and scream in his face. Baseball play-ers know how to argue with umps; baseball managers even kick dirt on them. Earl Weaver steals third base and won't give it back; Tom Landry folds his arms.

12. Vince Lombardi was never ashamed that he said, "Winning isn't everything. It's the only thing."

13. Football coaches talk about character, gut checks, intensity and reckless abandon. Tommy Lasorda said, "Managing is like hold-ing a dove in your hand. Squeeze too hard and you kill it; not hard enough and it flies away."

14. Big league baseball players chew tobacco. Pro football line-men chew on each other.

15. Before a baseball game, there are two hours of batting prac-tice. Before a football game, there's a two-hour traffic jam.

16. A crowd of 30,000 in a stadium built for 55,501 has a lot more fun than a crowd of 55,501 in the same stadium.

17. No one has ever actually reached the end of the restroom line at an NFL game.

18. Nine innings means 18 chances at the hot dog line. Two halves means B.Y.O. or go hungry.

19. Pro football players have breasts. Many NFLers are so frea-kishly overdeveloped, due to steroids, that they look like circus geeks. Baseball players seem like normal fit folks. Fans should be thankful they don't have to look at NFL teams in bathing suits.

20. Eighty degrees, a cold beer and a short-sleeve shirt is better than 30 degrees, a hip flask and six layers of clothes under a lap blanket. Take your pick: suntan or frostbite.

21. Having 162 games a year is 10.125 times as good as having 16.

22. If you miss your favorite NFL team's game, you have to wait a week. In baseball, you wait a day.

23. Everything George Carlin said in his famous monologue is right on. In football you blitz, bomb, spear, shiver, march and score. In baseball, you wait for a walk, take your stretch, toe the rubber, tap your spikes, play ball and run home.

24. Marianne Moore loved Christy Mathewson. No woman of quality has ever preferred football to baseball.

25. More good baseball books appear in a single year than have been written about football in the past 50 years. The best football writers, like Dan Jenkins, have the good sense to write about some-thing else most of the time.

26. The best football announcer ever was Howard Cosell.

27. The worst baseball announcer ever was Howard Cosell.

28. All gridirons are identical; football coaches never have to meet to go over the ground rules. But the best baseball parks are unique.

29. Every outdoor park ever built primarily for baseball has been pretty. Every stadium built with pro football in mind has been ugly (except Arrowhead).

30. The coin flip at the beginning of football games is idiotic. Home teams should always kick off and pick a goal to defend. In baseball, the visitor bats first (courtesy), while the host bats last (for drama). The football visitor should get the first chance to score, while the home team should have the dramatic advantage of receiving the second-half kickoff.

31. Baseball is harder. In the last 25 years, only one player, Vince Coleman, has been cut from the NFL and then become a success in the majors. From Tom Brown in 1963 (Senators to Packers) to Jay Schroeder (Jays to Redskins), baseball flops have become NFL standouts.

32. Face masks. Right away we've got a clue something might be wrong. A guy can go 80 mph on a Harley without a helmet, much less a face mask.

33. Faces are better than helmets. Think of all the players in the NFL (excluding Redskins) whom you'd recognize on the street. Now eliminate the quarterbacks. Not many left, are there? Now think of all the baseball players whose faces you know, just from the last Series.

34. The NFL has—how can we say this?—a few borderline godfathers. Baseball has almost no mobsters or suspicious types among its owners. Pete Rozelle isn't as picky as Bowie Kuhn, who for 15 years considered "integrity of the game" to be one of his key functions and who gave the cold shoulder to the shady money guys.

35. Football has Tank and Mean Joe. Baseball has The Human Rain Delay and Charlie Hustle.

36. In football, it's team first, individual second—if at all. A Rich Milot and a Curtis Jordan can play 10 years—but when would we ever have time to study them alone for just one game? Could we mimic their gestures, their tics, their habits? A baseball player is an individual first, then part of a team second. You can study him at length and at leisure in the batter's box or on the mound. On defense, when the batted ball seeks him, so do our eyes.

37. Baseball statistics open a world to us. Football statistics are virtually useless or, worse, misleading. For instance, the NFL quarterback-ranking system is a joke. Nobody understands it or can justify it. The old average-game-per-attempt rankings were just as good.

38. What kind of dim-bulb sport would rank pass receivers by number of catches instead of by number of yards? Only in football would a runner with 1,100 yards on 300 carries be rated ahead of a back with 1,000 yards on 200 carries. Does baseball give its silver bat

to the player with the most hits or with the highest average?

39. If you use NFL team statistics as a betting tool, you go broke. Only wins and losses, points and points against and turnovers are worth a damn.

40. Baseball has one designated hitter. In football, everybody is a designated something. No one plays the whole game anymore. Football worships the specialists. Baseball worships the generalists.

41. The tense closing seconds of crucial baseball games are decided by distinctive relief pitchers like Bruce Sutter, Rollie Fingers or Goose Gossage. Vital NFL games are decided by helmeted gentlemen who come on for 10 seconds, kick sideways, spend the rest of the game keeping their precious foot warm on the sidelines and aren't aware of the subtleties of the game. Half of them, in Alex Karras' words, run off the field chirping, "I kick a touchdown."

42. Football gave us The Hammer. Baseball gave us The Fudge Hammer.

43. How can you respect a game that uses only the point after touchdown and completely ignores the option of a two-point conversion, which would make the end of football games much more exciting.

44. Wild cards. If baseball can stick with four divisional champs out of 26 teams, why does the NFL need to invite 10 of its 28 to the prom? Could it be that football isn't terribly interesting unless your team can still "win it all"?

45. The entire NFL playoff system is a fraud. Go on, explain with a straight face why the Chiefs (10-6) were in the playoffs but the Seahawks (10-6) were not. There is no real reason. Seattle was simply left out *for convenience.* When baseball tried the comparably bogus split-season fiasco with half-season champions in 1981, fans almost rioted.

46. Parity scheduling. How can the NFL defend the fairness of deliberately giving easier schedules to weaker teams and harder schedules to better teams? Just to generate artificially improved competition? When a weak team with a patsy schedule goes 10-6, while a strong defending division champ misses the playoffs at 9-7, nobody says boo. Baseball would have open revolt at such a nausatingly cynical system.

47. Baseball has no penalty for pass interference. (This in itself is almost enough to declare baseball the better game.) In football, offsides is five yards, holding is 10 yards, a personal foul is 15 yards. But interference: maybe 50 yards.

48. Nobody on earth really knows what pass interference is. Part judgment, part acting, mostly accident.

49. Baseball has no penalties at all. A home run is a home run. You cheer. In football, on a score, you look for flags. If there's one, who's it on? When can we cheer? Football acts can all be repealed. Baseball acts stand forever.

50. Instant replays. Just when we thought there couldn't be any-

thing worse than penalties, we get instant replays of penalties. Talk about a bad joke. Now *any* play, even one with no flags, can be called back. Even a flag itself can, after five minutes of boring delay, be nullified. NFL time has entered the Twilight Zone. Nothing is real; everything is hypothetical.

51. Football has Hacksaw. Baseball has Steady Eddie and The Candy Man.

52. The NFL's style of play has been stagnant for decades, predictable. Turn on any NFL game and that's just what it could be— any NFL game. Teams seem interchangeable. Even the wishbone is too radical. Baseball teams' styles are often determined by their personnel and even their parks.

53. Football fans tailgate before the big game. No baseball fan would have a picnic in a parking lot.

54. At a football game, you almost never leave saying, "I never saw a play like that before." At a baseball game, there's almost always some new wrinkle.

55. Beneath the NFL's infinite sameness lies infinite variety. But we aren't privy to it. So what if football is totally explicable and fascinating to Dan Marino as he tries to decide whether to audible to a quick trap? From the stands, we don't know one-thousandth of what's required to grasp a pro football game. If an NFL coach has to say, "I won't know until I see the films," then how out-in-the-cold does that leave the fan?

56. While football is the most closed of games, baseball is the most open. A fan with a scorecard, a modest knowledge of the teams and a knack for paying attention has all he needs to watch a game with sophistication.

57. NFL refs are weekend warriors, pulled from other jobs to moonlight; as a group, they're barely competent. That's really why the NFL turned to instant replays. Now, old fogies upstairs can't even get the make-over calls right. Baseball umps work 10 years in the minors and know what they are doing. Replays show how good they are. If Don Denkinger screws up in a split second of Series tension, it's instant lore.

58. Too many of the best NFL teams represent unpalatable values. The Bears are head-thumping braggarts. The Raiders have long been scofflaw pirates. The Cowboys glorify the heartless corporate approach to football.

59. Football has the Refrigerator. Baseball has Puff the Magic Dragon, The Wizard of Oz, Tom Terrific, Big Doggy, Kitty Kaat and Oil Can.

60. Football is impossible to watch. Admit it: The human head is at least two eyes shy for watching the forward pass. Do you watch the five eligible receivers? Or the quarterback and the pass rush? If you keep your eye on the ball, you never know who got open or how. If you watch the receivers . . . well, nobody watches the receivers. On TV, you don't even know how many receivers have gone out for a

pass.

61. The NFL keeps changing the most basic rules. Most blocking now would have been illegal use of the hands in Jim Parker's time. How do we compare eras when the sport never stays the same? Pretty soon, intentional grounding will be legalized to protect quarterbacks.

62. In the NFL, you can't tell the players without an Intensive Care Unit report. Players get broken apart so fast we have no time to build up allegiances to stars. Three-quarters of the NFL's starting quarterbacks are in their first four years in the league. Is it because the new breed is better? Or because the old breed is already lame? A top baseball player lasts 15 to 20 years. We know him like an old friend.

63. The baseball Hall of Fame is in Cooperstown, N.Y., beside James Fenimore Cooper's Lake Glimmerglass; the football Hall of Fame is in Canton, Ohio, beside the freeway.

64. Baseball means Spring's Here. Football means Winter's Coming.

65. Best book for a lifetime on a desert island: *The Baseball Encyclopedia.*

66. Baseball's record on race relations is poor. But football's is much worse. Is it possible that the NFL still has NEVER had a black head coach? And why is a black quarterback still as rare as a bilingual woodpecker?

67. Baseball has a drug problem comparable to society's. Pro football has a range of substance-abuse problems comparable only to itself. And, perhaps, The Hells Angels'.

68. Baseball enriches language and imagination at almost every point of contact. As John Lardner put it, "Babe Herman did not triple into a triple play, but he did double into a double play, which is the next best thing."

69. Who's on first?

70. Without baseball, there'd have been no Fenway Park. Without football, there'd have been no artificial turf.

71. A typical baseball game has nine runs, more than 250 pitches and about 80 completed plays—hits, walks, outs—in 2½ hours. A typical football game has about five touchdowns, a couple of field goals and fewer than 150 plays spread over three hours. Of those plays, perhaps 20 or 25 result in a gain or loss of more than 10 yards. Baseball has more scoring plays, more serious scoring threats and more meaningful action plays.

72. Baseball has no clock. Yes, you were waiting for that. The comeback, from three or more scores behind, is far more common in baseball than football.

73. The majority of players on a football field in any game are lost and unaccountable in the middle of pileups. Confusion hides a multitude of sins. Every baseball player's performance and contribution are measured and recorded in every game.

74. Some San Francisco linemen now wear dark plexiglass visors inside their face masks—even at night. "And in the third round, out of Empire U., the 49ers would like to pick Darth Vader."

75. Someday, just once, could we have a punt without a penalty?

76. End-zone spikes. Sack dances. Or, in Dexter Manley's case, "holding flag" dances.

77. Unbelievably stupid rules. For example, if the two-minute warning passes, any play that begins even a split second thereafter is nullified. Even, as happened in this season's Washington-San Francisco game, when it's the decisive play of the entire game. And even when, as also happened in that game, not one of the 22 players on the field is aware that the two-minute mark has passed. The Skins stopped the 49ers on fourth down to save that game. They exulted; the 49ers started off the field. Then the refs said, "Play the down over." Absolutely unbelievable.

78. In baseball, fans catch foul balls. In football, they raise a net so you can't even catch an extra point.

79. Nothing in baseball is as boring as the four hours of ABC's "Monday Night Football."

80. Blowhard coach Buddy Ryan, who gave himself a grade A+ for his handling of the Eagles. "I didn't make any mistakes" he explained. His 5-10-1 team was 7-9 the year before he came.

81. Football players, somewhere back in their phylogenic development, learned how to talk like football coaches. ("Our goals this week were to contain Dickerson and control the line of scrimmage.") Baseball players say things like, "This pitcher's so bad that when he comes in, the grounds crew drags the warning track."

82. Football coaches walk across the field after the game and pretend to congratulate the opposing coach. Baseball managers head right for the beer.

83. The best ever in each sport—Babe Ruth and Jim Brown—each represents egocentric excess. But Ruth never threw a woman out a window.

84. Quarterbacks have to ask the crowd to quiet down. Pitchers never do.

85. Baseball nicknames go on forever—because we feel we know so many players intimately. Football monikers run out fast. We just don't know that many of them as people.

86. Baseball measures a gift for dailiness.

87. Football has two weeks of hype before the Super Bowl. Baseball takes about two days off before the World Series.

88. Football, because of its self-importance, minimizes a sense of humor. Baseball cultivates one. Knowing you'll lose at least 60 games every season makes self-deprecation a survival tool. As Casey Stengel said to his barber, "Don't cut my throat. I may want to do that myself later."

89. Football is played best full of adrenaline and anger. Moderation seldom finds a place. Almost every act of baseball is a blending

of effort and control; too much of either is fatal.

90. Football's real problem is not that it glorifies violence, though it does, but that it offers no successful alternative to violence. In baseball, there is a choice of methods: the change-up or the knuckleball, the bunt or the hit-and-run.

91. Baseball is vastly better in person than on TV. Only when you're in the ballpark can the eye grasp and interconnect the game's great distances. Will the wind blow that long fly just over the fence? Will the relay throw nail the runner trying to score from second on a double in the alley? Who's warming up in the bullpen? Where is the defense shading this hitter? Did the base stealer get a good jump? The eye flicks back and forth and captures everything that is necessary. As for replays, most parks have them. Football is better on TV. At least, you don't need binoculars. And you've got your replays.

92. Turning the car radio dial on a summer night.

93. George Steinbrenner learned his baseball methods as a football coach.

94. You'll never see a woman in a fur coat at a baseball game.

95. You'll never see a man in a fur coat at a baseball game.

96. A six-month pennant race. Football has nothing like it.

97. In football, nobody says, "Let's play two!"

98. When a baseball player gets knocked out, he goes to the showers. When a football player gets knocked out, he goes to get X-rayed.

99. Most of all, baseball is better than football because spring training is less than a month away.

Greg Monroe

COLLEGE BASKETBALL

By *MITCH ALBOM*

From the Detroit Free Press
Copyright © 1987, the Detroit Free Press

It doesn't matter, all the money and the music and the new clothes and the computers. College is still about kids making their parents proud. It always has been.

The last time Greg Monroe's father came to see him play basketball, Greg was a freshman in high school. It was the first game he would get to start, and Greg recalls his father's only advice: "Do what you gotta do."

That was it. One game. In the games that followed, in the years that followed, through the high school championships and county all-stars and freshman and sophomore and junior years at Syracuse University, all those nights, all those tournaments, Greg Monroe never played before his father again, never saw him waiting in the tunnel after the gym had emptied.

Instead, he "did what he had to do." When the games were over, he visited the hospital, where Walter Monroe would spend the better part of seven years. A stroke put him there. Another stroke robbed him of his speech. Then cancer struck, brain cancer, and yet he somehow survived, he lived for years in that bed, and his son grew up and brought him newspaper clippings and videotapes of his blossoming basketball career.

"We communicated a lot through eye contact," Greg Monroe said. "Every now and then he'd try to mumble a few words. Usually he just smiled, and I guess the smile was telling me, 'Don't worry about it, keep your head up, don't let this situation bother you.'

"That's the kind of guy he was. Very strong."

And then, last summer, Walter Monroe died.

On Saturday afternoon, Greg Monroe was introduced to a thunderous roar inside the sold-out Superdome. The Syracuse Orangemen were in the semifinals of the NCAA tournament, one game from the championship finale. Monroe, a stocky player with sleepy eyes, is their starting guard and team co-captain.

The game began and Monroe got the Orangemen's first shot. He went up calmly from the right of the key and buried a three-pointer. And in the stands behind the Syracuse bench, his mother, Mary Monroe, quietly applauded. To almost everyone else watching, he was another college ball player on another magic carpet ride to glory. "Lucky kid," they would mumble, eyeing the screaming fans and the national attention.

Mary Monroe knew better. She knew of the daily hospital visits, of the agonizing silence, of the slow ooze of life that those things bring about. Her son had dedicated this season to her and her late husband. And so well had he played, that his teammates dubbed him "Money" —as in "Money in the bank."

And Saturday, Money delivered. He hit several key three-point baskets; he shut down Providence's Billy Donovan, the man deemed most dangerous in this contest; and then, with under 12 minutes remaining and Syracuse mired in a sudden slump, Money stole the ball from Providence's Delray Brooks, ducked his head and drove the length of the court, dishing off for a basket and getting fouled in the process. The play was worth three points and that, more than any single occurrence, turned the tide back in Syracuse's favor.

The Orangemen would win, 77-63. They are going to the NCAA final, the top of the mountain. And as the last seconds ticked away, it was Monroe dribbling past defenders, his shirt dangling out of his shorts. Do what you gotta do. He had scored 17 points. The TV announcers named him player of the game.

The buzzer sounded and as his teammates leaped up and down, he walked off the court quietly. One more to go for his team. One more for his personal quest.

When the game was over, there was no father to congratulate Greg Monroe, but his mother was there, and she kissed him. And when this is all over, whatever happens Monday night, Monroe plans to go to the Rochester, N.Y., cemetery where his dad is buried. He'll go alone. No crowds, no cameras.

"I'll just have a quiet moment there with him," he said. "It'll be the end of my college career and I'm sure he'd be very pleased to know that I graduated on time, that we had a chance to go to the Final Four, that me and my Mom are coping as best we can."

So it really doesn't matter, all the hype and the attention and even the final score. College is still college. It is largely about one thing. "I just hope my father's proud of me," Greg Monroe said before leaving, and somewhere, no doubt, he is.

Boules Fever

GENERAL

By *PHIL HERSH*

From Chicago Tribune Magazine
Copyright © 1987, Chicago Tribune

By early June, the cherry harvest in northern Provence is well underway. Cherries and the migrant workers who pick them seem to hang from every tree. Open-backed Citroen trucks laden with overflowing crates of cherries crisscross the region. Every grocery, large and small, has baskets filled with cherries *du pays*—from the region —that vary in size, roundness and color according to their exposure to the sun. In this part of southeastern France, they are the first sweet taste of summer.

It is at this time that Caromb, a town of 2,800 in the foothills of Mont Ventoux, has its annual two-day cherry festival. Strange to say, but nowhere in Caromb is there any evidence of the fruit whose rich abundance is being celebrated. Festival posters advertise a grand ball, a parade of antique cars and other attractions typical of a country fair. The main street of the town is lined with carnival games of chance, a merry-go-round and booths selling pizza, brochettes, ice creams and sweets made from just about everything but cherries.

There is, instead, another Provencal specialty evident in such profusion that it appears to be the object of everyone's attention in Caromb. It is *la boule*, the metal ball used in the game of *boules*. Made of iron, steel and occasionally bronze, the balls are 3 to 4 inches in diameter and weigh from 1½ to almost 3 pounds (in tournament play the size and weight of the balls are determined by the official rules of a French national federation). That this product is not grown but manufactured, not gathered but thrown out on a playing field does not make it any less a sign of summer in Provence. Nothing is more part of the nature of Provence, nothing a better way to celebrate the climate with which the Provencal has been blessed than playing boules.

"Boules was born in this region because of our sun," says Robert Vachet, a retired schoolteacher who is a former French champion in the sport and president of the prominent boules club in nearby Carpentras. "The Provencal is a person who likes to talk, who likes to have friends, who likes to live outside. Boules allows him to do all three."

The games played with the balls—either by one individual against another or by two opposing teams from two to four players each—are part of the bowling family and quite similar to the Italian *bocce* and the Anglo-American lawn bowling. They are generally known as "*boules*" but include variations like *sport-boules* (or *la lyonnaise*), *petanque* and *jeu provencal*. To watch a game of boules on a bright afternoon or warm evening, paying particular attention to the players and not the outcome, is to feel some of the rhythms in a land that nourishes ancient customs as well as annual harvests.

If Provence is "the empire of the sun," as native poet Frederic Mistral called it, the game of boules could be seen as the imperial amusement—if it weren't such a favorite of both commoner and elite alike.

In petanque, the version played most widely, the game is played almost anywhere but ideally on a field roughly 20 feet wide by 30 feet long. The player or team that wins the right to start the game, by mutual agreement or a coin toss, does so by rolling the target ball or mark—a wooden ball about an inch and a half in diameter called a *but* or *cochonnet*—between 19 and 32 feet from the players. Each player has two balls (or as many as four if playing one-on-one), and the object is to throw these balls—with an underhand motion but with the palm facing down—as close as possible to the cochonnet. Hitting the cochonnet and knocking the balls already thrown either away from or closer to it are allowed. These moves, in fact, are part of the game strategy, and teams include two kinds of specialists: those skilled in getting balls close to the cochonnet and those at knocking opponents' balls away from it.

Points are counted after all the balls have been thrown, each ball closer to the cochonnet than the next closest of the opposing side getting the point. The side that's ahead then starts the next round by rolling the cochonnet toward the other end of the field. The first side to score 11 points wins a game. Because only one point may be scored in each round, a full game is often lengthy, and three-game matches, in which 13 points are needed to win the deciding game, even more so.

All-day festivals, like the one in Caromb, are the perfect venue for boules. Three of the eight listings on Caromb's two-day calendar of events are boules tournaments. The click-click of the metal balls is everywhere, as if every male in town were auditioning to play Captain Queeg in "The Caine Mutiny." Most of the tournament matches take place below the town's main square, on the dusty, sloping ground surrounding Caromb's 15th century church.

Between games, the players head for the Cafe La Mirande, where the scores are tallied and the good spirits maintained with beer or preferably, *pastis*, a drink made by mixing the yellow licorice-flavored aperitif of the same name with water. All the country's major boules tournaments are sponsored by manufacturers of pastis, among them Ricard and Pernod. Many boules clubs, like Vachet's Societe de L'Industrie, are headquartered in a bar.

"In the past," Vachet explains, "boules and Provence were the same thing. Now it goes beyond the borders, even of France. The game has always been a mixture of French and Provencal customs, like pastis and water. But it should always have more pastis than water."

Outside the Cafe La Mirande, the smell of roses and oregano mingle. In the distance, on the higher slopes of the 6,000-foot Mont Ventoux, the lavender is in full bloom, giving the mountain a robe of pale purple. It is an unusually cool June day, the mid-afternoon temperature in the high 70s, but the sun is shining brightly. Later in the summer the players and spectators will seek the comfort of the shady trees and cool pastis to make it through the games that are played on tongue-dragging days.

The Provencal indeed lives out of doors. But he is no fool nor mad dog nor Englishman. His customs, his literature, even his games are based on both *enjoying* and coping with the climate.

Explaining the differences between literature in the north and the south of France, the early 19th century writer, critic and theorist Madame de Stael wrote, "The poets of the south never cease to blend the image of coolness, of leafy woods, of limpid brooks with all the feelings of life . . . to blend the idea of a friendly shadow which must preserve them from the burning intensity of the land."

To a visitor, a boules tournament does not seem to generate much heated competition. The major impression a spectator has is of groups of people mainly standing around, gesturing, talking and drinking. And that, of course, is exactly what the players are doing. These are the Provencal passions, and these are games of boules a la Provencal.

★　　★　　★

Vaucluse, one of the six departments, or administrative regions, of Provence, has the highest annual average temperature in France. In summer, when the temperature is rarely below 85 degrees, the sun takes on a special intensity in the cloudless skies. Mont Ventoux, called "the giant of the Vaucluse" because it looms over the entire area, shimmers in waves of dry summer heat, its rocky outline blurred by the haze.

Such a climate attracts thousands of sun-starved Parisians and northern Europeans to the area every year. There is plenty of room for them in the sparsely settled Vaucluse, an area slightly larger than Rhode Island but with a population of only 340,000, compared to nearly 1 million in Rhode Island. The people are spread thinly across its valleys, its round-topped hills, its high plateaus and mountain ranges.

Many of its villages retain a sense of splendid isolation, despite modern communications and highways. A bowler from one town is unlikely to know the name of a frequent rival from a few miles away. Marcel Buou, president of the boules club in the Vaucluse village of Venasque, says there are few links between *boulistes* in neighboring towns, which he refers to as *"autres pays"*—other countries.

Boules games—particularly the petanque version, which originated at the turn of the century in the Provencal seaside town of La Ciotat—blend perfectly with village life throughout the region. In the Vaucluse are 150 boules clubs, 10,000 registered bowlers and perhaps another 30,000 who play without formal team or club affiliations. One is likely to find a set of boules in the garage of almost every house. Boules is widely popular because of its simplicity, its minimal expense and its even more minimal physical demands.

"You always carry your boules in the car," Buou says. "After a meal, there is always time for a match."

A wide map pocket or the console near the gear shift in the car of a Provencal is likely to be filled with several boules, ready to be used in an impromptu match. People from all over Europe bring a set of boules when they vacation in Provence.

"No matter where you go—the country, the mountains, the seashore—you play boules," Vachet says.

A set of three boules costs between $25 and $50, and most serious boulistes own two sets. Boules oxidize, and sometimes they break, but they often outlast the buyer, which seems appropriate for a lifetime pursuit.

"Here it is the same thing as fishing or hunting," says Bernard Zelez, a candymaker in Carpentras. "There are a lot of retirees in the boules environment."

"The game constitutes a social program," says Vachet, 57. "It prevents the older people from curling up and dying."

Age is hardly a barrier against rolling a ball that weighs under three pounds. Neither is the lack of vigorous physical conditioning; Zelez played a minor tournament on the campground outside Carpentras with a broken collarbone in a sling. This is a game in which it seems almost *de rigueur* to play with a cigarette dangling nonchalantly from one's lips. Some players use a magnet on a string to pick up their boules, meaning they never have to stoop to conquer.

Whether boules is a game or a sport is a question that has long been argued, in the manner of similar debates about golf, bowling and horseshoes. Coming down on the side of sport in his book "C'est ca, la Petanque," Andre Desplais recalled "losing 466 grams (slightly more than a pound) and having his calves so overtired" from standing through a lengthy tournament that he couldn't sleep all night. Tournaments can drag on from midday to midnight, but players are allowed to sit between matches and take frequent refreshment breaks.

A French bouliste can play in regional, national and international championships. A few players are good enough to become near professionals at the sport. At most tournaments, however, the rewards are merely social.

"No one is unbeatable," says Buou, who is also the postmaster in Venasque, a village of 526 inhabitants some eight miles east of Carpentras. "I could reasonably compete with the champion of France. That would be impossible in tennis, which I also play."

Boules, according to Vachet, cuts across class distinctions, even if it seems to attract few members of the BCBG, or the *bon chic, bon genre* crowd, the French version of preppies. The best evidence of the sport's egalitarianism is linguistic. French has both a familiar and formal form of the pronoun "you"; the familiar *tu* is normally used only when addressing family members, close friends and children.

"In a boules match, you say *tu* to each other immediately," Vachet says.

Friendship is easy to maintain in most boules tournaments because the prizes are hardly worth fighting over. The first-place award for the Carpentras tournament in which Zelez played—$12 for a three-man team—would have barely covered the price of a couple of drinks and a snack. One of the food trucks that pulled up to the campground offered sausage sandwiches for $1.75 and $2 each and brochettes for $2. Another truck had five varieties of pizza at $4 to $5 for an entire pie or $1 a slice. A bar sold beer and wine for 60 cents, pastis for 70 cents and soft drinks for $1.

This tournament was both typical and unusual for Provence. It was, like most, small in reward and scope—100 teams were entered, including several female teams in a sport that has admitted women only in the past decade. That it was being played outside town, on a field next to the stables for the Carpentras race track that is used one week a year, was a sign of the changing times in the region.

Not long ago boules had such an upper hand in Provence that the streetcars in Marseille would stop for games that were being played on both sides of the tracks. That was before Marseille became a city of a million people and seemingly twice as many cars.

"Cars have been killing boules," Vachet says. "All the little squares are being used for parking."

         ★   ★   ★

The automobile has certainly been responsible for the near death of jeu provencal, which demands a playing field at least 82 feet long. That is more than twice as long as the regulation area for petanque, which can be played informally in the nooks and crannies that pass for open spaces in Provence, especially in the many picturesque villages that cling to the edges of cliffs. Furthermore, it is next to impossible to play boules on paved surfaces because on them the balls roll too far and too fast.

"In some cities, keeping areas for boules is a political issue," Vachet says. "It is good for our area to have games going on so that the tourists can see the traditional life of Provence."

In Carpentras, a city of 25,000, the grace of God is literally responsible for keeping Place Marotte, the square across from the Bar de L'Industrie, unpaved. The Carmelite convent that owns the square has decided to let it remain a haven for boulistes, who can be seen playing there every afternoon. The brothers Tournyaire, Rene and Jacques, alternate playing days so that one of them can play while the other runs the newsstand they own. That arrangement has worked so well for the brothers that when they got together as a team for last year's regional tournament, they won the championship.

The pressure to create more parking spaces, combined with the apparent desire to play boules year-round, led to the opening recently of an indoor bouladrome in Carpentras. But the venture was short-lived. The locals found it absurd to pay for what they had always done for free, and they never really thought the game was meant to be played in the winter, at least not in the south.

"In a bouladrome, the game loses its folklore side and becomes a business," Buou says.

It is precisely the game's lack of presumption and accouterments that makes it such a natural part of the life in Provence. On any summer Sunday one can stumble across a game in the most unlikely place, like the parking area and picnic ground outside the pilgrimage church of St. Gens, a local saint of the Vaucluse. In grass so high the cochonnet disappears from view and even the boules are barely visible and on a slope so steep the long grass was needed to slow the balls, a group of elderly men dressed in their Sunday best are ending their picnic with a game. Such a scene assuages any misgivings that boules is being turned into an artificial tourist attraction, like a sound-and-light show.

During the cherry harvest, there are no marriages, no baptisms and no official boules matches in Venasque because the town is so small nearly everyone is occupied with the cherry-picking. On a June Sunday, only children can be seen playing on the spot where the local club, La Boule Sarrazine, holds its weekly tournaments.

Skill in the game is passed from one generation to another, even though they rarely play together. When Buou plays in Venasque, on a field next to the 10th century walls built to repel the Saracens, his 3-year-old grandson immediately tries to pick up a boule and throw it. "I've already given the boules virus to my daughter," Buou says. Some boules clubs have gone so far as to hire instructors to teach the game to youngsters, but most let it develop according to a well-established rhythm.

"Boys start playing in school and keep playing until they are about 16 or 17," Buou says. "Then there is a short break, during which the passion for the mating game becomes stronger. At about 22 or 23, they get married—and start playing again."

That pattern is being changed as equality between the sexes comes even to Provence. There are now mixed teams—two men and a woman—and husbands can be seen playing pick-up games with their wives.

"It's not right for only the men to have ways to amuse themselves," Vachet says. "The women began by watching, and now it is almost a mixed sport. Where there is a tournament for men, there is almost always a parallel tournament for women."

In July and August, when nearly all French take their vacations, a bouliste based in Carpentras can play one tournament a day in areas within a 30-mile radius of the town. Visitors with their own boules are welcome in major and minor tournaments, for which entry fees usually run between $2 and $10. One need not be a licensed club member to compete. In some tournaments entries are by teams; in others teams are formed by lot—*a la melee*—from individual entrants. Spectators are also welcome—even expected and encouraged. The season's major Provencal tournament, Ricard La Marseillaise, held each July in Marseille, draws thousands, Buou among them.

"You may think it's odd to go to watch a game like this, but every bouliste likes to," Buou says. "As we watch, we play the game along with the others."

Most boulistes will not mind being photographed as they play, although it is both wise and polite to ask for their permission, unless one is far enough away to preclude any disturbance of the players' concentration.

*   *   *

To find out about boules in the Vaucluse, one need only read Rene Recolin's twice-weekly column, which he writes under the *nom de plume* Ratamiaou, in the newspaper *Le Provencal*. The column, titled "De La Rafle a L'Estanque," lists upcoming events on Fridays and gives results on Wednesdays. Recolin has also become something of a cultural historian by recording the legendary anecdotes and *bon mots* that attract spectators to boules tournaments.

In the most picturesque—and slightly risque—tradition, a losing team that is shut out has to *"faire Fanny,"* which can almost be understood without translation: to kiss the backside of a legendary lady of the evening. Legend holds that the custom began when a boules club in Lyon, north of Provence, recruited the lady to cooperate in dishonoring the loser. For reasons of both propriety and hygiene, the kiss later came to be delivered upon an image—painted, sculpted or molded in metal or clay—of the notorious lady.

"One can say that boules is less dangerous than Formula 1 automobile racing," wrote the author of a book on the cult of Fanny. "One can really say that. But a total defeat in boules is more humiliating. Because death doesn't follow. Just humiliation. . . . That is why I no longer play boules. I'll watch the others come face-to-face with their fate and risk their honor."

In a recent column Recolin showed his empathy for such unfortunate losers. "There were several 'Fannys' over the weekend," he wrote, "but as it is early in the season, they can go unmentioned."

"For the Provencal, an essential part of the game is the human side—the exchanges, the ripostes," Vachet says.

Unfortunately, much of the repartee is lost in translation, even for a Frenchman visiting from elsewhere. Many local players speak the native dialect, Provencal, which closely resembles the Latin from which it was derived. Provencal, the language of the medieval troubadors, has been making a comeback after nearly disappearing because of an edict in 1539 that mandated the speaking of French in the south.

What even the unsophisticated spectator can understand is the body English of the bouliste. Some players crouch to throw the ball with a backhand flip. Others throw with their bodies leaning in various angles. The gyrations begin in earnest when the outcome of each throw is already apparently out of the player's hand.

"Watch the bouliste closely," says a book titled "Self-Portrait of the French," "and you will read on his face all the tribulations preying on his soul. He is under the simultaneous influence of two of the most powerful motivators of the human heart: fear and hope.

"He has just thrown his last ball. As it rolls in front of him, you can follow its movement in his countenance. He broods over it, he protects it with his gaze, he advises it, he would like to see it obey his voice. He hurries it along or slows it, according to whether a mountain or a ravine stops its passage or precipitates its descent. He encourages it with gestures: a push with the shoulder, a check with the hand. Perched on tiptoes, arm extended, face animated by a pack of different emotions, he communicates through bizarre body movements. One could say that his soul has passed into his boule."

Temper, Temper

by Jerry Lodriguss of the Philadelphia Inquirer. Football fans and union picketers were in a fighting mood outside Philadelphia Veterans Stadium before the NFL's first replacement game during the players' strike. Copyright © 1987, Jerry Lodriguss, Philadelphia Inquirer.

Agony of DeFeet

by Ernest T. Coleman of the Danville Commercial-News. Missy Weber from Ford Central High School in Piper City, Ill., has sympathy pains for her teammate, Kristy Jackson, who hurt her ankle during the Illinois state high school basketball tournament. Copyright © 1987, Ernest T. Coleman, Danville Commercial-News.

Kevin Allen:
A Life in Ruins

PRO FOOTBALL

By *PAUL DOMOWITCH*

From the Philadelphia Daily News
Copyright © 1987, Philadelphia Newspapers Inc.

"When I came out of college, I had some doubts about my potential. But now, I know I can compete. I know I can hold my own against anybody. I just have to go in with the right mental attitude. There's naturally going to be a little bit of pressure. But I've always done well under pressure. I've always excelled when my back's been to the wall."

—Kevin Allen, May 6, 1985

"We gave him every opportunity. . . . We did everything in the world to try and make a player out of Kevin Allen. We didn't have much success."

—Buddy Ryan, October 3, 1986

A man is born and a man dies. What he does with the time in between is up to him.

Not so very long ago, Kevin Allen had big hopes for his time in between. On a clear day when he still could see forever, Allen peered into the future and saw everything he ever wanted, everything he ever dreamed about, right there within his grasp. And he was determined not to let it slip through his fingers.

"I don't want to end up like a lot of guys who were broke as soon as they were done playing," Allen told the *Daily News* shortly after the Eagles made the offensive lineman from Indiana University the ninth pick in the first round of the 1985 draft. "I want to plan for the future. I want to be able to relax when I'm done playing and enjoy the things I've done."

He had plans and he had dreams, but now Kevin Allen has nothing. His future came crashing down on top of him 15 months ago, when he staggered drunkenly onto a Margate, N.J., beach and raped a 31-year-old Massachusetts woman.

Now, Allen's football career is over, most of the money he made from it is gone, and what is left of his life lies in shattered pieces inside Southern State Correctional Facility, where Allen is serving a 15-year sentence for the Labor Day 1986 attack.

Allen is trying to reverse the guilty plea he entered last February and receive a trial. Regardless of how the appeal turns out, however, one thing is certain: Allen's life never will be the same again.

"It's weird," said Allen's lawyer, Walter Lesnevich, "how five minutes on a beach can turn your life around. One minute you're a football star, the next minute you're a rapist."

That time spent on the beach put Allen in prison, but it was not the only reason his life turned around. A three-month investigation by the *Daily News* determined that Allen's life had begun to unravel long before that.

It began to unravel a year and a half earlier, around a table in a room at Veterans Stadium. It began to unravel on the fateful April day that the Eagles decided to make him their first-round pick in the 1985 draft.

"The kiss of death," Allen's agent, Peter Johnson, has said, "was the day the Eagles drafted Kevin Allen."

The Eagles went into the 1985 draft looking for a savior. What they got was a player who was not nearly as good as they thought he was, and one who ultimately would end up being crushed by the weight of his own failure.

From the moment he was drafted until the moment he was released 17 short months later, Allen's life was one calamity after another.

There was the routine drug test the day after the draft that revealed Allen had used cocaine, sources now have told the *Daily News*. There was the 35-day training camp holdout. There was the 3½-sack nightmare against the New York Giants in his NFL debut and his benching four weeks later.

There was the minicamp in Tampa at which he arrived 35 pounds overweight and the two training camp workouts that he slept through. There was the never-ending ridicule from Coach Buddy Ryan. There were the cramps and the dehydration and the eventual exile to the Eagles' non-football injury list less than a week before the attack on the beach.

And finally, almost mercifully, there was his release, just three days before his October 3 arrest.

Allen was not good enough to fulfill the Eagles' expectations. But maybe more significantly, he was not strong enough to deal with their disappointment. He was a 6-foot-5, 285-pound mountain of a man. But inside that huge body was a child, a child who was easily influenced and often incapable of making his own decisions, a child who seemed lost—and earmarked for tragedy—from the moment he arrived in Philadelphia.

"Kevin just couldn't handle the stigma of being a No. 1 pick," said Johnson, who negotiated Allen's four-year, $1.65 million contract. "The plain fact of the matter is, he shouldn't have been a No. 1 pick. He wasn't tough enough physically or emotionally."

"Kevin was, to a great extent, a victim of circumstances," said Lynn Stiles, the Eagles' director of player personnel in 1985 and now an assistant coach with the San Francisco 49ers. "He was put into one of the most difficult situations a player can possibly be put into. He was thrown into the lion's den against the No. 1 defense in pro football (the Giants) with just nine days of training camp under his belt and never recovered.

"It was ridiculous for it to have ever occurred. Then he became somewhat of a whipping boy, which didn't do a lot for his self-esteem.

"Kevin was the kind of kid who never seemed to be able to help himself. From the start, he seemed to be headed nowhere fast. Maybe if somebody had taken the time to give him a little bit of help or encouragement or direction at the end there, maybe things might've turned out different, I don't know. I guess we'll never know."

★   ★   ★

Albert Allen never will know, either. He never will know whether there was something, anything, he could have done differently that might have prevented what has happened to his son. But the father's guilt that Albert Allen now feels makes him suspect that there was.

Albert Allen grew up in the Cincinnati projects. He grew up poor and he grew up hard, but he grew up.

"When you grow up in the projects," he said, "you survive by the law of the jungle. You either get involved in a gang or run home every day. Because of my size, I didn't have to do either."

Albert Allen made it out of the projects and into a pleasant, middle-class neighborhood in the Cincinnati suburbs. He spent nearly two decades working for General Motors. And he vowed that his children never would have to grow up living by the law of the jungle. He vowed to screen them from the world's evils and unpleasantness.

But now, as his only son sits inside a New Jersey prison, Albert Allen wonders if maybe he protected his children too much.

"Sometimes, I want to blame myself for what's happened to Kevin," the father said. "I didn't want to happen to him what I had to do. He never ran the streets. He never had time to get into trouble when he was growing up.

"He was kind of naive about a lot of things; not very street-smart. He's learned a real sad lesson in life. And he's learned it the hard way."

"Kevin trusted a lot of people," said Eagles offensive lineman

Ken Reeves, Allen's closest friend on the club. "I guess, looking back, maybe too many."

Allen was a follower, not a leader. He was a three-sport star at Cincinnati's Northwest High School and a four-year starter at Indiana, and yet never once was a team captain.

"He wasn't a leader, he just wasn't a leader," said Eric Moore, who played and roomed with Allen at Indiana for four years. "He wasn't the captain of our team. He was a first-round draft choice and he wasn't the captain of the team. I bet there aren't too many first-round draft choices that weren't captains of their team.

"But that's just the way Kevin was. He was a motivator. He'd get in the huddle and say, 'Run the ball to my butt.' But he wasn't a leader."

"Kevin had a lot of ability," said George Belu, Indiana's offensive coordinator. "But you had to watch him. When you sat on him and structured everything for him, he never bucked. He would work hard. But you always had to keep after him.

"I remember something a good friend of Kevin's once told me. He said if Kevin had one flaw, it was that he always had to have somebody around to influence him, somebody to tell him what to do."

In Cincinnati, that somebody was his mother and father. At Indiana, it was Moore, a walk-on center from Bloomington, Ind., who would become Allen's best friend.

"I took care of Kevin in college," said Moore, now a middle school teacher and football coach in Columbus, Ind. "He was a simple kid. We had this old, torn-up Nova we used to drive around in. We went everywhere together. I'm like a son to his family and he's like one to mine.

"When he got drafted, he wanted me to move to Philadelphia and take care of him. That's how dependent he was on me. I feel so bad right now that I didn't do it. If I had been there, he never would've gotten involved with Scott Cartwright."

★   ★   ★

If there is one common thread in the saga of Kevin Allen's demise, it is Scott Cartwright.

Cartwright, a 25-year-old unemployed schoolteacher from Scranton, was there at the beginning and he was there at the end. He was Allen's roommate for most of the 17 months that Allen was with the Eagles. He also was Allen's companion that night on the Margate beach. Cartwright is serving a seven-year prison sentence for beating the woman's male companion, Joseph Milone, and serving as Allen's accomplice in the rape.

Allen's parents and friends blame Cartwright for not only triggering the incident on the beach, but for just about every other bit of misfortune that has befallen Allen in the last 2½ years.

"He used Kevin," Albert Allen said. "The biggest mistake Kevin ever made was getting involved with that guy."

"It was like this huge cancer hit Kevin when he met

Cartwright," Eric Moore said. "All Cartwright did from the day he met Kevin was sponge off him. He did nothing for him. All he did was introduce him to the wrong people, get him involved in riffraff stuff. Every bad situation you could get him into, he got him into."

"He was always wanting him to spend his money on something. He kept taking him down to Atlantic City. He got him to spend thousands and thousands of dollars buying these Corvettes and putting new engines in them.

"You can't blame everything on him because he didn't make Kevin do all those things. But when you've got somebody who takes you out and gets you drunk every night . . . if Kevin had a preacher for a roommate, he would've been going to church. You do as is being done."

Cartwright, a 1984 graduate of East Stroudsburg State College, met Allen shortly after the 1985 draft, while working as an intern in the Eagles' marketing department.

"His basic job was to call up and set up interviews for advertising for our program book," said Bobby Caesar, the Eagles' former marketing director. "But he wasn't getting enough leads. He was more infatuated with being around the players than he was with working. So I eventually let him go."

Cartwright, who, like Allen, declined to be interviewed by the *Daily News*, enjoyed hanging around the players, but not all of them necessarily enjoyed hanging around him. He quickly earned a reputation around the locker room as a person to avoid.

"I didn't know Scott that well," Reeves said, "but I had heard from other people that he wasn't really a guy you'd want to hang around with."

"Scott wasn't a bad guy," said linebacker Mike Reichenbach, who went to school with Cartwright at East Stroudsburg. "Everybody thinks he was a troublemaker. But Scott wasn't as much a troublemaker as he was a schemer. He was always looking for an angle on something. He was always looking to get ahead."

Cartwright worked for the Eagles for less than three months before Caesar let him go. But it was long enough to enable Cartwright to strike a friendship with Allen and eventually become his roommate.

"When Scott still was working for the club, he used to run draft picks back and forth from the airport and stuff like that," Reichenbach said. "As Kevin was coming in and out of town for workouts and stuff before he signed, Scott got to know him.

"He carted Kevin all over the place. He was like his chauffeur. That's how they started to first hang around with each other. Scott would take Kevin out to places. They got along well.

"Kevin wasn't a real outward guy, wasn't a decision maker. He used Scott as his mouthpiece, because Scott was a talker. He was one of those guys who wasn't afraid to go right up to somebody and start talking to them."

"I kept telling Kevin the guy was bad news," Eric Moore said. "And he'd just say, 'Well, move in with me and I'll get rid of him.' He was always ready to kick him out. But he'd say, 'Well, I'm waiting for him to get this job and then he's going to leave.'

"He never pushed him out the door. And just when he might be thinking about it, Cartwright would clean the house up or something and buddy up to him again."

★   ★   ★

With the exception of the Eagles, few NFL clubs regarded Allen as a first-round prospect going into the 1985 draft.

He came from a troubled college program at Indiana that went through three head coaches and lost 33 of 44 games while Allen was there. At 6-5 and 285 pounds, he looked like a first-rounder. And on occasion during his senior year, he even played like one. But not often enough to convince most of the league's player personnel people that he deserved to be the ninth pick in the draft. Or even the 49th.

"He never should have been taken that early, never," said New Orleans Saints player personnel director Bill Kuharich, who had Allen rated as only the 12th best tackle in the '85 draft class. "He was a good height-and-weight guy. But he was a very inconsistent performer his senior year. He had a problem run-blocking. As far as pass-blocking, he was good some plays, bad some plays.

"He clearly was a reach. It was an example of a player being drafted out of need more than ability."

"He was an up-and-down guy," said New England Patriots player personnel director Dick Steinberg, who had Allen rated, at best, as an early third-round pick. "He was a very inconsistent player. A classic boom-or-bust guy. He was 6-5 and 285 pounds, had a 109 IQ and could run a 5-flat (40-yard dash) on grass. He had very good athletic ability. The question was his competitiveness.

"He was the kind of player that you stay away from unless you are desperate enough to feel you have to take a chance."

Two and a half years ago, the Eagles were desperate enough to feel they had to take a chance. They were coming off three consecutive losing seasons, they had an impatient, new owner, Norman Braman, who was making playoff noises, and they had a head coach, Marion Campbell, who knew he was working without a net.

Campbell wanted an offensive tackle in the worst way. He wanted someone who could provide immediate help to an offensive line that had given up 60 sacks and been the centerpiece of the league's worst running game the year before.

The three best offensive tackles that year, in the minds of most NFL personnel people, were Bill Fralic, of Pitt; Lomas Brown, of Florida; and Ken Ruettgers, of Southern California. Fralic was expected to be claimed quickly (he was the second player selected, by Atlanta), but the Eagles went into the draft reasonably confident that either Brown or Ruettgers, or maybe even both, still would be on the board when Philadelphia would select.

But the Eagles guessed wrong. The Detroit Lions, who had the sixth pick, grabbed Brown. Then, in a move that caught the Eagles totally unaware, Green Bay traded up with Buffalo, which had the seventh pick, and took Ruettgers.

That left the Eagles hurriedly searching for a Plan B. There still were plenty of blue-chip players on the board: wide receivers Eddie Brown (Miami), Jerry Rice (Mississippi Valley State) and Al Toon (Wisconsin) still were available, and so were defensive backs Jerry Gray (Texas), Derrick Burroughs (Memphis State) and Richard Johnson (Wisconsin) and defensive end Kevin Brooks (Michigan).

But Campbell was determined to take an offensive tackle.

"The decision (to draft a tackle) had been mandated before the draft ever began," Stiles said. "After Brown and Ruettgers were taken, we could have opted for the best available athlete, or maybe even traded down.

"But there was such an overwhelming desire to fortify that position that it weighed heavily on the decision making."

The next two highest-rated tackles on the Eagles' draft list after Fralic, Brown and Ruettgers were Allen and Ohio State's Jim Lachey. Lachey was rated slightly higher, but he had been a guard for most of his college career.

Ken Iman, the Eagles' offensive line coach then, flew to Columbus, Ohio, a few weeks before the draft and watched Lachey work out. Iman's conclusion: Lachey would have difficulty making a quick transition to tackle in the NFL and probably would not be able to help the Eagles right away. (Note: Iman was incorrect. Lachey, who was drafted by the San Diego Chargers just three picks after the Eagles took Allen, made the NFL's all-rookie team as a tackle and was a Pro Bowl alternate in each of his first two seasons.)

That left Allen.

*   *   *

The Eagles flew Allen to Philadelphia on Draft Day and smiled proudly and insisted he was every bit as good as Bill Fralic or Lomas Brown or Ken Ruettgers or Jim Lachey. Marion Campbell shook Allen's hand and Norman Braman put his arm on the kid's shoulder, and as the cameras clicked, both of them predicted a long and glorious future for Allen in Philadelphia.

"He's ready to play," Campbell said on Draft Day. "I expect him to come in and make a real big mark with us this year."

But things would begin to turn sour very quickly.

The day after the draft, Allen and the rest of the Eagles' draft choices were given physical examinations. The physical included a drug test. According to two different sources, Allen's turned up traces of cocaine.

The drug test result made Allen's contract negotiations, which already were expected to be lengthy and difficult, even more lengthy and difficult. Braman, who had bought the Eagles two months earlier from Leonard Tose for $65 million, already had vowed to restore "fiscal sanity" to his club. And the knowledge that his No. 1 draft pick had used cocaine at least once made Braman only more determined to hold the line on salaries.

"That was one of the reasons (the negotiations) took so long," said one source. "After he tested positive, (the Eagles) demanded a drug clause in his contract. They also wanted to come way down on his signing bonus because of it, too. Braman didn't want to give any guaranteed money to a guy he suspected might have a drug problem."

Eagles president Harry Gamble would neither confirm nor deny that Allen had tested positive for cocaine. He said the only thing that held up the club's negotiations with Allen was money.

"The only issue we ever had a problem with was arriving on the dollar and cents figure," Gamble said. "That was the only issue in the negotiations."

Allen missed 35 days of training camp, easily the longest holdout by a rookie in club history. He did not sign until August 20, less than two weeks before the start of the season.

Nevertheless, with just a handful of practices under his belt and only faint acquaintance with the Eagles' blocking schemes, Allen opened the season as the club's starting left tackle.

His pro debut was a nightmare. The Giants' Lawrence Taylor and Leonard Marshall manhandled him. They crashed around and through him for 3½ sacks in a 21-0 Giants victory. Things did not get much better in the next three weeks, either. Finally, after Allen had given up 8½ sacks in four games, Campbell benched the shellshocked rookie. But the damage was done.

"I don't think he was ready," Reeves said. "That first game (against the Giants) really shot his confidence. It took a toll on him. Once your confidence level drops, you start questioning yourself and your ability. I think that's what happened to him."

"Two games into the season, our No. 1 and No. 2 (quarterback Randall Cunningham) draft choices were starters," said tight end John Spagnola. "That bothered me. It bothered me because I thought that '85 team was a good team. I didn't think we needed to be throwing guys out there before they were ready.

"It hurt both players. But Randall was able to overcome it. Maybe Kevin wasn't."

Allen was not used to failure. Until Campbell demoted him, the last time Allen had ridden a bench was his freshman year in high school. He had spent most of his life listening to people tell him how good he was. Now, suddenly, he was being forced to deal with the possibility that he was not good enough.

"Kevin's biggest problem was that it was very easy for him to become satisfied," Moore said. "He was a content person. He wasn't aggressive. When he lost his starting job with the Eagles, instead of being determined to win it back, he just admitted, 'I've been beat out.' "

What Allen needed was someone to rebuild his confidence, some-one to push him and keep after him and make him work the way George Belu and head coach Bill Mallory did in Allen's senior year at Indiana. What he got was Buddy Ryan.

Ryan, who replaced Campbell as the Eagles' head coach after the '85 season, was not terribly interested in the state of Allen's confidence, particularly after Allen showed up at Ryan's first offseason minicamp 35 pounds overweight.

Ryan constantly ridiculed Allen, once calling him "a big ol' fat kid who could probably play for somebody if all they want him to do is stand around and kill grass."

Rather than try to prove Ryan wrong, Allen took the barbs to heart. "The more Buddy Ryan told him he was pitiful," Moore said, "the more Kevin believed it. He began thinking he wasn't a very good football player."

                    ★   ★   ★

For one ever-so-brief moment at the beginning of training camp last year, it appeared that maybe, just maybe, the worst might be behind Kevin Allen.

Ryan stopped ridiculing him long enough to pencil him in as his starting left guard as camp opened. But the promotion was all too brief. Allen was hospitalized for cramps and dehydration his first day at West Chester and promptly demoted.

The cramps and dehydration continued throughout training camp, and the more practices Allen missed, the shorter Ryan's patience grew. The last straw came in late July, when Allen slept through a pair of workouts.

"We don't worry about Kevin Allen," Ryan said then. "You all check on him if you're interested. I don't know where he is, and I don't care."

The Eagles tried to find out the cause of Allen's cramps and dehydration. They sent him to an internist and then to a specialist at the University of Pennsylvania Hospital. But they could find nothing wrong with him.

Allen's cramping and dehydration problem dated back to his college days at Indiana. "I can remember when he was a freshman," said Bill Montgomery, the Hoosiers' longtime strength coach. "He was 296 as a freshman. We were just stretching and he started getting cramps in his stomach.

"He had a lot of trouble with that. But we just thought that it was because he wasn't a runner. He didn't like to run. He wasn't in real good cardiovascular shape."

Eric Moore thinks the problem might have been caused by anabolic steroids, which he says Allen started using in college.

"I think he might've used them to the point where they affected his water tissue level," Moore said. "All he needed to do was stay off of them for a while. But in the NFL, they've made it so if you don't take steroids, you don't make the team."

Eagles trainer Otho Davis said he suspected Allen used steroids. But Davis doubts they were behind the cramping and dehydration problem.

On August 26, just six days before the attack on the beach, the Eagles placed Allen on their non-football injury list. They also made an appointment for him to take one last series of tests on Labor Day at Columbia Presbyterian Hospital in New York City.

Those tests, like all of the other ones, were inconclusive. No one could find a medical reason for Allen's cramps. Finally, on September 30, three days before Allen and Cartwright would be charged in the Labor Day attack, the Eagles released Allen.

The Eagles insisted then, and still insist now, that Allen's release had nothing to do with his involvement in the attack, although both club and police sources confirmed that the Eagles knew Allen was a prime suspect in the attack within days after it happened.

"The way he was performing, there was no use keeping him," Ryan said.

"It was strictly a football decision," Gamble said. "There was no medical reason found for the problem he was having. The results of the (Columbia Presbyterian Hospital) test showed there was no major medical problem causing the cramps.

"We felt we did what we should have done morally, which was try to find out what the problem was. But once it was determined that it was not the result of some medical disorder, we made a decision to let him go."

The Eagles still aren't through with Allen, though. He has filed a grievance against the club with the National Football League Players Association, charging that the Eagles released him while he was suffering from a football-related injury. He is asking for his 1986 salary, which was $175,000. The grievance will be heard by an arbitrator on March 1.

★   ★   ★

Kevin Allen's football career ended before it ever began, and so, too, did his dreams. He said he wanted to plan for the future. Instead, he sits in a New Jersey prison dwelling on the past and wondering how a life that once seemed so right could have gone so very wrong.

"He has learned a real sad lesson in life," said his father. "And he has learned it the hard way."

Allen has learned it the hard way and he has learned it the expensive way. Because, in addition to everything else, Allen is broke.

Just two years after signing one of the largest contracts in Eagles history, the money is gone. He received nearly $700,000 from the Eagles before he was released. But according to several sources familiar with his financial situation, little of it is left.

"It's gone," one source said. "Where, I don't know. But it's gone. About the only thing he's got left to his name is his car (a 1986 Corvette)."

"Part of being a man is stepping up to things and knowing your responsibilities and understanding the big picture," Lynn Stiles said. "I'm sure now, in retrospect, he has a better idea of how to do that.

"He wrote me a letter recently. He said he's going to try to get his life squared away. That's the one great thing about a democracy. Yeah, he's going to have to pay for what he did. But if he can keep his perspective, he's at least going to have other opportunities to function in society."

Pete Rose, Manager

BASEBALL

By *PAUL ATTNER*

From The Sporting News
Copyright © 1987, The Sporting News

Most nights after games, while he is driving home, Pete Rose listens to one of those call-in sports programs on which some fan will ask an outrageous question about his managing and the host will make a wise-guy reply. And if Rose had a phone in his car, he'd dial it right away and straighten everyone out real fast.

"Twenty seconds," Rose said. "Give me 20 seconds, and they wouldn't even want to ask the question. That's how they would feel after hearing my answer."

Rose wants every fan of the Cincinnati Reds to understand the game. After all, doesn't he patiently explain his thinking to the media day after day? Doesn't he use his various radio shows as tactical forums, Professor Pete's Baseball School in Progress? Still, the questions persist. When he was playing, hardly anyone ever second-guessed Peter Edward Rose. Who could doubt a guy who would run over his best friend—and his best friend's mother—if they dared block the plate? But being a legend isn't enough when you become a manager. Geez, doesn't anyone know this game anymore?

"Ah, hell, he loves it," said Bob Trumpy, who is host of one of Rose's radio shows and is both a friend and sometimes critic. "He thrives on this stuff. If no one asked him why he did things he wouldn't want the job. I'm convinced of that." Rose stared at Trumpy and laughed.

"But I'm going to straighten you out about something," Rose told him, "and when I finish, you'll know exactly what was going on, and you'll agree with me. You know the situation: why I left Teddy Power in the other night at Houston."

"I thought you were crazy," Trumpy said.

Power, a reliever-turned-starter and one of Rose's pet projects, was locked in a scoreless duel with Nolan Ryan. Through seven innings, Power had allowed only one hit and thrown just 71 pitches. In the top of the eighth, the Reds had two on and no outs with Power due up. Rose let him bat, looking for the sacrifice. But Ryan threw a wild pitch, moving the runners over. Power eventually struck out. Then, leadoff hitter Tracy Jones grounded to third, the runner was tossed out at home and the rally fizzled. The Reds finally won in 10 innings, but Power didn't figure in the decision.

"Everyone wanted to know why I didn't pinch hit for Power," said Rose, who then rattled off the reasons: His bullpen was tired, Power was tossing the game of his life and had thrown so few pitches, Ryan probably would overpower a pinch-hitter and, besides, Ryan was near his pitch limit and was about to come out.

"I wanted Teddy to get that win," Rose said. "Do you know what that would have done for his confidence?"

Trumpy nodded, but he wasn't totally embracing the game according to Pete.

"You are always telling us that you play for the win on the road and a tie at home," Trumpy said. "In that situation, I figured you had to be wondering how many chances you were going to get against Ryan."

"All I know is that if Tracy hits a fly ball, we score and we win, 1-0, and Ted gets the decision," Rose said. "That's what you want to see happen."

Trumpy got off easy. The two men enjoy each other, and Rose respects him. Not so with another call-in host, who once was asked the age of Rose's wife.

"Which one?" the host replied, and everyone chuckled.

Rose was listening, and the next time he saw the broadcaster, he confronted him. "As far as I know, I only have one wife," he said. "I paid half a million dollars to get rid of the other one. So why did you say that?"

The broadcaster apologized.

"He thought it was funny," Rose said. "But why should he have fun at my expense? They don't think I am listening."

*   *   *

All his baseball life, Pete Rose has made sure no one laughed at him. So what if he wasn't blessed with the greatest natural ability? He combined guts, determination and stunning single-mindedness to make himself into one of the game's biggest stars. He went from a player no one wanted to the man who replaced Ty Cobb in the record books.

But that was Pete Rose, player. Pete Rose, manager, now that was a different story. Maybe no one exactly laughed when Rose became Cincinnati's player-manager in August of 1984, but it was difficult to take the situation seriously. The Reds were a team in trouble, with next-to-last-place results on the field and declining support in the stands. Why not bring back this native son, one of the stars of the old Big Red Machine, and let him pursue Cobb at home? It couldn't hurt attendance, nor could the team possibly do much worse even if directed by a man with no managing experience. When and if he passed Cobb's career hit total, he'd probably gracefully retire, so things could get serious again in Cincinnati.

Three years later, Rose is having the last laugh. This spring, with his playing career at last on temporary hold, Rose has turned Cincinnati into a high-flying pennant contender following two straight second-place finishes. The Reds, blessed with a combination of talented youth and solid experience, are a good team with the help of Rose, not despite him. What began as, in many eyes, a gimmick has turned into a wonderfully successful move for both the franchise and Rose.

"I look for him to set records in managing. I really do," said Tigers Manager Sparky Anderson, who managed the Big Red Machine. "Now that he's started, I wouldn't be surprised if he managed 20 to 25 years. If you know Peter, then you know he has a fire in him that doesn't stop burning."

Certainly, that fire is burning hotly this season. Rose was as surprised as anyone by Cincinnati's success in 1985, and a pathetic April eliminated any realistic championship hopes in 1986. But the Reds' fast start, coupled with the maturity of his young players, the emergence of Eric Davis as a bona fide star and a rock-solid bullpen has Rose convinced this is the year Cincinnati reclaims its role as a National League power.

"If we don't win, I'll be very disappointed," he said. "We were overachievers the last two years. This year, we should be in contention all the way."

Rose is talking while sitting in the Reds' dugout hours before the start of a game. Some habits never change. He always arrived early when he was a player; as a manager, he's usually the first one at the park. During spring training this year, to beat the rush-hour traffic in Tampa, he thought about showing up at 6:30 a.m. But he reasoned: "What good does it do to get there before the clubhouse guy?"

But some things do change. Once, there was no easier, funnier interview in baseball than Pete Rose. Walk up to him, turn on a tape recorder and let him write the story. He's still cooperative, but things are a lot more serious these days. Managing has made him more introspective and more defensive, especially with the local media. During spring training, he was so abrupt and formal after games that reporters covering the team yearned for the old days, when he made them laugh all the time.

Managing will do that to anyone's personality.

"Usually, when you take a star of (Rose's) magnitude, they don't want to be criticized or booed or anything like that, and I don't blame them," Anderson said. "They've been cheered all their lives. Why should they start taking that abuse?"

Yet Rose runs counter to the baseball cliche that says great players don't necessarily make successful managers. Bill Bergesch, the Reds' general manager, remembers talking to Mickey Mantle about becoming a manager. Mantle told him he couldn't. "How can I tell them how to do something when I don't know how I did it myself?" Mantle asked. But Rose hasn't forgotten his roots. He got to the top through hard work; nothing came easy. So when a player messes up, he can empathize, not wonder why he has been burdened with such fools.

So it follows naturally that Rose is, without question, a player's manager. There has to be a line separating the players from the boss, but Rose's is as informal as it can be. After all, until last August, when he took his last major league at-bat, he was still a player. And even now, when he is in undeclared retirement, he continues to roam the clubhouse like a player, teasing and needling his players as if he was a teammate and protecting their rights like the most zealous team captain a squad could elect.

"You can say things to Pete that you can't say to other managers," said pitcher Bill Gullickson. "He messes with me the same way he did when I played with him. You can clown with him, but you still respect him."

Dave Parker and Rose were discussing a reconstructed scoreboard at Riverfront Stadium.

"Looks like my television at home," said Rose, glancing up at the huge screen.

"It would have to be that big to get your whole head in," said Parker, not missing a beat.

No one laughed harder than Rose.

"There isn't anyone in this clubhouse who doesn't like him," said Davis, the extraordinarily gifted young player. "If there is, they are doing a good job of hiding it. Pete isn't like one of those managers who puts himself on a shelf and comes down just for games. He is one of us."

Here's another cliche Rose is violating. "You know that bull about managers who say 'I don't care if they like me as long as they respect me?' Well, that's crap. I want them to like me," Rose said. "Otherwise, it would be like living everyday with someone you hate. I don't want them to see me walk by and say, 'That lousy SOB.'"

Of course, with the type of talent Cincinnati has, it's easy to be happy. "You ever see a clubhouse unhappy that is hitting .300 as a team?" Rose asked.

But what's fascinating about Rose, the manager, is that he is so different than Rose the player. As a player, Rose was glaringly simplistic. No philosophizing, no great pronouncements. Each day was a crusade against the pitcher, against the opponent, against time. You played hard, you played to win and you came out again the next day earlier than anyone else and started all over again.

As a manager, Pete Rose is anything but simplistic. He's deeply involved with strategy, motivation, scouting reports and development, concerned about results over the long run, not the short term. He scoffs at managers who say they are thinking ahead innings at a time, but one of his coaches, Tommy Helms, says Rose "is always three or four batters ahead, always planning stuff out."

Helms, who was a teammate of Rose's in Cincinnati, says something else about Rose the manager: "The most surprising thing to me is his patience. The way he played you wouldn't expect that. But he is very, very patient as a manager."

Rose has been so patient that it also has become his greatest fault. He has stayed with veterans when it might be time for them to retire and he especially has stayed with starting pitchers when it was beyond time for them to be yanked. Although he says Anderson had the biggest influence of any of his former managers, Rose certainly never would be accused of being another Captain Hook.

"He might have managed (pitchers) with his heart before," Gullickson said. "Sometimes you need to be taken out at just the right time."

Tom Hume, a former Reds pitcher now with Philadelphia, said Rose "might've waited a batter too long to replace a pitcher sometimes because he was still wondering whether or not to do it. He knew everything else about the game already, but that was something he had to learn like any other manager."

Rose also was looking at the big picture, trying to build the confidence of his still shaky starting rotation. But this year, with John Franco as his bullpen stopper and Frank Williams, Rob Murphy and Ron Robinson also performing well in relief, starters aren't getting as much chance to bail themselves out.

Yet Rose still shows tremendous loyalty to his regulars. When he was a player, he wanted his managers to stick with him, build him up, give him a chance. What pitcher wants a manager to cave in after a bad inning or two? Or what hitter wants to be benched in the middle of a mini-slump? Rose, the manager, remembers all that.

"Pete likes to joke that he probably made more outs than anyone in history," said second baseman Ron Oester. "He remembers what it was like to be a player. That's what makes it great to play for him."

Montreal's Jay Tibbs, a former Reds pitcher, says Rose's ability to keep his word is also impressive. "Some managers say things at a time just to make you feel better," Tibbs said. "They don't mean what they say. Not Pete."

It's not hard to play for Rose. He has two rules: Be on time, and play hard. "Dave Bristol was one of my favorite managers," he said, "but he had too many rules." When Rose rejoined the Reds, the man he replaced, stern Vern Rapp, had banned beer from the plane, littered the clubhouse with slogans and rules and enforced a coat-and-tie policy while traveling. Rose's Reds get a couple of cases of beer on trips, don't need ties and know they only have to bust their rear ends to please their manager. And the slogans? They came tumbling down as soon as Rose showed up. In their place appeared a television set.

"I want it to be a fun clubhouse, where the players want to come early," Rose said. "I don't want them leaving for the park at 4:15 for a 5 o'clock deadline. It's fun to be able to watch the Kentucky Derby or Monday night football or another game. If we had cable at our park, we could be watching the Cubs all the time, scouting them."

Said Parker, the huge outfielder and one of Rose's most important team leaders: "Pete is actually lenient. But he's worked hard to make himself a better manager. He's not above second-guessing himself. I mean, you *want* to play for him."

As a manager, Rose says he is a product of every person for whom he has played and every situation he has encountered in baseball.

"I'll manage according to my material," he said. "It would be dumb to force people to do what they can't."

But it also is a strength to recognize what your players can do best and then give them the freedom to do it. In Cincinnati's case, Rose has given the Reds the freedom to become the N.L.'s most potent offensive team.

"We don't have a lot of signs, and we don't bunt very much," Davis said happily. "He doesn't take the bat out of your hand. He wants us swinging."

Didn't Rose, the player, want to be swinging? And running? The Reds, thanks to a productive farm system, have a host of young, quick players with power and speed. Rose gives five or six of his best baserunners the green light to steal on their own; he helps at other times by calling the hit-and-run when baseball strategy least dictates it. It's no accident that the Reds hustle and dirty their uniforms.

"An action manager," Parker said.

Added Helms, "He's always taking the opportunity to score a run. He's not afraid to be aggressive that way. He'll give you a chance to hit on 3-and-0."

Isn't this something: a baseball manager who isn't afraid to gamble, to go against accepted thinking.

"I'm not going to stay predictable," Rose said. "I don't worry about what the guy in the other dugout is doing."

Rose has been so refreshing as a manager that even statistical whiz Bill James hasn't been able to figure him out. In the latest edition of his "Baseball Abstract," James wrote: "The controversy over whether Rose should retire has largely obscured the fact that, as a manager, Rose is one of the most intriguing and impressive in the league. Rose's style is not easy to characterize. . . . Most managers can be classified either as tacticians or emotional leaders. None of the National League's emotional leaders, such as (Tom) Lasorda and (Chuck) Tanner, has the impact on his team's outlook that Pete does. . . . Yet, while he certainly is not an intellectual, Rose is just as much a tactician as he is an emotional leader."

Until this year, because of the debate over his playing future and the presence of mentor George Scherger in the dugout, it was never clear how much of what we were seeing with the Reds was Rose and how much was the influence of others. After all, Rose readily admits he knew nothing about managing when he took over the Reds. He relied heavily on Scherger, who also had tutored Anderson. Scherger would sit with Rose in the dugout and bounce strategy options off him. And when the Reds were on the field, he would keep track of details while Rose played first base.

"I thought of George Scherger as being the manager," said Gary Redus, a former Reds outfielder who is now with the White Sox. Redus has been the only player to have a major run-in with Rose. Frustrated over his lack of playing time, Redus said out loud what others had been thinking: Rose was taking up a spot on the roster that should go to a younger player, so wouldn't it be great if he retired? The outburst got Redus traded and flamed a controversy that still hasn't been doused completely.

Well, Scherger has retired, and his dugout spot has gone to Helms. And Rose is no longer an active player, although he also hasn't officially retired. Without question, he is making the moves now—and there is no question the Reds' hierarchy would like to see him remain an ex-player.

"The big change in Pete is that he is devoting 100 percent of his attention to managing the team," said Bergesch, who was hired after Rose returned to the Reds but has since developed a close working relationship with him. "He doesn't have George around, and now the whole thing has been forced on him. He's managing the moves now, the strategy, and he's very good at it.

"The game has grown so big that it is tough to manage a club and worry about 24 players and also worry about himself. It's too much to ask of an individual. I think he handled it extremely well, but I would like him just managing the club. As hard as he tried, he still had to devote time to his playing. Now I feel he is so much better."

Rose readily admits he is a better manager now than before, but he credits the improvement to experience—"knowing my personnel better"—and not to his reduced duties.

"If I say that not playing has helped, which I don't believe, I'd be eliminating anyone from ever having an opportunity to be player-manager," he said. "If anything, as a player-manager I was involved more. I was always into the game as a player. After a game, I could tell you what happened on every pitch. On the bench sometimes you can think too much and not just react."

When the Reds got off to a miserable start last April, Rose was on the disabled list. But somehow, his playing future and the Reds' problems became entangled, and he thought the local press "laid me out. If they wanted to blame me as a manager, fine, but not as a player. I wasn't even playing."

Near the end of the season, Rose told Cincinnati writers that he had been "a hell of a lot fairer with them than they had been to me." The writers are convinced that fall-out from the retirement controversy contributed to Rose's abruptness this spring. And he still indicates he could return, at 46, if the Reds need a pinch-hitter or offensive help.

Regardless, Rose's baseball future is set, although he says he never thought about managing as a player. Yet he indirectly prepared himself by quizzing his managers incessantly, digging into the nuances of the game. But they never told him about the emotional drain.

"It devours you 24 hours a day," he said. "When you were a player, you were directly responsible for yourself. As a manager, you are responsibile for 24 players. You have to work at it because you have to be fair and you have to communicate and you have to look at them as 24 individuals, like they are."

Managing, says Rose, is nothing more than handling people.

"I don't know any more about baseball than you or Tommy Lasorda or Whitey Herzog, maybe less. But I know a little. And I know my job is to break down the squad, determine what each guy does best, then use them in situations where each guy feels valuable and part of the team. Baseball is nothing more than situations, anyway, and using each guy at the right time. And I know there's not going to be a player who said I am not fair with them, that I didn't give them a chance."

Fairness is important to Rose. He has never understood how the Reds could have declined to sign him after the 1978 season, letting him move to Philadelphia. He never wanted to leave Cincinnati and, deep down, as the franchise declined under Dick Wagner, he hurt for the fans. He took a substantial pay cut to come back as a player-manager after using a 90-minute phone call—"I wish I had called collect"—to convince former general manager Bob Howsam that he wasn't considering managing just to continue his pursuit of Cobb's record.

"You play for a guy for 11 years (as he had for Howsam), and he still doesn't know you," Rose grumbles even now. "The sacrifices I made as a player to help us win—that wasn't going to change. But he was convinced I was going to keep my name in the lineup no matter what. I wanted to come back and make them winners again and get people into the stands."

Reuven Katz, Rose's agent, originally suggested the dual role to the reluctant Howsam, who wanted Rose to stop playing. But hasn't the decision turned out splendidly? Rose was nearing the end of his playing career at Montreal; the move to Cincinnati gave him a chance to pass Cobb. The Reds were floundering when they signed Rose; their attendance benefited from his pursuit of Cobb's record, and now their reputation as an elite team has been revitalized. In the process, Rose became the first manager to make $1 million (in 1986), and he still remains the game's highest-paid leader at $800,000. No wonder everyone is smiling at Riverfront Stadium.

There's one more thing, however. "They say that managers take a job to get fired," Rose said defiantly. "Well, I didn't take this job to get fired. I'll walk away first."

Better talk to Sparky first.

"Pete showed me his Tums the other day," Anderson said, "and I said that was nothing. I've graduated into Gelusil."

Rose laughed. "Well," he said. "I take that before I go to bed."

After he listens to the call-in shows.

The Long Night of John Avila

HIGH SCHOOL FOOTBALL

By *BILL BRUBAKER*

From the Washington Post
Copyright © 1987, Washington Post Co.

Nothing seemed terribly wrong on the evening of September 11 when John Avila staggered off a high school football field in Alexandria, complaining of dizziness. It had been a warm and humid evening, after all. It was the third quarter of a fiercely contested game between J.E.B. Stuart and Thomas Edison. It was the first time Avila had gone "both ways" on the Stuart varsity, and he had participated in every offensive and defensive play. So when Avila wobbled to the team bench, John Dwyer, the Stuart trainer, was not alarmed. "I thought maybe John had just gotten his bell rung," Dwyer recalled.

In the moments that followed, the reality of Avila's condition became frighteningly evident. Far from having his "bell rung"—being disoriented after a blow to the head—Avila was losing consciousness. Dwyer waved an ammonia capsule under his nose. There was no reaction. He shone a penlight in Avila's eyes. No reaction. Dwyer then turned to a student manager: "Call the ambulance."

As he attempted to disperse the crowd that had formed around the bench, Tom Arehart, the Stuart football coach, was scolded by a gray-haired man who had a distressed look on his face. "He said, 'You should never have played this boy both ways,'" Arehart recalled. "I said, 'Sir, I don't know who you are, but we just do the very best we can with our football players.'"

The man gently lifted Avila's head, as if to give it support. "I didn't realize who the man was until I heard him trying to talk to John," Arehart said. "The man was saying, 'My son, my son.'"

More than seven weeks have passed since Moises Avila watched his son—his only son—collapse at that Friday night game. Today,

John Avila, co-captain of the Stuart Raiders' football squad, lies comatose in the intensive care unit of Alexandria Hospital, the victim of an acute subdural hematoma, a blood clot caused by ruptured veins between the skull and brain.

The prognosis for Avila's recovery is chilling: If he survives, his doctors say, he will live in what they call a "primitive, vegetative" state.

"The doctors tell me there is little hope for my son," Moises Avila said in a recent interview, his eyes welling with tears. "But we still have hope that John will recover, that one of these days he'll wake up."

The tragedy that struck 17-year-old John Avila has focused attention on one of the most troublesome questions in all of sport: Are catastrophic injuries inevitable in high school football?

Of the 931,176 boys who participated in the sport last season, 17 died and five suffered irreversible brain and spinal cord injuries. This season, six high school football players have died. Although catastrophic injuries are proportionately rare, at least one football-related death has occurred each year since 1931, when statistics were first kept.

Stuart and Fairfax County school system officials said they have not determined the exact cause of Avila's injury. "The game films don't show an obvious play in which John was hurt," Arehart said. "I don't know what happened. I'm not a doctor. It could have happened on the field or he could have slipped in the shower at home. I just don't know."

Avila's neurosurgeon, Aldo Rosemblat, said there is little doubt the injury was sustained during the game. "A subdural hematoma is caused by trauma," he said. "I received a guy dressed in full football gear in the emergency room. Did it happen because he fell in his bathtub or did it happen on the football field? You answer the question."

In many ways, John Avila—5 feet 8, 170 pounds—was the quintessential high school athlete. In the fall, he prided himself on finishing first in the wind sprints and having the most nicks, or "battle scars," on his helmet. In the spring, he worked tirelessly as a member of the Stuart baseball team—even though he was a second-string catcher who rarely played.

Avila was not a particularly noteworthy football player. He was strong, he was determined, he was intelligent. But he was not big, he was not fast, he was not what major college recruiters would call a "prospect."

Clearly, Avila played high school football because he loved high school football—not because he expected to become a Sooner or a Trojan or a Buckeye.

"John had other plans: He wanted to go to medical school to become a dermatologist," Moises Avila said.

He was speaking over a bowl of soup in the Alexandria Hospital cafeteria, having just spent several hours in the presence of his co-matose son.

"We worried about John playing football," Moises Avila continued. "John was strong but many of the other players were bigger and taller. I would tell John, 'If the other players are taller or heavier than you, don't try to stop them because maybe you will not make it.' But John said, 'No, father, I can't do that.' "

Moises Avila sighed. "John told me that the game of football was like a fight. He said: 'You have to kill the other guy, and the other guy has to kill you. You know, you have to hit hard.' I told him I didn't like it. But John liked it. So he played."

Like many of his classmates at J.E.B. Stuart—a school of 1,527 students, named after a Confederate general—John Avila comes from a family of immigrants. Moises Avila closed his carpentry shop in Bogota, Colombia, to bring his wife and two daughters to the United States in 1968. "We wanted more opportunity for ourselves and our children," he explained. "And we knew that if things didn't work out we could always go back to Colombia."

Avila worked in the construction business in New York, then New Jersey, and things worked out. A son was born to the Avilas in 1970, and they moved to Northern Virginia seven years later. Although they spoke Spanish in their home, Moises and Teresa Avila encouraged their children to adopt what they called "the American ways."

John Avila adopted that most American of sports: football. He played on several youth league teams, then became a two-way performer on the Stuart junior varsity. Explaining why Avila played linebacker and offensive guard, Arehart said: "John liked to hit. He was a very intense player."

When he joined the varsity last fall, Avila was told he could start on offense but not defense. "I said, 'John, you can't start on defense because I've got to get more people involved in the program,' " Arehart recalled. "John was disappointed. He kept bugging me to play him both ways."

That opportunity came this fall when an injury sidelined one of Stuart's top defensive players. "When I told John he'd also be playing linebacker in our second game, he beamed," Arehart said. "John was on cloud nine."

Not so with Avila's father. On the night before the second game, Moises Avila told his son he did not want him to play "on both sides." Although he knows little about football, Moises Avila said he knows plenty about soccer "and how you can get very tired if you are playing too much."

John Avila told his father not to worry, that he was in excellent physical condition. "John wanted to play, so what was I going to do?" Moises Avila said with a helpless shrug. "I told John to be careful."

★   ★   ★

On the evening of September 11, a crowd of 1,500 gathered to watch Stuart play Edison. Several minutes before the 8 o'clock kick-off, Stuart co-captains Avila and Mark Maldonado walked onto the Edison field for the coin toss. "John was funny, as he always was," Maldonaldo recalled. "He said, 'Do you want me to call it?' I said, 'Yeah, you call it.' Then he looked at me and said, 'All right, what do I call? Heads or tails?' "

Edison took a 7-6 lead at the half. Although he had participated in every offensive and defensive play, even helped out on a special team, Avila did not appear tired.

"John prided himself on not getting tired," Arehart said. "He was kind of a workaholic."

"John's tough," said Stuart defensive end George Lambiris, a close friend of Avila's. "I mean, he would never get hurt or anything. And if he did, he wouldn't dare say he was hurt."

Edison's game plan was simple: run the ball straight at 'em. In the second half, the strategy worked. "We were averaging about six yards a carry," an Edison coach recalled. "There was a lot of hitting going on."

During Edison's first possession of the third quarter, Avila collided with an opposing lineman "helmet to helmet, shoulder pad to shoulder pad," according to Stuart Athletic Director Dave Morgan. When he returned to the huddle, Avila clutched his stomach. "I've got cramps, I've got cramps," he was heard to say.

Several players waved to the sidelines, trying to attract the attention of Dwyer. The Stuart trainer noticed the waving but did not believe anything was wrong. "Nobody was lying on the ground, nobody was holding a knee," Dwyer would later explain. "There wasn't any indication that somebody was in distress."

A Stuart player attempted to call time out, but play was about to resume. The ball was given to an Edison tailback, who was tackled by several Stuart defenders. Although the tailback was down, Avila fell onto the pile. "You teach the kids to make sure the runner doesn't fall forward to get a couple extra yards," Arehart said.

While his teammates returned to the huddle, Avila remained on the ground. After a few seconds, he stood up, then lowered his head. "I can't see, I can't see," he was heard to say.

Avila walked off the field, dropping his mouthpiece. Moises Avila, watching from the stands, did not believe his son was in trouble. "I thought, 'Thank God. He's now coming off the field to relax a little bit,' " Moises Avila recalled.

Avila removed his helmet and staggered to the team bench. He seated himself near the 50-yard line, leaned forward and placed his forearms on his thighs.

"He had the blank stare that comes from someone who'd got their bell rung," Dwyer remembered.

Dwyer approached the bench to assess Avila's condition. It was approximately 9:35 p.m. Dwyer said the conversation went as follows:

Dwyer: "What's wrong?"
Avila: "I feel dizzy."
Dwyer: "Is there anything else wrong?"
Avila: (Silence).
Dwyer: "Do you have a headache?"
Avila: (Silence).
Dwyer: "John, were you on the bottom of the pile?"
Avila: "No."
Dwyer: "Do you know what the score is?"
Avila: "No."

When Avila failed to answer several other questions, Dwyer laid him on the bench. Now Moises Avila was worried. "I thought, 'Oh my God, he's very tired. Maybe something happened,' " he recalled.

Dwyer walked to his training table, about 10 yards away, to get an ammonia capsule. When he returned, Avila was lying on the ground behind the bench. "I was told he was put down there by some players," Dwyer said. "They thought he was vomiting and they didn't want him to aspirate."

When Avila did not respond to the ammonia, Dwyer instructed a team manager to call the emergency medical technicians who were stationed nearby with an ambulance. Team physicians are not required to attend games and, since Stuart's doctor was not there, Dwyer directed another manager to locate Edison's physician, Gerard Engh.

With the game in progress, Engh walked around the perimeter of the field to reach the Stuart bench. "No one had told me there was any dramatic urgency," Engh recalled, "so I didn't go running across the field."

When Engh arrived, Avila was barely conscious and secretions were dribbling out of his mouth. Engh placed Avila flat on his back, tilted his head to the side and inserted an airway tube in his mouth so he would continue to breathe normally.

Within seconds, Avila lost consciousness and his pupils dilated—an indication of abnormal brain activity. Then Avila suffered what Engh described as a muscular seizure.

At approximately 9:40, an EMT arrived to assess the injury. "Where's the ambulance?" Moises Avila was heard to say. "Why is it taking so long?" It is standard procedure for an EMT to evaluate a patient's condition before summoning an ambulance.

An ambulance arrived between one and two minutes later, according to Engh and Dwyer. Avila was suctioned, connected to an electrocardiogram monitor and a blood pressure cuff was wrapped around his arm. But the ambulance was not moving. Engh turned to the EMTs. "Why aren't we moving?"

An EMT responded that regulations did not permit him to transport a patient until he was stabilized by paramedics, according to Engh. The EMTs had already called for an advanced life support ambulance.

Engh told the EMTs he would take full reponsibility if they left immediately for Alexandria Hospital. At approximately 9:45, the EMTs agreed to leave. (Fairfax County Emergency Medical Services chief Doug Casey said in an interview that an EMT team leader has the option of waiting for paramedics or leaving immediately with a doctor. Engh said he does not believe Avila's condition was affected by the time elapsed.)

A light rain fell as the yellow and white ambulance pulled out of the Edison parking lot, its sirens sounding. They arrived at the hospital about 10 minutes later. Avila was comatosa.

As Avila was being treated, Engh, an orthopedist, attempted to reassure Moises and Teresa Avila and their daughter, Patty. "I related the story of an Edison football player who'd had surgery for a head injury about seven years ago," Engh said. "I told them that this boy had come out of it OK."

After the game (won by Edison, 27-14), Arehart, Dwyer and Morgan joined Avila's family in the hospital waiting room. "I had the feeling John was going to make it OK," Arehart remembered.

*   *   *

All optimism faded several minutes later when Rosemblat walked into the waiting room, closed the door and informed Moises and Teresa Avila that their son was severely brain damaged.

"I told them that really he had about a 5 percent chance of really making it," Rosemblat recalled. "I also told them that in neurosurgery, the worst thing that can happen to you is not actually to be dead but to survive in a very handicapped condition."

In addition to the subdural hematoma, or blood clot, Avila also suffered from a venous infarct (extensive destruction of brain tissues below the hematoma) and hydroxcephalus (excessive spinal fluid within the brain), according to Juan Jammes, a neurologist who later treated Avila.

Although the prognosis was poor, Rosemblat told Moises and Teresa Avila that since their son was an otherwise healthy 17-year-old who still had brain stem activity, an operation could be attempted to relieve the pressure on his brain. The Avilas agreed.

Shortly before midnight, Avila was transferred to the operating room, where over a 4½-hour period, Rosemblat performed a craniotomy, in which he removed the subdural hematoma and a portion of the skull, relieving pressure on the brain. The surgery did not change Avila's condition appreciably.

At approximately 4:30 a.m., Rosemblat returned to the waiting room, where, speaking in the Spanish of his native Argentina, he told the family that as the swelling in Avila's brain peaked anything could happen, including brain death.

"He was using the example of Karen (Ann) Quinlan, the girl who was in a coma for I don't know how many years," Patty Avila recalled. "He gave us an example that John was going to be like her, that he would be surviving but with an artificial life."

Rosemblat also asked the family if they would be willing to donate the boy's organs if he became brain dead.

"When he talked about that, I cried and I started shaking," Avila's mother remembered.

★   ★   ★

At 8 that morning, Arehart, who had neither slept nor showered, addressed the Stuart varsity and junior varsity teams.

"It looks as bad as it can look," Arehart recalled telling the players. "I don't think John is going to live." Arehart cried as he spoke to the players. "I know I have to be strong for you guys," he continued. "But I'm human, too."

Two days later, on September 14, several hundred students gathered for a prayer service at St. Anthony's Catholic Church in Falls Church.

Stuart principal John Randall read from the Book of Ecclesiastes. "There is a place and time for everything," he began. ". . . A time to be born and a time to die. . . . A time to weep, a time to laugh . . . ."

Later, Lambiris stood before his classmates to read from the First Letter of Peter. He began tentatively, blinking back tears. "All of you should be . . . sympathetic," he said. "Loving toward one another." He had not been at the pulpit 10 seconds when he paused in midsentence, bowed his head and cried.

"I felt like I was going to fall down," Lambiris would say later. "It wasn't that I was nervous—I wasn't because I knew most everybody there. It was just that, I felt this was the end. I felt we were doing this service because it was the end of John. That was hard to accept. It was also hard to accept that football could have done such a thing to John Avila."

In the days that followed, Lambiris thought often of his friend. He remembered the Sunday nights they would spend in Georgetown, making the scene. He remembered the laughs Avila would get in the school cafeteria, imitating singer Janet Jackson. And he remembered the fights they would pick with each other—silly fights, the kind brothers would sometimes have.

Several days after the prayer service, Lambiris made an emotional visit to the Alexandria Hospital ICU. "I know this sounds dumb, but I had something to tell John," he said. "It was about those fights. They weren't serious fights, but I felt guilty about them. It was weird, but I felt really guilty."

When no one else was around, Lambiris leaned forward and spoke to his friend. "John, you know, we got into a lot of fights with each other," he recalled saying. "But you know that I care about you, John. And I know that you care about me, too."

Lambiris wasn't the only Stuart player who had difficulty coping with the trauma.

"We all felt, if we had done this or done that, maybe. . . ." Maldonado explained. "Some players thought, maybe if I would have made that block, he wouldn't have gotten hit, or maybe if I would have made that tackle before he did. . . ."

"I'm worried about some of the guys," Arehart said early that week. "Some of these guys just aren't talking."

On September 16, Arehart invited Joan Mayer, a psychologist for the Fairfax County school system, to meet with his team. At a closed-door session, 35 players—whites, blacks, Asians and Hispanics —sat in an oval, their heads hung low, their faces pained.

At first, the players seemed reluctant to share their thoughts. Then, gradually, they spoke: of regrets they had for not assisting Avila when he complained of stomach cramps ("I should have called a time out," one player said), of Avila's compassion for his teammates ("He never laughed at other guys' mistakes"), of playful moments outside of school (one boy spoke of pulling down Avila's shorts in a pizza restaurant) and of the violent nature of football ("I hit hard but I don't try to kill anybody," one player advised his teammates).

After an hour and a half, Mayer asked the players how they would like to end the season.

"On a positive note," one said.

"With everybody thinking of John with a big smile," another suggested.

Mayer offered a closing thought. "You're going to be the closest team in Fairfax County this year, no matter how many games you win or lose," she said. "That's something that John Avila has given to you."

★   ★   ★

Could anything have been done to prevent this tragedy? "Unfortunately, I can't think of anything," Dave Morgan said, echoing an opinion shared by other Stuart and Fairfax County officials.

Avila's helmet was in perfect condition, these officials said. His preseason physical indicated he was in excellent health, they said. His coaches had taught him the proper tackling and blocking techniques, they said. A doctor, trainer and ambulance were present at the game, even though none is required under Virginia High School League rules. As for playing both ways, that is a common practice in high school football, particularly at lower-enrollment schools.

Moises Avila said he believes the injury may never have occurred if his son had been better rested. Arehart said he has had other two-way performers in his program, and he has no regrets about having played Avila both ways. "He wasn't a scrawny little kid who was terribly out of shape and had terrible techniques," Arehart said. "He was one of our best-conditioned players."

Engh, who has been Edison's team physician for 17 years, said he doesn't believe the injury was related to Avila playing both ways. "But playing both ways can be a problem if a coach doesn't use good judgment," he said. "These boys do get tired."

Engh is more concerned with the violent tackling he has witnessed at recent high school games. "Somebody's going to have to look at the rules," he said. "The head-to-head contact, the way people are tackling today, there's more violence than there used to be. When the tackler is putting his helmet into the other kid's helmet, it's almost like delivering a knockout punch. Their aim is for the head. And that worries me about the game."

Spearing—head-first tackling—was outlawed by the National Federation of State High School Associations in 1976. To emphasize this prohibition, the VHSL recommends that its member schools send each player and his parents a written warning concerning the dangers of improper blocking and tackling.

"Do not use (your) helmet to butt, ram or spear an opposing player," the warning states. "This is in violation of the football rules and can result in severe head, brain or neck injury, paralysis or death to you and possible injury to your opponent. There is a risk these injuries may also occur as a result of accidental contact without intent to butt, ram or spear. NO HELMET CAN PREVENT ALL SUCH INJURIES."

Moises Avila said he never received any warnings from Stuart about his son's safety. Arehart said, "We didn't give that (printed warning) to the players but we talk constantly to our players about safety. A warning is inside their helmet and we tell the players, 'It's a contact sport.' "

Could a head-first tackle have caused Avila's injury? "That's a possibility," Arehart said. "But John's technique was as good as anybody I've ever coached." The coach added that, although players are warned of the dangers of spearing, at times head-first tackling cannot be avoided.

"The kids are taught the right way to tackle, but sometimes they'll inadvertently butt helmets," he said. "That's just something you're not going to take out of the game."

Catastrophic injuries: Are they inevitable in high school football?

"Let me repeat a quote from the movie 'War Games,' " Rosemblat said. "The quote is: 'The only way to win the game is not to play.' "

        ★   ★   ★

Three weeks after Avila's injury, an 11th grader at Stuart, Manny Fierro Jr., quit the football team at his father's request. "Just seeing what happened to John brought a lot of conflicts in my mind," said Manny Fierro Sr., who has acted as a liaison between the Avila family and representatives from the school, hospital and news media.

"Seeing John's parents in the hospital, I said to myself, 'My God, what a helluva situation we could get into. This could happen to us.' "

Moises Avila estimates that his son's medical and doctor bills already have exceeded $100,000. What his medical insurance doesn't cover, a Fairfax County liability policy may pick up—if the family agrees never to file suit against Stuart, Fairfax, the VHSL or the national federation.

"I'm not thinking about any of that now," Moises Avila said the other day. "I'm only thinking about the health of my son."

Every day, Moises and Teresa Avila visit the intensive care unit of Alexandria Hospital, where their son (whose weight has dropped 40 pounds) is being maintained by a respirator, tracheotomy, gastrostomy, foley cather and central venous line.

At times, they see their boy move his head from side to side, a reflex against pain. "Is there hope?" they ask the doctors and nurses. Speaking in Spanish, Rosemblat has told the Avilas again and again that there is little hope, that for all intents and purposes their son, as they once knew him, no longer exists.

"The doctor tries to talk to us in simple words so we can understand John's condition," Moises Avila said. "In one conversation, Dr. Rosemblat told us, 'El murio en el compo de futbol (he died on the football field).' "

Moises Avila shook his head. "I understand what the doctor is saying," he said. "He doesn't want us to hope any more. But we hope. We still hope. We hope that someday our son will wake up."

Saving History Of Black Athletes

GENERAL

By MIKE LITTWIN

From the Baltimore Sun
Copyright © 1987, the Baltimore Sun

Ocania Chalk is 60 years old and lives alone in a run-down trailer in this rural outpost that time forgot. He has no phone, he has no car and he bikes three miles up and three miles back each day to the post office and general store. The townspeople know him, as one neighbor put it, as "that colored man on the bike."

Chalk does not ride the bike for exercise, or for the amusement of the general populace. He has a purpose. Chalk would hope to be known as one who helped preserve the largely forgotten history of the black athlete. It is his obession. It is, literally, his life.

"Blacks don't have the sense of history, sadly enough," Chalk says. "Our history is largely oral. If you want to know what happened 50 years ago, you go to the oldest man in the county. That's part of our heritage, dating back to Africa.

"But the old men are dying, and then what will we have? Our history will be gone forever, and that would be a terrible loss."

Chalk is a writer and historian, dedicated to preserving the memories of such men as Battling Siki, a Senegalese boxing champion, and Joe Lillard, the last black to play in the National Football League before Paul Brown opened the doors again in the late '40s. He has found proof that Bud Fowler, in the 1870s, was the first black to play professional baseball and one of perhaps 60 blacks who played in the 19th century. He has documents and pictures, born of years of tireless research, also of tireless biking to the library in Rock Hill, 14 miles away. Chalk believes this knowledge is important, and he wants to share what he has learned. But the sharing, he finds, is often more difficult than the learning.

"I do the research and write the books and then send them out,"

Chalk says. "Sometimes they keep them for a year and still send them back."

He writes fiction, none of it published. He writes histories, two of them finding their way to print. He figures he has penned two dozen manuscripts, and he is writing more.

"I believe that if you write something worthwhile, it will eventually be noticed," he says.

He smiles.

"Eventually," he says again.

Chalk has his research and writing and, crucial to any writer, he has hope. He also has Arthur Ashe, the former tennis player, who is writing what Chalk calls the definitive history of black sports. Chalk is his willing researcher.

"Arthur is a fine, intelligent man who is putting together a great work," Chalk says. "But his research, well, it could be better."

Chalk's tiny bedroom/office—cooled only by a table-top fan in the August swelter, illuminated by a single light—is clearly a writer's workshop. The typewriter rests on a table/desk. The bookshelves are filled with well-worn volumes, a few of his own hand. The drawers yield his manuscripts. Letters, some of them rejection slips, are taped to the wall. Some might call the setting romantic, but only if they didn't live there. Chalk, dressed in brown work clothes, knows better.

In one article about Chalk, it was suggested that his lifestyle was eccentric. Chalk finds the characterization humorous.

"He thought I was eccentric because I didn't have a phone and I didn't have a car," says Chalk, laughing. "I'm poor, dirt poor. Not eccentric. I can't afford to be eccentric."

But strange?

Driven, maybe. And if, in these times, being driven by forces other than those economic is strange, then Chalk is downright weird.

"I don't do this for money—obviously," he says. "I do it because I enjoy the research and because I'm a writer."

He was once a Washington, D.C., civil servant who spent most of his time in the Library of Congress. He knew every corner, every clerk, every inch of microfilm.

"Information is free," he says. "You have to know where to find it."

He was a fixture there until the Civil Service decided that Chalk was a servant only to his research, to which he dedicates most of his working hours.

"It's almost impossible to get fired by the Civil Service," he says, "but I managed to do it."

Soon afterward, he moved to McConnells, where his father left him five acres of land, a trailer and a house, which he leases. He supports himself on the rent, which allows him to continue his research.

An example: To find Lillard, the last black football player, he wrote to Iowa, where Lillard was born, and New York, where he died. He couldn't get a copy of a birth certificate, but he did find a copy of the death certificate, which included an address of Lillard's daughter. She had moved, but the U.S. mail found her, and Chalk began a correspondence which resulted in a history of Lillard.

Chalk, whose next project is the history of the black soldier, is a fount of knowledge on black sports history. He can tell you how in one Kentucky Derby there were 14 black jockeys, noting that "there were plenty of blacks until the white money took over." He can list every black quarterback, and here he shows that historians are not always dispassionate.

"I love football, but I can't stand to watch it anymore when I know that the best man doesn't always get the job," he says. "Not allowing blacks to quarterback in the NFL (there are two today) is comparable to baseball's exclusion of blacks during World War II when 4-F's were playing but able-bodied black men were denied the same opportunity."

If you get him warmed up, the topic will move anywhere. To Al Campanis: "It's the owners who are to blame, not Campanis." To buoyancy: "Swimming was a major sport in Dakar in West Africa." To black quarterbacks: "Frederick Douglass 'Fritz' Pollard was a black coach of the Hammond (Ind.) Pros in 1923. He got to be the quarterback because he put his own damn self in the game."

Chalk has written "Pioneer of Black Sports" and "Black College Sport." He's trying to find a French translator for his manuscript on Battling Siki. He has a short story out that several magazines are studying, and Chalk, who lives to tilt at windmills, is hopeful.

"I don't know if I'll ever get rich," he says, "but I would like to sell a story so I can buy a 10-speed bike. Those hills will get to you after awhile."

Leonard Stuns Hagler With Split Decision

BOXING

By *RICHARD HOFFER*

From the Los Angeles Times
Copyright © 1987, the Los Angeles Times

Sugar Ray Leonard's enormous bravado, which was nearly offensive in the pre-fight buildup, became a promise fulfilled Monday
night when, after what was essentially a five-year layoff, he returned and upset boxing's dominant champion, Marvelous Marvin
Hagler. The sheer audacity of what he attempted was somehow
matched by the strategic elegance with which he did it.

The comeback, culminated before the largest world audience to
ever see a bout, had been judged foolhardy by most. The symmetry
of their careers, their destinies so intertwined, somehow forgave the
circumstances of the obvious mismatch. They deserved each other
five years ago, but this was better than never.

Still, only those who believed in time travel gave Leonard any
chance against Hagler. Leonard would have to return five years, to a
time when hands were fast and legs tireless, to meet the foreboding
Hagler on anything near equal terms.

Well, he wasn't the welterweight of 1982, when he first retired
after eye surgery. But there was more about Leonard than his tas-
seled shoes that recalled his time of greatness. For 12 tactically brilliant rounds, he circled and countered, confusing and confounding
the bewildered middleweight champion, until he had secured a split
decision.

Though the judges did not entirely agree on what they saw—Lou
Fillippo had it 115-113 for Hagler, Dave Moretti 115-113 for Leonard, and JoJo Guerra 118-110 for Leonard—the only person near the
ring in the parking lot at Caesars Palace to voice any genuine surprise at the decision was Hagler himself. "I beat him and you know
it," he said immediately afterward. "I stayed aggressive. C'mon. I

won the fight."

But Leonard's game plan never let Hagler in the fight. He circled outside, daring Hagler to stalk him, occasionally entangling the champion in a brisk flurry. Hagler missed monumentally as he chased Leonard. Although neither was hurt or in any danger of going down, it was clear that Leonard was hitting more than Hagler and gaining angles on a man not particularly known for his balance.

"Hit and run, stick and move, taunt and intimidate," explained Leonard, facing the press in a jaunty yachtsman's cap afterward, "a variety of things."

It was not always pretty and may have disappointed the nearly 300 million people watching, in that it lacked boxing's conclusive conclusion. But it was not ugly, as even Leonard's attorney, Mike Trainer, had predicted when the comeback was announced a year ago.

Richard Steele, the referee, said: "Maybe he fought him the only style he could win with."

Leonard, of course, knew better than to lead Hagler into any kind of brawl. Hagler (62-3-2, 52 KO) had leveled Thomas Hearns, the last fighter to try that, in just three rounds. In fact, he did fight Hagler the only possible way.

And he fought him that way the entire night. Leonard (34-1, 24 KOs) danced outside from the first round. The clinching was plentiful. And at times, Leonard leaned back into the ropes, imitating the last great popular champion, Muhammad Ali. It was obviously frustrating for Hagler. His long looping rights missed by feet, it seemed. Once he threw a punch, followed it into a ring post, while Leonard bobbed and returned to the center of the ring.

Leonard gave him head feints, his hands dropped, offering his chin disdainfully. Once, in the seventh round, Hagler threw three large right hands in a row. They sailed wide, tremendous arcs in the desert air.

Leonard was masterful in his attempt to frustrate Hagler. In the fourth round, Leonard mocked his opponent with a bolo punch to the stomach.

Hagler, of course, would not be unnerved in the way that Roberto Duran was, when Leonard frustrated him into submission. Still, he was mad, and the two often crossed stares at the bell, and several times had to be escorted to their corners. Hagler was often exhorting his long-time nemesis, "C'mon, c'mon, c'mon," he kept repeating.

"Once," said Leonard, shrugging his shoulders, "he called me a sissy."

In the later rounds, when Leonard was obviously and desperately tired, Hagler began to close the distance between the fighters. In the ninth round, Leonard appeared in trouble in his own corner, but he battled out of it with a vicious fury. At times, he seemed to die against the ropes. Or was he inviting Hagler in for that staccato counter-punching?

In that ninth round, the best of the fight, Leonard four times ensnarled Hagler in some reckless flurries.

It was dangerous and, considering the scoring up to that point, unnecessary. In the 11th round, Leonard got cute. He got up on his toes, smirked as he circled the champion, and threatened yet another bolo punch.

In the 12th and final round, with Hagler continuing to miss, Leonard mocked him by raising his right glove, apparently in anticipation of victory.

Inasmuch as this fight is expected to pull in more than $60 million, a record gross, there will undoubtedly be some who felt they didn't get their money's worth. Yet Leonard, who received a flat guarantee of $11 million to Hagler's $12 million (plus a percentage of the gross), certainly made an effort to earn his.

For, he won with as much grit as wit. At the fight's end, he collapsed into the arms of his handlers. Those legs, suspect going into the fight, hadn't failed him until then.

Leonard, 30, had fought just 12 rounds in six years but his year of conditioning apparently dissolved the ring rust that so affects boxers. Of the unlikeliness of his achievement, Leonard said: "It's the first time a young guy came back against an old guy." Previous examples of failure do not apply.

Hagler, 32, was obviously disappointed, and he referred very quickly to the trouble he has with judges in Las Vegas. He lost his first title bid on a controversial draw with Vito Antuofermo here. But he admitted that Leonard, who he had pursued for years, fought a "courageous fight." He could pursue him, but it doesn't look like he'll ever catch him.

Hagler, who was stopped short of his 13th title defense in the sixth and final year of his reign, must now hope for a rematch. Leonard will not likely be quick to oblige, if at all. In the ring he said, laughing, "depends on the contract." But later, he refused to guess one way or the other as to what he'd do.

The decision certainly creates some interesting matchups, and it will be fun to speculate on the combinations. Hearns, who has lost to both, will want in on the action. Permutations abound. If Hagler and Leonard remain true to their peculiar destinies, they are likely to chase each other around for years more, until finally, they really are too old for this kind of thing.

Paterno's Still the Paterno of Yesteryear

COLLEGE FOOTBALL

By *JERRY GREEN*

From the Detroit News
Copyright © 1987, the Detroit News

The journey takes a lifetime—from English D1 to No. 1. Joe Paterno spoke in the familiar voice: "I thought they were going to introduce me as General Paterno." He stood at the podium and he was tilted slightly to the left. He scratched the words as he spoke. It was good. It was the same as it was almost 40 years ago.

In those days, Joe Paterno was a skinny kid with olive skin out of Brooklyn. He'd been in the big war and he'd walk around the campus at Brown with his hands jammed into the pockets of his old Army fatigue jacket. He had a slow, loping walk. His body slanted to the left. He didn't look much like an athlete. He was an old soldier back in college and he was a very serious guy. He didn't have much size. And he had a sharply pointed face and a mop of black hair. That's how Paterno looked the first time I saw him coming across the pathways of that old, tree-studded university campus back in Providence, R.I. That's pretty much the way Paterno looked Tuesday as coach of Penn State at the Fiesta Bowl, where his team is playing for another national championship.

We were classmates together at Brown. We were required to take English D1. All incoming freshmen had to take it. One hour a day for the semester and you were supposed to learn how to write.

On Saturday, for four seasons after classes, Joe Paterno played football for Brown. He played for Rip Engle, who coached at Brown before going off to Penn State and a measure of immortality.

The memory recalls that Paterno was never really a great quarterback. He was scrawny. He was slow. He had a weak arm. His passes wobbled.

But they somehow reached the target.

Joe Paterno had one knack as a football player. He had the uncanny quality for winning, for simply scratching away at Harvard, or Yale, or Princeton.

Stanley Woodward, the sports editor of the *New York Herald Tribune*, characterized Paterno in one column paragraph one day in the late '40s: "He can't run. He can't pass. All he can do is win."

It was enough. Paterno's team went 7-2 our junior year and 8-1 when we were seniors. Brown was the Ivy League power.

Tuesday morning Paterno spoke of John Shafer, the other quarterback in the Penn State-Miami Fiesta Bowl.

"Shafer's a guy who goes out and makes the plays," Paterno said. "He keeps our guys together. He doesn't beat you. Eventually, he'll find some way to win."

An old classmate said to himself: "That was Joe Paterno, in college."

There was the Saturday in 1948 when Paterno took the train down to Princeton. Princeton had him—us—whipped after three quarters, 20-6. Paterno scratched out a touchdown. Brown got the ball back and Paterno scratched it down the field again. He was maybe 20 yards away and a solitary guy, Bill Altieri, was at the far corner of the end zone. Paterno threw it.

Tuesday morning, he remembered.

"Altieri caught the ball," Paterno said. "I threw the pass. It went end-over-end. I used to run punts back. In those days, you could fair-catch the ball and kick it back. I fair-caught the next punt. I did that. That's how Joe Condon could kick the field goal."

Joe Condon, another old soldier, kicked it 40 yards. The ball twisted and fluttered. But it made it, between the wooden goal posts, in the final minute of the game. The final score was 23-20. We won. Joe Paterno won it. Somehow.

Thirty-eight years later, it remains the best football game I ever saw.

The next Monday morning we were back in Providence. Paterno slouched across the campus. His hands were stuffed into his Army fatigue jacket. He was tilted left. He marched past Sayles Hall toward Hope College, on to the English Lit. course. The professor asked a question. Paterno sat in the back row, with the athletes. He answered the question in the scratchy, Brooklyn voice.

Now it was Tuesday morning in December 1986. Paterno was in a gray suit, button-down shirt, necktie. It was three days before the Fiesta Bowl for the national championship. His picture graces the cover of the year-end *Sports Illustrated.* He is celebrated as SI's sportsman of the year. He is the most visible, most famed Brown graduate, class of 1950.

Joe Paterno left the podium, shuffling, slanting slightly to the left. He spoke again and the voice was just as it was when he called signals himself and when he discussed the writings of Hemingway.

Somebody asked him about the roguish players from Miami, Vinny Testaverde and the others. They have come to the Fiesta Bowl in Army boots and splotched jackets. They are criticized for presenting an unsavory, angry image.

"My problem is I can't decide who are the good guys and who are the bad guys," Paterno said.

There was a vision—Joe Paterno, tilted left, under the trees, crossing the campus at Brown. His hands were stuffed into the pockets of his old Army jacket.

Hit Parade

by Bernard Brault of La Presse newspaper. Montreal's John Kordic delivers a solid left to the jaw of Toronto's Wendel Clark during a fight in a National Hockey League game. Copyright © 1987, Bernard Brault, La Presse.

Four's a Crowd

by Marcia Rules of the Daily Courier-News in Elgin, Ill. Green Bay fullback Brent Fullwood is the helpless victim of a Chicago Bears defensive thrust as he falls short of the goal line during 1987 action. Copyright © 1987, Marcia Rules, Daily Courier-News.

PRIZE-WINNING WRITERS IN BEST SPORTS STORIES 1988

Norm Clarke (Big Gamble: Betting and Broncomania) has been the major league baseball writer and sports projects editor of the *Rocky Mountain News* since September 1984. Before joining the *News*, Clarke worked for the Associated Press for 12 years and was the AP's Olympics coordinator for the 1984 Summer Games. While with the AP, Clarke was nominated for a Pulitzer Prize for coverage of the 1978 West Virginia scaffolding disaster which killed 52 steelworkers. A newspaperman since 1963, Clarke was sports editor of the *Billings* (Mont.) *Gazette* and a three-time winner of Montana's sportswriter of the year award. He is making his first appearance in *Best Sports Stories*.

Jere Longman (Chaney Has Held On to His Dream) has been a staff writer at the *Philadelphia Inquirer* for six years, the last three as a feature writer and before that three years as the paper's beat writer for the Philadelphia Eagles of the National Football League. He is presently a feature writer specializing in football and basketball at both the college and professional levels. Longman is making his first appearance in *Best Sports Stories*.

Rick Reilly (A Ring and a Prayer) has been writing about sports for 10 years, the last three with *Sports Illustrated*. The Boulder, Colo., native began his career with the *Boulder Daily Camera* after graduation from the University of Colorado and later worked for the *Denver Post* and *Los Angeles Times*. Reilly won two national awards at the Associated Press Sports Editors convention in 1984 and won the top feature award at the Associated Press Editors convention the same year. Reilly lives in Littleton, Colo., and is making his fourth appearance in *Best Sports Stories*.

Bob Verdi (Special Olympics: Something Special) has been a sports columnist at the *Chicago Tribune* for 20 years and appears weekly in *The Sporting News*. He is a 10-time winner of the Illinois Sportswriter of the Year award and has won several Associated Press and United Press International sportswriting awards.

OTHER WRITERS IN BEST SPORTS STORIES 1988

Mitch Albom (Greg Monroe) has been a sports columnist at the *Detroit Free Press* for the last three years. In 1987, Albom was named the nation's top sports columnist by the Associated Press Sports Editors for column writing in newspapers of more than 175,000 circulation. A former columnist and feature writer for the *Fort Lauderdale News/Sun Sentinel*, Albom is making his second appearance in *Best Sports Stories*.

Paul Attner (Pete Rose, Manager) has been a national correspondent for *The Sporting News* since 1984. The former *Washington Post* staff writer is a 1969 graduate of California State University at Fullerton and was selected Alumnus of the Year by the university's School of Communications in 1986. Attner, the author of three books, has won numerous sportswriting awards, including three first places in the annual Pro Football Writers Association of America writing contests and a first-place award in the U.S. Pro Basketball Writers annual contest. He is active in both writing associations and is making his second appearance in *Best Sports Stories*.

Ron Borges (He Fought His Way Up), a sportswriter for the *Boston Globe*, has spent the last 13 years in pursuit of professional athletes from coast to coast. He began his career at one of the smallest weekly newspapers in Massachusetts, the now defunct *Martha's Vineyard Grapevine*. He worked for the *Sacramento Union*, the *Oakland Tribune* and the *Baltimore News-American* before joining the *Globe* staff in 1983. Borges was the 1984 winner of the Associated Press Sports Editors award for best feature story and is appearing in *Best Sports Stories* for the fourth time.

Thomas Boswell (He Gave His All, Which Was a Lot and Why is Baseball So Much Better Than Football?) is a reporter for the *Washington Post* and a contributor to such publications as *Golf Magazine, Esquire* and *Playboy*. The 1969 Amherst College graduate is one of the most respected baseball writers in the country and has written two books on the sport, *How Life Imitates the World Series* and *Time Begins on Opening Day*. Boswell is a former winner of the American Society of Newspaper Editors first prize for sportswriting and a three-time winner in *Best Sports Stories* competition. He is making his ninth appearance overall in *Best Sports Stories*.

Bill Brubaker (The Rise and Gall of Walters and Bloom and The Long Night of John Avila) is a staff writer for the *Washington Post*, specializing in project and investigative stories. Brubaker, who was born in New York City and reared in Miami, Fla., was previously employed by the *Hollywood* (Fla.) *Sun-Tattler*, the *Miami News*, the *New York Daily News* and *Sports Illustrated*. A man whose enjoyment of travel has taken him to some 60 countries on five continents, Brubaker is making his second appearance in *Best Sports Stories*.

Gene Collier (Playing at Home Can't Help the Bears) is a sports columnist for the *Pittsburgh Press*. The 1975 Penn State graduate and Coaldale, Pa., native began his career with the *Pittstown Mercury* before moving to the *Camden Courier-Post*, the *Philadelphia Journal* and the *Pittsburgh Post-Gazette*. Collier joined the *Press* in 1984 and is making his second appearance in *Best Sports Stories*.

Paul Domowitch (Kevin Allen: A Life in Ruins) is a special projects writer for the *Philadelphia Daily News*, where he has worked since 1982. Before becoming a special projects writer, Domowitch covered the Philadelphia Eagles of the National Football League for three years. A 1976 graduate of Wilkes College and a native of Wilkes-Barre, Pa., Domowitch started his career at the *Midland* (Tex.) *Reporter-Telegram* before joining the *Fort Worth* (Tex.) *Star-Telegram*, where he covered the Texas Rangers baseball team.

John Feinstein (Navratilova Still Shows Championship Qualities) grew up in New York City and received a history degree from Duke University in 1977. After working as a summer intern at the *Washington Post*, he was hired as a metro staff reporter before moving to the sports department. During his 10 years in Washington, he has covered police, courts and state politics on the news side and pro soccer, college football and basketball, major league baseball and tennis on the sports side. He currently covers college basketball and tennis. Feinstein, who won last year's commentary category in *Best Sports Stories* and is making his fifth appearance overall in the anthology, has written two books on college basketball. His first, *A Season on the Brink—One Year With Bob Knight and the Indiana Hoosiers*, was published in the fall of 1986 and his second, a chronicle of the 1987-88 season, is scheduled for publication in November 1988.

Mike Fish (Gansz: A Closer Examination) is a general assignment reporter for the *Kansas City Star and Times*, where he has worked since September 1980. A 1974 graduate of Ithaca College, Fish writes about various sports in the Kansas

City area, with his present emphasis being the National Football League's Chiefs. He is making his first appearance in *Best Sports Stories.*

Lew Freedman (Straight Pool: Rack 'Em Up) is sports editor of the *Anchorage Daily News.* A 1973 graduate of the Boston University School of Public Communication, he worked for the *Philadelphia Inquirer,* the *Florida Times-Union* and the *Syracuse Herald-Journal* before joining the *Daily News* four years ago. He is making his first appearance in *Best Sports Stories.*

Steve Friedman (Falling Star) is managing editor of *St. Louis Magazine.* He attended Stanford University and worked at the *Columbia* (Mo.) *Daily Tribune* before joining the magazine. He is making his first appearance in *Best Sports Stories.*

David Granger (The Anatomy of an At-Bat) has been an editor at *Sport* magazine since August 1986. Granger has a master's degree in English from the University of Virginia and worked as a senior editor at *Family Weekly* before moving to *Sport.* He is making his first appearance in *Best Sports Stories.*

Jerry Green (Paterno's Still the Paterno of Yesteryear) has been a sports columnist for the *Detroit News* since 1973. Prior to '73, Green covered pro football for the paper after working seven years with the Associated Press, two of those years as the AP's Michigan sports editor. He also has worked for the *New York Journal-American* and *Long Island Star-Journal.* Green is the author of two books, *Year of the Tiger* and *The Detroit Lions—Great Years, Great Teams.* He is making his third appearance in *Best Sports Stories.*

Mark Heisler (James Lofton's Trying Times) currently works for the *Los Angeles Times* after earlier stints with the *Rochester* (N.Y.) *Times-Union* and the *Philadelphia Inquirer.* The Springfield, Ill., native has at various times covered the Philadelphia 76ers of the National Basketball Association, baseball's California Angels and Los Angeles Dodgers and the Los Angeles Raiders of the National Football League.

Phil Hersh (Boules Fever) handles special assignments, including the Olympics, for the *Chicago Tribune.* Hersh, a 1968 graduate of Yale University, previously worked for the *Gloucester* (Mass.) *Daily Times,* the *Baltimore Evening Sun,* the *Chicago Daily News* and the *Chicago Sun-Times.* The 1986 winner in the commentary category of *Best Sports Stories,* Hersh is making his sixth appearance in the anthology.

Brian Hewitt (Harry Caray) has covered sports as a staff writer for the *Chicago Sun-Times* since July 1976. Hewitt, who received a master's degree in journalism from Northwestern University in 1973 and a bachelor of arts degree from Stanford University in 1972, was a sportswriter for Pioneer Press publications from 1973 to 1976. A native of Princeton, N.J., Hewitt is a regular contributor to *Sport* magazine and has won several suburban journalism awards. He is making his first appearance in *Best Sports Stories.*

Richard Hoffer (Double Trouble and Leonard Stuns Hagler With Split Decision) has been writing features and covering a variety of sports for the *Los Angeles Times* for the last nine years. The Miami (Ohio) University graduate previously worked for the *Massillon* (Ohio) *Evening Independent,* the *Riverside* (Calif.) *Press-Enterprise* and the *Cincinnati Post.* Hoffer, who also holds a master's degree from Stanford University, was the 1985 winner in the *Best Sports Stories* reporting category and is appearing in the anthology for the sixth straight year.

Candace Lyle Hogan (What's in the Future for Women's Sports?) is a free-lance writer who lives in New York City. A former managing editor of *The Runner* magazine, Hogan has reported on Title IX and women's sports since 1973. She is making her first appearance in *Best Sports Stories.*

Tony Kornheiser ('Doc': An Aviator for the Ages) is a columnist for the *Washington Post.* He previously was a staff reporter for *Newsday* and *The New York Times.* His work has appeared in such publications as *Sports Illustrated, The New York Times Magazine, New York, Rolling Stone, People* and *Esquire.* Kornheiser won the feature-writing competition sponsored by the Associated Press in 1977 and 1981 and was the news-feature winner in *Best Sports Stories* in 1979.

Mark Kram (Bad Boxers) has been a sportswriter for the *Philadelphia Daily News* since March 1987. Before joining the *News,* Kram worked for both the *Detroit Free Press* and the *Baltimore News-American.* He is making his first appearance in *Best Sports Stories.*

Franz Lidz (Spar Wars) is a staff writer for *Sports Illustrated* based in Philadelphia. Lidz, a graduate of Antioch College, effectively mixes the off-beat with sports and approaches life in much the same manner. Lidz has been a disc jockey, a soda jerk, an improvisational actor, a South American wanderer, a Boston cabbie and a bus driver near Baltimore. He is making his third appearance in *Best Sports Stories.*

Mike Littwin (Saving History of Black Athletes) is a columnist for the *Baltimore Sun.* A University of Virginia graduate, Littwin joined the *Sun* in August 1986 after working for seven years as a feature writer and columnist for the *Los Angeles Times.* Earlier in his career, Littwin worked for the *Newport News Times-Herald* and the *Virginian-Pilot* in Norfolk, Va. He is making his sixth appearance in *Best Sports Stories.*

Joan Mellen (Workin' On the Chaney Gang) is a professor in the English department at Temple University in Philadelphia. She teaches creative writing in the graduate program as well as film and literature. Mellen is currently working on her 10th book, this one about Indiana University basketball coach Bob Knight. It will be her first book on a sports-related topic.

Scott Ostler (A Day of Little Challenges) is a syndicated columnist who writes for the *Los Angeles Times.* A Brigham Young graduate, Ostler joined the *Times* in 1977 and has been voted California sportswriter of the year in five of the last six years. He is co-author of *Winning Times,* a book about the National Basketball Association's Los Angeles Lakers.

Edwin Pope (Blacks in Sports) has been sports editor of the *Miami Herald* for 21 years, and a sportswriter for 48 years. He began at age 11 for the *Athens (Ga.) Banner-Herald* and worked for United Press International and the *Atlanta Constitution* and *Atlanta Journal* before moving to Miami in 1956. He has won a record three Eclipse Awards for writing about horse racing and a record three National Headliners Club awards for best sports columns.

Ron Rapoport (Young's Views Never Shaded), currently a sports columnist for the *Los Angeles Daily News,* was for 10 years a sports columnist for the *Chicago Sun-Times,* the publication in which his *Best Sports Stories* entry appeared. Rapoport, who holds a degree from Stanford University and did graduate work at the Columbia University School of Journalism, was the 1984 winner of the National Headliner Award for "consistently outstanding sports columns." Prior to his work at the *Sun-Times,* Rapoport worked for the *Los Angeles Times, Associated Press* and *Sport* magazine. He is making his seventh appearance in *Best Sports Stories.*

Randy Rieland (co-author of The Secret Life of Jerry Smith) is a senior editor at *The Washingtonian* magazine. He is former editor of *Pittsburgh Magazine* and *Regardie's,* a business magazine in Washington, D.C. Before that, Rieland worked as a reporter with the *Baltimore Sun* and the *Pittsburgh Press.*

Jay Searcy (The Power and the Kingdom of Joe Paterno) is a senior writer for the *Philadelphia Inquirer,* a paper for which he was executive sports editor for 10 years before returning to writing in 1986. Searcy has been writing and editing sports stories for 30 years and was twice named Tennessee sportswriter of the year. Searcy, who also has worked for the *Chattanooga Times* and *The New York Times,* is making his third appearance in *Best Sports Stories.*

Bill Utterback (Steroids: Deadly Deception) has worked for the *Pittsburgh Press* since October 1985, primarily covering the National Football League. He is a graduate of the University of Pittsburgh at Johnstown and previously wrote about sports for the *Greensburg Tribune-Review* and the *Beaver County Times.*

PRIZE-WINNING PHOTOGRAPHERS IN BEST SPORTS STORIES 1988

Louis DeLuca (Jump For Joy) has been a staff photographer for the *Dallas Times Herald* for the past four years. He began his career with the *Shreveport* (La.) *Journal,* moved to the *Chicago Sun-Times* in 1983 and to Dallas a year later. DeLuca has won in *Best Sports Stories* competition on three other occasions: in 1987 for best black and white feature photo, and in 1984 and 1986 for best black and white action photos. He was the 1982 Photographer of the Year in Louisiana, Texas and New Mexico and was runner-up for that honor in 1985.

Larry Steagall (Stranglehold) has been a newsphotographer for 10 years, the last four with the *Sun* in Bremerton, Wash. The Seattle native enjoys going to SuperSonics, Seahawks and Mariners games every chance he gets. Steagall is making his first appearance in *Best Sports Stories.*

Judy Walgren (A Heady Play) has worked as a photographer at the *Dallas Morning News* since August 1987. Walgren graduated from the University of Texas in 1986 with a degree in photojournalism and did an internship with the *News* and another with the *Odessa* (Tex.) *American* before joining the *News* full-time. She is making her first appearance in *Best Sports Stories.*

OTHER PHOTOGRAPHERS IN BEST SPORTS STORIES 1988

Larry Alpaugh (Teamwork) is the chief photographer for the *Transcript-Telegram* in Holyoke, Mass. He began his career in 1983 as a part-time sports photographer for the *Salisbury Daily Times* in Salisbury, Md. Alpaugh worked briefly at a regional sports magazine, *Shore Sports,* in 1984 before returning to the *Daily Times* as chief photographer. He is making his first appearance in *Best Sports Stories*.

Bernard Brault (Hit Parade) is a staff photographer for *La Presse* newspaper who also does free-lance work out of Canada. Brault, who lives in Longueuil, Quebec, began his career in 1976 as a staff photographer for a local newspaper before taking the free-lance route four years later. His work has appeared in several Quebec sports magazines and he has contributed to such wire services as *United Press Canada, Reuters* and *Canadian Press*. Brault, who began contributing to *La Presse* in 1984, has earned numerous citations for his work and gives seminars on sports photography a couple times a year. He is making his third consecutive appearance in *Best Sports Stories*.

Robert Bunch (Helping Hands) is a free-lance photographer living in Dallas. The East Texas State graduate previously worked at the *Tyler* (Tex.) *Morning Telegraph* and *Bryan* (Tex.) *Eagle* before going free-lance. Bunch is making his first appearance in *Best Sports Stories*.

Ernest T. Coleman (Agony of DeFeet) is a staff photographer for the *Danville* (Ill.) *Commercial-News*. He previously worked part-time at the *Orange Coast Daily Pilot* in Costa Mesa, Calif., while attending California State University at Fullerton. Coleman is making his first appearance in *Best Sports Stories*.

Ralf-Finn Hestoft (Go Go Girls) is a staff photographer for the *Kankakee* (Ill.) *Daily Journal* and is a partner in The Image Group, a commercial photography studio. Hestoft, who also is associated with the Picture Group photo agency, holds a bachelor's degree in political science from Northwestern University and is making his first appearance in *Best Sports Stories*.

Dave Kraus (Tough Luck) is a staff photographer for the *Tulsa Tribune*. After graduating from the University of Kansas in May 1981, Kraus worked at the *Tribune* as an intern over the summer and joined the staff full-time in August of that year. He has since been named Oklahoma News Photographer of the Year five times, the National Press Photographers Association Regional Photographer of the Year twice and is making his second appearance in *Best Sports Stories*.

Jerry Lodriguss (Temper, Temper) is a staff photographer for the *Philadelphia Inquirer* who specializes in sports. A New Orleans native, Lodriguss worked for newspapers in the New Orleans area after graduating from the University of New Orleans with a degree in communications. He also has free-lanced for publications such as *Sports Illustrated, Sport, Time* and *U.S. News and World Report*. He is making his first appearance in *Best Sports Stories*.

Dennis "Buzz" Magnuson (Safe!) was brought up in a family of photojournalists. His father, Chet, was a news photographer with the *Minneapolis Star* and then with the Associated Press until his death in 1957. Buzz's older brother, Dick, was a photographer for the *St. Paul Pioneer Press Dispatch* for many years. Buzz, who started work for the *Pioneer Press* in 1955 and is still there at age 55, is making his sixth appearance in *Best Sports Stories*.

John F. Rhodes (The Yawner) has been a staff photographer for the *Dallas Morning News* for the past 15 years. He graduated from East Texas State University in 1972 and has been with the *Morning News* ever since. Rhodes has covered three Super Bowl games and his photo of Cowboys tight end Jackie Smith dropping a certain touchdown pass in Super Bowl XIII was recognized by the Pro Football Hall of Fame as the "Pro Football Photograph of the Year" in 1978.

Wayne Roper (Follow Through) is the chief photographer for the *Brantford* (Ont.) *Expositor*. He joined the paper's photography department four years ago after 16 years as a writer/photographer for the *Expositor*. Roper has won four Canadian Press awards in the past four years and is making his first appearance in *Best Sports Stories*.

Marcia Rules (Four's A Crowd) is currently a staff photographer at the *Daily Courier-News* in Elgin, Ill. She started her career in 1978 as a free-lance photographer at the *News-Sun* in Waukegan, Ill., and also had a six-month stint at the *Milwaukee Journal*. Rules is making her first appearance in *Best Sports Stories*.

Arlene Schulman (Machine Gun) is a New York-based free-lance writer and photographer who has published many features and photo essays. Her work has appeared in such journals as *The Village Voice*, the *New York Daily News*, the *New York Post*, the *Toronto Star*, the *Boston Globe*, and *Inside Sports* magazine.

Dale E. Tait (12 Straight) is the team photographer for the National Basketball Association's Milwaukee Bucks and is the owner of Photo/Graphic's Ltd. of Milwaukee. His work is regularly published in *The Sporting News*, *Basketball Digest* and *Hoop Magazine* and he also has been a stringer for United Press International since February 1987.

Billy Weeks (Something Special) has been a staff photographer for the *Chattanooga Times* for three years. He also worked two years at the University of Tennessee at Chattanooga while attending that school. Weeks, who enjoys photographing nature and wildlife as well as sporting events, is making his second appearance in *Best Sports Stories*.

THE PANEL OF JUDGES FOR BEST SPORTS STORIES 1988

Brian Brooks is an associate professor of journalism at the University of Missouri and coordinator of the school's editing programs. The former reporter and editor at the *Memphis Press-Scimitar* and *Columbia Missourian* managing editor is co-author of *News Reporting and Writing* and *The Art of Editing*, best-selling textbooks in their fields.

George Kennedy is an associate dean at the University of Missouri School of Journalism. Before moving to Columbia, Kennedy spent 7½ years as a reporter and editor with the *Miami Herald* and two summers as a writing coach for the *San Jose Mercury*. He is co-author of *News Reporting and Writing* and *The Writing Book*, two college and professional textbooks.

Bill Kuykendall is an associate professor and director of the photojournalism sequence at the Missouri School of Journalism. He formerly was director of photography at the *Seattle Times* and a frequent speaker on photojournalism and photo department management. Kuykendall also directs the international Pictures of the Year competition.

Daryl Moen is a professor at the University of Missouri and director of mid-career programs at the university's School of Journalism. He is a former managing editor of the *Columbia Missourian* and two other dailies. Moen also is co-author of *News Reporting and Writing* and *The Writing Book* and author of *Newspaper Layout and Design*.

Byron Scott is the Meredith professor of journalism and director of the service journalism program at the University of Missouri. He has worked as a newspaper reporter and magazine editor in Miami, Chicago, New York, Washington and Long Beach. Scott formerly headed the magazine sequence at Ohio University's Scripps Journalism School.